THE BONHOEFFER PHENOMEN

Dietrich Bonhoeffer

THE BONHOEFFER PHENOMENON

Portraits of a Protestant Saint

STEPHEN R. HAYNES

Fortress Press

Minneapolis

THE BONHOEFFER PHENOMENON
Portraits of a Protestant Saint

Frontispiece: Bonhoeffer icon by Lewis Williams, © 2003. Image courtesy of www.trinitystores.com.
Cover design: Brad Norr Design
Book design: Ann Delgehausen
Author photo: Cyndy Hubbard

ISBN: 0-8006-3652-X

The paper used in this publication meets the minimum requirements of American National Standard for Information Sciences—Permanence of Paper for Printed Library Materials, ANSI Z329.48-1984.

Manufactured in the U.S.A.
08   07   06   05   04   1   2   3   4   5   6   7   8   9   10

Für Alyce

CONTENTS

PART TWO
INTERPRETING THE BONHOEFFER PHENOMENON

[Bonhoeffer] was a representative figure, graced with just enough greatness to fulfill our expectations of what a representative Christian ought to be . . . It is not just that anybody died a victim to Nazism. A representative Christian died.

    —THE CHRISTIAN CENTURY

Can a theologian be both popular and legitimately understood?

    —JAMES PATRICK KELLEY

The heart of Bonhoeffer's spiritual legacy to us is not to be found in his words, his books, but in the way he spent his time on this earth.

    —ROBERT COLES

There is always the danger of romanticizing a martyr, of turning him into a religious hero, which must be avoided. Bonhoeffer could not have imagined anything more revolting.

    —JOHN D. GODSEY

PREFACE

M ost people," Robert Ellsberg writes, "possess an instinctive ability to recognize heroic sanctity when they see it."[1] The verity of Ellsberg's claim was evident in a recent on-line discussion of sainthood among religious "seekers." When asked what modern figures they would propose as "saints," that is, notable human beings whose lives instruct us, participants in the discussion nominated Mother Teresa of Calcutta, Albert Schweitzer, Fr. Guido Sarducci of *Saturday Night Live* fame, Bill W. (the founder of Alcoholics Anonymous), and Sir Laurens van der Post (the biographer of C. G. Jung). Yet the very first candidate to be named was Dietrich Bonhoeffer. Indeed, Bonhoeffer's stature in the contemporary religious imagination is impressive evidence for Ellsberg's assertion that, regardless of religious background, most people possess an instinctive capacity to recognize sanctity in others.

For over half a century Bonhoeffer has assumed a variety of roles in the religious imagination—seer, prophet, apostle, hero, bridge, martyr, and even saint. The pages that follow argue that exploring this last role is the key to understanding the others, that is, that Bonhoeffer's reception is helpfully illuminated by the concept of sainthood. In calling Bonhoeffer a "saint" I am not arguing that he would qualify for beatification had he been a Roman Catholic. Neither do I mean that he was a "saintly" man, though he most certainly was. Nor do I intend "saint" as a solecism for "martyr," though assertions of his martyrdom are a crucial component of Bonhoeffer's sainthood. Nor am I observing that some authors cast Bonhoeffer in the suprahistorical realm of hagiography, or that Bonhoeffer himself had a "complex love-hate relationship with the phenomenon of sainthood.[2] Rather, I wish to argue that in significant ways Bonhoeffer *functions* as a saint. Clues to this function will be sought in the master narrative of Bonhoeffer's life—which reflects the very patterns that animate traditional saints' "lives"—and in various aspects of the Bonhoeffer "cult," particularly pilgrimage, narration, dramatization, and commemoration.

As we shall see, Bonhoeffer's unofficial sainthood is sanctioned by a diverse group of scholars, writers, publishers, retailers, and travel agents who are devoted to his legacy. They produce popular biographies, church bulletin inserts, and "Christian fiction"; they sponsor films, plays, musical productions, radio dramatizations, and traveling art exhibitions; they promote Bonhoeffer tours through Germany and Poland. Most of these publications and activities are historically faithful and in good taste; all emerge from genuine admiration. Even so, the saintly image of Bonhoeffer to which they contribute interferes with objective assessments of his life and thought. Specifically, the Bonhoeffer cult *domesticates* his legacy by placing it in the service of contemporary questions, needs, and concerns whose connection with his own time and place are sometimes tenuous and often more symbolic than real; and it *sanctifies* the theologian's memory by making criticism of his life and thought seem disrespectful or even sacrilegious. As will be explored at the conclusion of this study, the problems of domestication and sanctification are brought into sharp relief by considering the ways Bonhoeffer serves as a guide for pro-life activism and post-Holocaust theology.

A CONFESSION

I must confess at the outset that I am more of a Bonhoeffer devotee than a Bonhoeffer scholar. I am, however, familiar with professional Bonhoeffer studies, whose ethos I first encountered nearly a decade ago. In November 1995 I read a paper on Bonhoeffer and Holocaust Education before the English Language Section of the International Bonhoeffer Society. My comments provoked spirited reactions from some of my auditors, mainly because I dared to question whether Bonhoeffer was in fact the guide for post-Holocaust Jewish-Christian relations he is generally assumed to be.[3]

While initially painful, the experience of being called to task by eminent Bonhoeffer scholars was extremely beneficial in the long run.

For it taught me that many who study Bonhoeffer do so from a desire to salvage something from the rubble of Christian civilization left in the wake of World War II and the Holocaust. As church historian John Conway has written, "largely because he seemed to be the one 'good German' whose witness could be held up for unstinting praise, and whose heroic martyrdom vindicated these ideas," hagiographical impulses are often at work when Bonhoeffer is remembered.[4] Addressing the International Bonhoeffer Society, I had entered an arena where the analytic and hagiographic impulses were in considerable tension, and I had failed to strike the proper balance.

I could appreciate this situation since my initial encounter with Bonhoeffer had occurred when I was a college student. As part of my preparation for leadership in an evangelical parachurch ministry I was asked to read *The Cost of Discipleship*. An eighteen-year-old with precious little knowledge of Christian theology or German history, I found the book opaque, but enthralling. I was particularly struck by its gnomic pronouncements, and I recall that one of these — "when Christ calls a man he bids him come and die" — was printed on the back cover of the paperback edition. For a while *The Cost of Discipleship* became something of a devotional text for me. Unconcerned with the history in which the book is inscribed, I read Bonhoeffer's words as timeless exhortations to Christian living. I highlighted passages that appeared to address my circumstances, but never finished the book.

My next engagement with Bonhoeffer came when I decided to pursue a master's degree in religion at Florida State University. John J. Carey's course in "Twentieth-Century Western Religious Thought" included a discussion of Bonhoeffer's theology, particularly the appropriation of his thought by the so-called death-of-God theologians. When I moved on to Emory University and a doctoral program in religion and literature, I bumped into Bonhoeffer yet again. Under the influence of my teachers, especially Walter Adamson in history and Jack Boozer in religion, I became intrigued by the interplay of political and religious thought in interwar Europe. This time I met Bonhoeffer with a special interest in his biography, in the relationship of his religious and political commitments, and in his fate under the Nazis.

These encounters with Bonhoeffer at different stages of my intellectual and spiritual development are indicative of a distinctive aspect of the Bonhoeffer phenomenon — the way different persons imagine different Bonhoeffers. When I identified with an evangelical subculture during my college years, I interpreted Bonhoeffer as a committed disciple full of wisdom about living for Christ "in the world." A few years later, when I was searching for spiritual moorings in a public university, I read Bonhoeffer as a theological visionary who had peered beyond the borders of Christian orthodoxy. When I met Bonhoeffer again, I had settled in the theological center and was seeking ordination in a mainline Protestant denomination. Not surprisingly, I read Bonhoeffer as a theological liberal who articulated a prophetic critique of modern culture.

When I returned to Bonhoeffer in 1995, I did so as a teacher of the Holocaust, a participant in Jewish-Christian dialogue, and a student of Christian images of the Jewish people. From this perspective I saw new things in Bonhoeffer—his lonely stand on behalf of Jews, his identity as a rescuer, and his struggle to revise the church's historic theological apprehensions of the Jewish people. As this volume and the one to follow reveal, I am still trying to make sense of Bonhoeffer from this perspective. I invite the reader to join me on that journey, probing the many facets of the Bonhoeffer phenomenon to divine his meaning for today.

ACKNOWLEDGMENTS

Any book this long in the making is supported by a large cast. In this case, the cast includes institutions, particularly Rhodes College and the Lilly Endowment, Inc., librarians Annette Cates and Kenan Padgett, students Amy Taylor, Amy Riddle McCallum, Jessica Maki Teague, and Stephen Ogden, colleagues Kenny Morrell, Tom McGowan, Tim Huebner, Richard Kyte, and Bernadette McNary-Zak, clergy colleagues Steve Montgomery and Gayle Walker, mentors John Carey and Richard Rubenstein, Bonhoeffer aficionado Phil Taylor, and scholars Barry Harvey, Burt Nelson, Michael Lukens, Ruth Zerner, Victoria Barnett, and Franklin Sherman, among others. None of these persons, of course, is responsible for any of this work's shortcomings, only for enriching the process through which it came into being.

My life has changed so much in the eight years since I started this project that I hardly feel like the same person. Through these changes God has provided three things to sustain me: close friends, particularly Kenny Morrell, John Jones, Eric Schaefer, and Steve Kinney, remarkable children, Christiana and Matthew, and a new bride, Alyce. A friend recently said about my wife that she is the sort of spouse academics dream of. Indeed, her love and support have made possible not only the completion of this book but the unexpected happiness of its author. For that and so much more, it is dedicated to her.

Today there are once more saints and villains.
— DIETRICH BONHOEFFER, *ETHICS*

Between East and West, Protestant and Catholic, Liberal and Conservative, clergyman and layman, theologian and activist, Calvinist and Lutheran, across the ecumenical spectrum [Bonhoeffer] has stood as a symbol.
— MARTIN E. MARTY

Like those indistinct ink blots in a Rorschach test, Dietrich Bonhoeffer's equivocal theological residue elicits wildly different interpretations. In the current enthusiasm to decode the anagram and declare "what Bonhoeffer really meant," we learn at least as much about the sleuths as about the mystery itself.
— HARVEY COX

Interpretations of the life and thought of Dietrich Bonhoeffer are like the answers elicited by a Rorschach test—no two commentators see the same things . . . What Bonhoeffer really meant and what he would have said had he lived has become a wideopen pastime, little previous experience required.
— PETER VORKINK II

INTRODUCTION

BEYOND THE HISTORICAL BONHOEFFER

Bonhoeffer's Reception

In a letter dated July 21, 1944, Dietrich Bonhoeffer wrote to his friend Eberhard Bethge:

> I remember a conversation that I had in America thirteen years ago with a young French pastor. We were asking ourselves quite simply what we wanted to do with our lives. He said he would like to become a saint (and I think it's quite likely that he did become one). At the same time I was very impressed, but I disagreed with him, and said, in effect, that I should like to learn to have faith. For a long time I didn't realize the depth of the contrast. I thought I could acquire faith by trying to live a holy life, or something like it . . . I discovered later, and I'm still discovering right up to this moment, that is it [sic] only by living completely into this world that one learns to have faith.[1]

There is great irony in this oft-quoted excerpt from Bonhoeffer's prison writings. For Jean Lassere (the "young French pastor" to whom Bonhoeffer refers) passed into virtual anonymity, while Bonhoeffer became a Protestant saint without parallel. And despite his disavowal of efforts "to live a holy life," Bonhoeffer's extraordinary existence is the foundation on which his sainthood rests. This book is an exploration of the Bonhoeffer phenomenon and the various ways it has received expression in the years since his death.

What distinguishes Bonhoeffer's reception from that of other modern religious figures? The first thing to note is the contrast between his relative obscurity during the years of the Third Reich and his celebrity in the years since. Second, despite being incomplete, occasional, and fragmented, Bonhoeffer's writings continue to invite serious engagement by theologians, philosophers, psychologists, and political scientists. In an ever-expanding series of articles, monographs, and dissertations, Bonhoeffer is compared with thinkers as diverse as Martin Luther, Karl Marx, Mahatma Gandhi, Ludwig Feuerbach, Friedrich Nietzsche, Martin Heidegger, Carl Jung, Adolf von Harnack, Pierre Teilhard de Chardin, Karl Barth, Rudolf Bultmann, Reinhold and H. Richard Niebuhr, Wilhelm Dilthey, Harry Stack Sullivan, Werner Elert, Friedrich Gogarten, Albert Camus, John Dewey, Jean-Paul Sartre, Yves Congar, Lawrence Kohlberg, Carl Rogers, Francis Fukuyama, Richard Rorty, Theodor Adorno, and Emmanuel Levinas.[2]

Third, this seminal intellectual figure enjoys a remarkable popularity among nonacademics. A respected observer of the Bonhoeffer phenomenon writes that "generally there has been much more interest in Bonhoeffer's life and thought outside the academy."[3] Indeed, this has been the case for some time. In 1962 Martin Marty noted that following Bonhoeffer's academic dissertations most of his theological writing had "the kind of lucidity that makes him understandable also among those not professionally trained in theology," and in 1968 James Patrick Kelley remarked on the many "popularizing works aimed at pastors and intelligent lay Christians."[4] Today references to Bonhoeffer's life and thought are just as likely to be found in popular magazines and church bulletins as in scholarly journals. Laypersons read his books, participate in e-mail discussion groups, and join societies devoted to extending Bonhoeffer's influence. Pastors of all theological persuasions refer to him in their sermons. And for those in search of inspiration for Christian living, Bonhoeffer's words are readily available in volumes compiled for devotional use. Indeed, the German theologian seems to offer something for everyone with an interest in religion or spirituality, regardless of age, even among members of the presumably antitheological "Generation X."[5]

We can compare Bonhoeffer's popularity with that of other twentieth-century theologians by perusing the offerings of an on-line bookseller. At the time of this writing Amazon.com listed 240 book titles dealing with Bonhoeffer, most of them in English and in print and many having a profoundly popular cast. Searching the same on-line database with the name "Paul Tillich" yielded nearly as many titles (209), yet the vast majority of these were specialized studies of interest primarily to scholars (including a good number of dissertations). Amazon.com listed seventy-four titles dealing with "Rudolf Bultmann," although many of these were out of print or of limited availability.[6] Furthermore, Bonhoeffer showed up on every list of the twentieth century's most influential religious books that was released around the turn of the millennium, whereas Tillich appeared only once and Bultmann not at all. Likewise, neither Bultmann nor Tillich made *Christian History*'s list of the most influential Christians of the twentieth century, while Bonhoeffer was voted among the top ten by both scholars and general readers.[7]

My choice of Tillich and Bultmann as points of comparison is not arbitrary. In *Honest to God* (1963) John A. T. Robinson identified Tillich, Bultmann, and Bonhoeffer as indispensable for "recasting the mold" of Christian faith in the postwar world.[8] As Robinson experienced a gradual epiphany under the influence of these German giants, he came to view them as representing the best hope for ensuring the gospel's continuing relevance. "For all their apparent difficulty and Teutonic origin," Robinson wrote, "they so evidently spoke not only to intelligent non-theologians but to those in closest touch with the unchurched masses of our modern urban and industrial civilization."[9]

As influential as were Robinson's predictions regarding the "Copernican revolution" in postwar theology, he missed the mark in at least two senses. First, Robinson imagined that Bonhoeffer's significance lay primarily in his thought—particularly his musings from prison concerning the modern world's failure to acknowledge the religious a priori and its rejection of God as a "working hypothesis."[10] However, to the extent that these letters are valued today, their importance rests largely on the fact that they originate from Bonhoeffer and are authenticated by his life and death. Second, Bonhoeffer continues to exercise the religious imagination in more obvious and permanent ways than either Tillich or Bultmann.

This observation seems self-evident at the outset of the twenty-first century, but in 1963 very few could have predicted that Bonhoeffer's influence would eclipse that of Tillich and Bultmann. Not only did these men enjoy the luxury of adjusting their theological positions in light of the profound social changes of the 1950s and 1960s (Tillich died in 1965, Bultmann in 1976), but both maintained relatively undisturbed academic careers. By comparison, Bonhoeffer, who died in 1945, was never able to devote himself exclusively to thinking and writing after 1933. In 1963 Robinson perceived Bonhoeffer's role as confirming what other, more productive and systematic religious thinkers were saying. Yet today Bonhoeffer possesses credibility among persons with little knowledge of or interest in Tillich, Bultmann, or Barth.

As was noted in the preface, any comprehensive study of Bonhoeffer's reception must attend not only to his unusual popularity, but to the interest and devotion he claims among distinct groups of admirers. Previous studies have observed Bonhoeffer's impact across the spectrum of religious thought. "His influence cuts across our customary theological, denominational, national and age-group divisions," wrote John Godsey in 1965.[11] Three years earlier, Martin Marty had commented on this very feature of the Bonhoeffer phenomenon:

> If he is read in both East and West, so, too he is studied in both Catholic (Orthodox and Roman) and Protestant Christian circles. Within Protestantism he has been regarded by some as a lineal descendant of the nineteenth century's liberal tradition . . . Others regard him as a sort of Lutheran Karl Barth, a neo-orthodox "radical conservative." Though fundamentalists are somewhat uneasy with his approach to the Bible, they admire the resultant exegesis, and the unflinching loyalty to Jesus Christ; meanwhile the liberal interest in Christian ethics is confirmed by his lifework.[12]

Wayne Whitson Floyd has observed that Bonhoeffer remains a man of "many faces"—the proponent of death-of-God theology, the conservative guardian of order, the liberation theologian, and the critic of the privileged church.[13] In fact, if anything has changed in the forty years since Marty commented on the remarkable ecumenicity of Bonhoeffer's influence, it is the extent of its penetration into the larger culture. In post-Christian societies with an abiding interest in "spirituality," Bonhoeffer is increasingly cast as a teacher of enduring "values," and there is little hesitation in interpreting him apart from the concerns of Protestant theology or the institutional church.

Explaining the Phenomenon

Having identified the distinctive aspects of Bonhoeffer's reception, we must inquire about the forces underlying them. Without doubt one of these is the inseparability of the Bonhoeffer narrative from the drama of the Third Reich. As John Godsey writes, a brief description of Bonhoeffer's life reads like a motion-picture ad:

> Take a young Protestant theological student from pre-Nazi Germany, reared with all the advantages of bourgeois existence; give him a year of life in the United States; then plunge him back into Hitler's Third Reich, and watch him struggle to be a Christian during the ensuing years of church controversy, Gestapo terrorism, and World War II. Dangle before his eyes the opportunity to escape from it all; witness his tormented decision and the final outcome.[14]

Robert E. Huldschiner describes the background for Bonhoeffer's life in more classical terms: "Germany between the wars, the advent to power of the little maniac with the barber's face and the Wagnerian conclusion to his Teutonic folly are like a contemporary version of Greek drama and Bonhoeffer is one of the cast."[15] Indeed, the era of "saints and villains" that determined the texture and duration of his life virtually ensures that Bonhoeffer comes to us in the figure of a hero.

His heroic figure is magnified by Bonhoeffer's involvement in the anti-Nazi resistance and his death as a result of Nazi brutality.[16] Since the modern imagination has made Hitler the epitome of Evil, Bonhoeffer the anti-Hitler naturally assumes the mythic role of warrior in the service of Good. The importance of Bonhoeffer's role as anti-Hitler is accentuated by the fact that so many Christians succumbed to fascism or to a spiritual proto-fascism that was impotent before the Nazi onslaught.[17] Similarly, the more that perpetrators of the Holocaust are demonized (as, for example, in the recent study by Daniel Goldhagen), the more we require saintly resisters to restore our faith in human nature. In other words, to the extent that we are fascinated and haunted by Nazi Germany, we are also drawn to Bonhoeffer.

Yet quite apart from the dramatic events in which it is inscribed, Bonhoeffer's life reveals a symbiosis between thought and existence that sets him apart from most public figures in his time and our own. Those who knew him repeatedly remark on this dimension of Bonhoeffer's legacy. Albrecht Schönherr writes that "it is for such a life of one piece, such an example that a young person longs."[18] And W. A. Visser 't Hooft notes the "impressive unity" formed by Bonhoeffer's life and writings: "Is not this hunger and thirst for reality, for becoming incarnate, for *living* the Christian life and not merely *talking* about it the real key to Bonhoeffer's message?"[19]

Such testimonies have ensured that images of integrity would dominate Bonhoeffer's public reception. "Unlike the lives of most theologians, Bonhoeffer's life was an extension of his beliefs," *Time* observed in 1960.[20] Five years later *Life* remarked that Bonhoeffer was "the example of what a modern Christian must be: a devout man whose life mirrored his beliefs, who accepted literally his own words that 'a Christian must follow Jesus unto death.'"[21] Why is there still an interest in Bonhoeffer? Eberhard Bethge asked in the preface to his monumental biography of 1967. Perhaps it is due to his "unusual combination of thought and action, of his life as martyr and theologian." Indeed, Bethge's magisterial work contributed to a widespread appreciation of the "fusion of theology and autobiography" in this man for whom "the drama of thought rivaled the drama of vocation."[22]

Nearly forty years later this perception of Bonhoeffer remains a prominent aspect of his reception. Noting that his life and thought "inform each other deeply," novelist Marilynn Robinson remarks that "to say this is to be reminded of the strangeness of the fact that this is not ordinarily true."[23] But we need not contrast Bonhoeffer with corrupt corporate executives to recognize his "impressive unity," for it emerges even in the presence of theologians such as Barth and Tillich (who never escaped rumors of marital infidelity) and Bultmann (who made a relatively easy accommodation with National Socialism). Indeed, the more Bonhoeffer's life is scrutinized, the more one perceives a rare integrity of word and deed.

After five decades of serious Bonhoeffer study there is no better explanation of his prominence in the religious imagination than the unusual integrity noted by so many commentators. The drama of his life and its unity of action and belief remain at the heart of the Bonhoeffer phenomenon.

Martyr or Theologian?

The powerful witness of Bonhoeffer's life ensured that from the beginning his influence in Europe and North America would be as much spiritual as academic, as grassroots as institutional, as likely to find expression in seminary common rooms as in professional journals. During the 1950s the European lay academies that convened the church's intellectual leadership found inspiration in Bonhoeffer's thinking and action. According to one commentator, "the radically modern, radically serving" spirit of these academies was "the offshoot of Bonhöffer's temper and articulate witness."[24] And in the 1960s Bonhoeffer helped open the eyes of German ministers "to the reality of Jesus Christ in this our world" and beckoned them to identify with the "humble and suffering presence of Christ in the world."[25] During this time a tendency to perceive Bonhoeffer's theology through a biographical lens led many to associate him with Albert Camus, another "prophet" whose writings were read against the background of his role in the anti-Nazi resistance.[26]

Even scholars were struck by the dual witness of Bonhoeffer's life and thought. German theologians such as Gerhard Ebeling, Jürgen Moltmann, and Helmut Thielicke were drawn to Bonhoeffer not only by his promising contributions to contemporary theology in the areas of Christology and hermeneutics, but by his sacrifice as well. And the Anglo-American "Bonhoeffer boom" of the late 1950s and early 1960s was fueled as much by interest in the theologian's personality as by his thought.[27] A case in point is John D. Godsey's *The Theology of Dietrich Bonhoeffer* (1960), the first comprehensive study of Bonhoeffer's theology in English. In portraying Bonhoeffer as an important theologian in his own right whose involvement in the German Church Struggle lent his voice a unique authority, Godsey highlighted Bonhoeffer's dual witness. Indeed, each chapter in his study of Bonhoeffer's theology began with a "biographical introduction." Illuminating Bonhoeffer's "life and witness," the book concluded on a doxological note: "The witness of

Dietrich Bonhoeffer is sealed. 'The blood of the martyrs is the seed of the church.'"[28]

The risks inherent in this approach were revealed when it became clear that some valued Bonhoeffer the martyr above Bonhoeffer the theologian. As the *Christian Century* concluded in 1965, Bonhoeffer, "great as he may have been or provocative as he certainly was, was not a sufficiently substantial thinker to have survived in memory had it not been for the manner of his death." In 1973 Henry P. Van Dusen epitomized this line of thinking when he wrote that "Bonhoeffer was not a great theologian, but he was a great Christian man . . . "[29] Such doubts concerning Bonhoeffer's stature as a thinker were no doubt intensified by his appeal among the young and restless. A 1965 *Christian Century* editorial noted that "many collegians have emulated Bonhoeffer because they feel that he more than any other thinker addressed the real world in which they live."[30] In 1967 Jaroslav Pelikan lamented that "college students who insist that they are not very religious stay away from Chapel and read Bonhoeffer; [while] theological students who are bored by traditional dogmatics have formed little Bonhoeffer coteries at various seminaries."[31] Strengthening Bonhoeffer's appeal among disaffected students was the burgeoning opposition to America's involvement in Vietnam, a force that "extended an appreciation for Bonhoeffer's life and its pattern of political opposition," particularly at the grass-roots level.[32]

Clearly, Bonhoeffer's popularity among those in search of heroes fueled a desire to distinguish his theology from his "life and witness." Concerned that excessive interest in Bonhoeffer's story could undermine his place among the theologians,[33] some sought to de-emphasize the biographical dimensions of his legacy by means of historical detachment or wider dissemination of his writings.[34] In this view, Bonhoeffer was "a theologian already popular for two decades before he could be clearly understood."[35] He came into full view only with the arrival of Bethge's definitive biography, which signaled the end of "guesswork," the replacement "once and for all" of a plaster saint with a real man, and the emergence of a consensus portrait of the German theologian.[36] Bethge's years of research and editing, it was believed, would make it possible to separate Bonhoeffer's theology from his life and rescue him from popularizers such as Robinson, radical distorters among the death-of-God group, and the psychological needs of the younger generation. The way was now clear for "more profound assessments of Bonhoeffer's contribution to Christian theology" from the likes of Andre Dumas, Clifford Green, Heinrich Ott, Larry L. Rasmussen, Ronald Gregor Smith, and John Phillips.[37]

This approach to Bonhoeffer, of course, assumed that it was possible and desirable to distinguish Bonhoeffer the theologian from Bonhoeffer the hero and martyr. But, as we shall see, Bonhoeffer's unique place in the history of modern religious thought must rest on assessments of his life as well as his thought. For most interpreters have found it impossible to ignore the nexus of belief and behavior revealed in Bonhoeffer's life.[38] Indeed, what continues to make Bonhoeffer so widely known, admired, read, and studied is his unique *combination* of innovative theology and committed living. The chapters that follow identify the ways this aspect of his legacy animates the dominant portraits of Bonhoeffer.

Beyond the Historical Bonhoeffer

This volume describes Bonhoeffer's reception in terms of four overlapping portraits drawn over the past half-century by scores of interpreters—professional and otherwise. I am not the first to note that Bonhoeffer's legacy is mediated in a variety of forms, or that Bonhoeffer himself was a paradoxical figure.[39]

The most complete description of Bonhoeffer's theological reception is James W. Woelfel's *Bonhoeffer's Theology: Classical and Revolutionary*, which appeared in 1970. Exploring "paths in Bonhoeffer interpretation," Woelfel demonstrated that Bonhoeffer's theological legacy had fallen into distinct constellations he called radical, liberal, and conservative. Yet Woelfel's analysis differs from my own in important ways. First, his work reflects standard receptions of Bonhoeffer through the 1960s, while, as we shall see, interpretive options have evolved considerably since that time. For instance, the lineaments of Woelfel's "liberal" Bonhoeffer were defined by arguments among Bultmannians and Tillichians, whereas "liberal" theology today is informed largely by liberation themes that were barely nascent when Woelfel wrote.

Second, Woelfel was concerned with varieties of "scholarly" interpretation, which made him methodologically inattentive to the popular

Bonhoeffer this book seeks to keep in view. The outlines of Bonhoeffer's conservative portrait, for instance, must be discerned largely from popular rather than scholarly sources. Third, Woelfel described the various categories of Bonhoeffer's theological reception in order to prepare the ground for judging their faithfulness to the historical Bonhoeffer and exposing "the most serious distortions and confusions of Bonhoeffer."[40] My objective, however, is to illuminate the contours of the Bonhoeffer phenomenon.

Given the bewildering plethora of interpretations that attach themselves to this man, there is understandable interest in recovering the historical Bonhoeffer.[41] And given his proximity to us in history, the survival of many who knew him, and the careful research of so many scholars, this seems a reasonable goal. Nevertheless, interpreters continue to claim Bonhoeffer as a "true" radical, liberal, or conservative. He is invoked as a champion of orthodoxy, neoorthodoxy, the theology of secularity, political and liberation theologies, religious pluralism, and postmodernism. In fact, one can find Bonhoeffer's name attached to virtually every mainstream theological movement that has flourished during the past three decades. "No name is invoked more frequently today in theological circles in America," J. Karl Ridd claimed in 1966, than that of Dietrich Bonhoeffer. "He is listed in support of one side or the other of virtually every question—and frequently is claimed by both sides."[42] This is no less true today.

Yet my goal is not to judge these competing claims against the standard of the "historical Bonhoeffer." Rather, it is to explore the ways this remarkable man is remembered, celebrated, and appropriated, the dominant images that emerge from scholarly and popular interest in Bonhoeffer, what these images reveal about the needs and concerns of his admirers, and the way these images elucidate and distort the Bonhoeffer legacy.

PART ONE

WHO IS

BONHOEFFER

FOR US?

[Bonhoeffer] seemed to run on ahead in the most varied dimensions . . . He was an impulsive, visionary thinker.

—KARL BARTH

Despite the fact that he has become an enigma, a fad, a saint, and in some cases an embarrassment in the two decades since his execution by the SS, [Bonhoeffer] still [has] his finger on the very issues which continue to torment us.

—HARVEY COX

Radical theologies, like other movements, need saints and Bonhoeffer seems tailor-made for the role . . . His prison writings, especially in the earlier edition, have a gnomic, inspirational quality which makes it possible, within wide limits, to read into them whatever one wishes and accounts for their becoming a modern classic among progressive Christians.

—GEORGE A. LINDBECK

SEER

THE RADICAL BONHOEFFER

Before the Radical Bonhoeffer

Craig L. Nessan has written that the Bonhoeffer who first encountered North American readers was a radical.[1] But Nessan's characterization applies to neither North America nor to Europe. While the prison writings garnered a great deal of attention when they appeared in German in 1951, like everything else in Continental theology at the time, they remained "shrouded in the smoke of battle round the two towering figures" of Barth and Bultmann.[2] While "friends" of Bonhoeffer gathered regularly and produced several volumes of essays under the title *Die mündige Welt* (1955–63),[3] he was understood in traditional categories until Hanfried Müller's *Von der Kirche zur Welt* claimed Bonhoeffer for socialism in 1961.[4]

The early reception of Bonhoeffer in Anglo-American circles was quite similar. When *Christianity and Crisis* announced Bonhoeffer's "martyrdom" in 1945, Reinhold Niebuhr described him as a neoorthodox thinker, "strongly under the influence of Barthian theology . . . [and] inclined to regard political questions as completely irrelevant to the life of faith."[5] *Life* recalled that Bonhoeffer had been an apologist for Barthianism during his days at Union Seminary.[6] Into the mid-1960s, in fact, Bonhoeffer was regarded as a dialectical theologian deeply influenced by the theology of crisis and its critique of "religion," yet serviceable for the neoorthodox religious establishment.[7]

While Bonhoeffer's *Letters and Papers from Prison* became the genesis for radical interpretations of his thought, the letters' initial reception forestalled appearance of the radical Bonhoeffer for some time.

Ronald Gregor Smith was both the first to publish Bonhoeffer's prison writings and the first to reflect on their theological significance. In *The New Man: Christianity and Man's Coming of Age* (1956) Smith identified *Letters and Papers from Prison* as containing resources for a modern doctrine of humanity consistent with the biblical tradition. He presented Bonhoeffer's questions and formulations as an "epoch-making turning point,"[8] and like the Anglo-American thinkers who would take up the letters a decade later, was concerned with the relationship of transcendence to concrete history and with constructing an anthropology appropriate to the late twentieth century.

Yet in elucidating the "powerful dialectic" of the worldliness of God, Smith arrived at conclusions quite familiar to orthodox Christians. "A faith which takes us not out of this world in its historicity," it was, it seemed to Smith "the very crux of our belief in the historical Incarnation."[9] The main commonality between this early gloss on Bonhoeffer's prison writings and their eventual appropriation by radical theologians was optimism, although for Smith "the real hope for the world" was not man's coming of age in a secular world but "the living encounter with God, within the structure of grace."[10]

John D. Godsey's *The Theology of Dietrich Bonhoeffer* (1960) acknowledged the importance of the prison writings by addressing the question that would vex Bonhoeffer studies during the following decade. The "problem" of Bonhoeffer's theology, Godsey wrote, is its "development during the final period, especially during the time of his imprisonment, and in the relation of the thought of this period to that of the two preceding periods."[11] The "clue" to solving this problem, Godsey argued, was Bonhoeffer's "steadfast concentration upon the revelation of God in Jesus Christ."[12] This reading of Bonhoeffer unmistakably reflected the neoorthodox paradigm that dominated American theology at the time and that continued to dictate Bonhoeffer's reception. Godsey saw Bonhoeffer, like Barth, as a theologian of the church, one who had, on the basis of a sound evangelical theology, "quite simply and clearly called the church to new obedience to the commandment of Jesus Christ."[13]

Emergence of the Radical Bonhoeffer

Beginning in the early 1960s, a few influential thinkers began to utilize Bonhoeffer's ideas to challenge the theological tradition in its liberal and neoorthodox forms. The radical Bonhoeffer caught on in America and Britain and by the early 1970s the German theologian was widely regarded as a radical critic of religion in the tradition of Freud and a soul mate of antigovernment activists such as Father Daniel Berrigan.[14] How do we explain this abrupt transformation from Bonhoeffer the dialectical theologian to Bonhoeffer "the symbol and personification of avant-garde theology"?[15] In part, it reflects the demise of the neoorthodox establishment. At the time, W. W. Bartley III pointed out that Bonhoeffer's star was on the rise at the very moment American Protestantism was in "desperate need" of a new voice:

> Barth, Brunner, Bultmann, Reinhold Niebuhr, Tillich—all have been famous since they were young men in the 1920s; and they are still today, in comparatively advanced old age, the only real major figures in Protestant thought, whose place is quite unthreatened by any serious competitors among the young. In the circumstances, a certain amount of boredom is understandable.[16]

As the "theologies of culture" elaborated by these thinkers became outdated, Bonhoeffer represented a clear alternative.[17]

Amid this changing of the theological guard the "gunpowder which exploded with a noise heard in many quarters" (Bethge) when Bonhoeffer's prison writings were introduced in Europe became audible in Anglo-American theological circles as well. In 1959 Peter L. Berger published a series of articles in the *Christian Century* entitled "Camus, Bonhöffer and the World Come of Age."[18] Like Camus, Berger wrote, Bonhoeffer had recognized modern man's capacity for freedom and had greeted it with "joy." As for secularization, Bonhoeffer would have us stop thinking about the process as a turning away from God and see it "as revealing God's gift of freedom and of the world to man."[19] While America's religious structures were still intact, in 1959 Berger predicted that the recent religious boom would be followed by a "collapse" involving the "rapid disintegration of religion." Reflecting the giddy confidence that would come to characterize secularizing interpretations of Bonhoeffer, Berger claimed that Nietzsche's prophecy of God's death had been fulfilled.

The lineaments of Bonhoeffer's radical portrait are evident in Berger's argument; yet the image of the radical Bonhoeffer did not catch on until John A. T. Robinson's *Honest to God* appeared in 1963.[20] Writing in a compelling first-person style, the Anglican bishop of Woolwich posed modern theology's challenges for thinking Christians who dwelt beyond the university and seminary. He began *Honest to God* by narrating his discovery of Tillich, Bonhoeffer, and Bultmann (in that order) and his gradual realization of the momentous challenge these theologians presented for contemporary Christianity. Robinson recalled his encounter with the "now famous passages about 'Christianity without religion'" from *Letters and Papers from Prison*, which had appeared in the *Ecumenical Review* in early 1952. "One felt at once that the Church was not yet ready for what Bonhoeffer was giving us as his last will and testament before he was hanged by the S.S.," Robinson wrote. "Indeed, it might be understood properly only a hundred years hence. But it seemed one of those trickles that must one day split rocks."[21]

Robinson quoted lengthy excerpts from the prison writings in which were expressed the "startling paradox" of Bonhoeffer's nonreligious understanding of God. He also utilized Bonhoeffer's categories in rethinking Christology for a new age. "What *is* Christ, for us today?" Robinson asked, paraphrasing Bonhoeffer. His answer was a thorough melding of Bonhoefferian and Tillichian concepts:

> Jesus is "the man for others," the one in whom Love has completely taken over, the one who is utterly open to, and united with, the Ground of his being. And this "life for others, through participation in the Being of God," is transcendence. For at this point, of love "to the uttermost," we encounter God, the ultimate "depth" of our being, the unconditional in the conditioned.[22]

Robinson felt free to communicate Bonhoeffer's message in such un-Bonhoefferian terms because he equated his assessment of "religion" with the critiques of "supranaturalism" by Tillich and of "mythology" by Bultmann. With one voice, Robinson believed these thinkers "in closest touch with the unchurched masses of our modern urban and industrial civilization" called Christians to a "Copernican revolution."[23]

It is difficult to overestimate the impact of Robinson's book in framing the theological discussions that would dominate the landscape of the 1960s, or in giving impetus to radical readings of Bonhoeffer. Attempting to explain to readers of the *New York Review of Books* "how Dietrich Bonhoeffer became really famous in America," W. W. Bartley III emphasized the remarkable response to Robinson's *Honest to God*.[24] According to Eberhard Bethge, the book allowed Bonhoeffer's reception in the English-speaking world to bypass the German obsession with relating Bonhoeffer's "non-religious interpretation of biblical concepts" to Bultmannian concerns. Rather, following Robinson, it was "religionless Christianity" that framed the questions.[25] Ironically, however, Robinson so closely linked Bonhoeffer with the giants of liberal Protestantism that a clear portrait of the radical Bonhoeffer did not emerge from *Honest to God*.[26]

The same year Robinson's book appeared, American theologian Paul van Buren placed Bonhoeffer in the service of an even more radical critique of Christian theology in *The Secular Meaning of the Gospel* (1963). The book opened with a quote from *Letters and Papers from Prison*:

> Honesty demands that we recognize that we must live in the world as if there were no God. And this is just what we do recognize—before God! God himself drives us to this realization.—God makes us know that we must live as men who can get along without Him. The God who is with us is the God who forsakes us (Mark 15:34)! We stand continually in the presence of the God who makes us live in the world without the God-hypothesis.[27]

With these words, van Buren claimed, Bonhoeffer described the reality of being Christian in a world "come of age," a world in which "men no longer believe in a transcendent realm where their longings will be fulfilled." In the process Bonhoeffer posed a question that continues to vex us: How can the Christian who is himself a secular man understand his faith in a secular way? Van Buren's answer called upon a variety of religious thinkers—Barth, Bultmann, Anthony Flew, and Ian Ramsey—and a method (linguistic analysis) that was "far removed from Bonhoeffer's thought." Yet Bonhoeffer's influence came to bear on van Buren's understanding of Jesus' freedom, "the characteristic which Bonhoeffer, in his last writings, found so impressive."[28] At the book's end, van Buren invoked Bonhoeffer once more: "Our method [of developing a "non-religious interpretation of biblical concepts"] is one which never occurred to Bonhoeffer, but our interpretation may nonetheless serve to justify his hope."[29]

Around this time, other professional theologians were seeking to develop a theology for what Nietzsche had called "the time of the death of God." Among these were Gabriel Vahanian (who was reflecting on the "death of God" as early as 1961 and in 1966 took up Bonhoeffer's claim that the age of religion had come to an end),[30] and Harvey Cox, whose seminal work *The Secular City* also appeared in 1966.[31] Unlike Vahanian, Cox did not directly engage Bonhoeffer's theology. He did, however, cite Bonhoeffer as a witness for his contention that Western Christianity had entered a new era defined by urban secularity. Cox maintained that since the ultimate roots of modern secularization were to be found in "biblical sources," Bonhoeffer's embrace of the secular should not shock us. For when he spoke of "man's coming of age" he was "merely venturing a tardy theological interpretation of what had already been noticed by poets and novelists, sociologists and philosophers for decades."[32]

Cox began the concluding chapter of his book with Bonhoeffer's observation from prison (April 30, 1944) that "we are proceeding toward a time of no religion at all . . . How do we speak of God without religion . . . How do we speak in a secular fashion of God?"[33] Bonhoeffer's query reminds us of incontrovertible facts, Cox argued: that we must speak of God and that the word "God bewilders or confuses modern secular man." But while Bonhoeffer's theology supplies "clues" and "hints" about how to address this Christian paradox, we should not look to him for the answer. Other American theologians were not so cautious in their assessment of Bonhoeffer's later writings.

William Hamilton and Thomas J. J. Altizer are the two names most often associated with death-of-God theology, in part because they co-authored *Radical Theology and the Death of God* (1966), the central text of the movement.[34] Yet the two men pursued "radical theology" in different ways and represent different orientations to the "death of God." Altizer is associated with "post-Christian theism," which claims it is possible to speak of God or the sacred only in ways that are "totally alien from historical Christianity and without reference to the past figure of Jesus of Nazareth." "Christian atheism," meanwhile, maintains that while God has been irretrievably lost, it is possible "to hold to the Jesus of history as the paradigm of human freedom, action, and optimism in a profane world."[35] Thinkers in this latter stream, particularly Hamilton and van Buren, gravitated toward Bonhoeffer.

Hamilton claimed that his own experience of the "death of God" included "the Bonhoeffer theme," which phrase he used to describe his development of Bonhoeffer's concept of man come of age.[36] Bonhoeffer's contribution to death-of-God theology in general Hamilton located in the theologian's "plea for a religionless Christianity in the prison letters":

> At no point is the later Bonhoeffer of greater importance to the death of God theology than in helping us work out a truly theological understanding of the problem of religionlessness. I take religion to mean not man's arrogant grasping for God (Barth) and not assorted Sabbath activities usually performed by ordained males (the moderate radicals) but any system of thought or action in which God or the gods serve as fulfiller of needs or solver of problems. Thus I assert with Bonhoeffer the breakdown of the religious a priori and the coming of age of man.[37]

Hamilton conceived his own theological project, in fact, as the logical filling out of Bonhoeffer's insight that God is no longer required as "a working hypothesis."[38] Yet the connection was tenuous, for Hamilton claimed that Bonhoeffer's importance for radical theology could not be tied up with "what [he] meant by religion"; rather, study of religionlessness had to be "carried out quite independent of the task, probably fruitless, of establishing just what Bonhoeffer meant."[39] It was precisely this attitude that led Hamilton afoul of those who did claim to know what Bonhoeffer meant. Indeed, that the death-of-God theologians went beyond Bonhoeffer when they spoke of "religion" was evident to anyone with even a passing familiarity with Bonhoeffer's spiritual life. Hamilton confessed that he did not see "how preaching, worship, prayer, ordination, the sacraments can be taken seriously by the radical theologian,"[40] while Bonhoeffer never ceased taking such matters seriously, even if their meaning was less clear in a nonreligious world.

Though differing from each other in important ways, the radical thinkers linked with the death of God—the "phrase that launched a thousand press releases"[41]—shared several fundamental convictions: that Christian theology was obligated to reinterpret the gospel in light of secularity and radical human freedom; that only by doing so could Christianity maintain its relevance for modern culture; that the most incisive theologians had been pointing in this direction for some time; and that chief among these "seers" was Dietrich Bonhoeffer. Yet as the radical theologians sought to enlist Bonhoeffer in support of their own programs of theological reflection, other interpreters (including those who had known Bonhoeffer and did not have a vested interest in the fate of radical theology) argued passionately that the death-of-Goders were badly misconstruing Bonhoeffer's theological legacy.

Responses to the Radical Bonhoeffer

By the mid-1960s radical appropriations of Bonhoeffer's prison writings were profoundly affecting perceptions of the German theologian and his intellectual legacy. *Letters and Papers from Prison* was regarded as a turning point in modern theology (Ronald Gregor Smith), its author an ally of Julian Huxley and "John the Baptist of the post-Christian age" (John A. T. Robinson), a dangerous theologian who must be read carefully (E. H. Robertson), "the apostle of Christian atheism, the troubadour of the new optimism, the St. George of the post-Christian era whose sword of the secular spirit has decapitated the two-headed dragon (at least two) of tradition and transcendence" (William Blair Gould).[42] Such characterizations suggested that images of the radical Bonhoeffer were beginning to dominate his reception.

In 1959, shortly after Peter Berger opined that Bonhoeffer's radical critique of religion meant that "any idea of the church as a sacred institution, set apart from the world, is ruled out," William H. Hudnut III responded that Berger's reading of Bonhoeffer represented a hardening of one facet of his thought into a solid core of antichurch polemic, a fallacy "compounded by taking certain statements made in the critical and (if you will) eschatological situation of nazi Germany and applying them to the American situation of a generation later."[43] This exchange set the terms for what would become a perennial argument regarding the radical Bonhoeffer: Was he the herald of a new age of secularism, honesty before God, and "Christian atheism"? Or were such readings of Bonhoeffer irresponsible, misleading, and dangerous?

When the argument rose to the level of debate, the crucial question became the degree of continuity in Bonhoeffer's thought. Reginald Fuller has referred to this as "the riddle of Bonhoeffer": Are his last writings to be interpreted as radical departures from or natural developments of his earlier theology?[44] Not surprisingly, attempts to answer the riddle have given rise to rival schools of interpretation, which Fuller names "ecclesiological-christological" (continuity) and "hermeneutical" (discontinuity). In the initial German response to Bonhoeffer, the hermeneutical approach was adopted by Gerhard Ebeling, while Eberhard Bethge and Jürgen Moltmann represented the ecclesiological-christological school.[45]

In Anglo-American theology, discontinuity was emphasized by David Hopper, the secularizing theologians, and some conservatives,[46] while John D. Godsey, John A. Phillips, Heinrich Ott, Andre Dumas, Ernst Feil, Peter C. Hodgson, John Gibbs, Paul L. Lehmann, Clifford Green, Thomas W. Ogletree, Larry Rasmussen, and others stressed continuity between Bonhoeffer's early and later thought. Where is this continuity to be found? For Phillips, Hodgson, Gibbs, Lehmann, Rasmussen and Godsey, Christology is the cord that binds together the Bonhoeffer corpus; for Ott it is the "reality theme"; for Dumas a Hegelian "structuring that combines self-knowledge with self-realization"; for Green the theology of sociality forged in his early work, and for Ogletree Bonhoeffer's focus on the church's relationship with and mission to the world.[47]

If those who emphasized continuity in Bonhoeffer's theological reflection gained the upper hand, it is because they showed more interest in Bonhoeffer's thought per se than in marshaling his authority to undergird their own positions. For instance, while *Honest to God* offered no in-depth analysis of Bonhoeffer's theology, Bishop

Robinson did assume that the fragments which caught his attention represented its "final flowering."[48] For his part, Paul van Buren admitted that he was "not primarily interested in Bonhoeffer, but in his paradox."[49] And in William Hamilton's landmark essay "Thursday's Child," where he considered whether the death-of-God theologians had discovered radical theology in Bonhoeffer and then in themselves, or in themselves and then rejoiced to find it in Bonhoeffer, Hamilton conceded that "the second is nearer the truth."[50]

Eberhard Bethge has lamented having been "too complacent in allowing certain sensational theses like the Death-of-God theologians to pass uncriticized."[51] Others did not commit that error, however. Contra the secularizers who were making so much of Bonhoeffer's prison writings, traditionalists claimed that he had neither left the Christian fold nor repudiated its beliefs and practices (as many of the secularizers themselves were doing). Bonhoeffer, they contended, was a tradition-grounded theologian who offered guidance for Christians trying to navigate the treacherous waters of secularity. In the cry of protest against the radical Bonhoeffer, three distinct responses could be heard: Bonhoeffer's last writings should be read in part as an expression of the physical and emotional pressure of life in a Nazi prison;[52] the radicals misinterpreted Bonhoeffer through glib associations with the thought of Tillich and Bultmann;[53] and they read Bonhoeffer's prison writings without regard for the rest of his theological corpus.

Naturally, orthodox theologians lamented radical theology's "destructive attitude to traditional Christianity."[54] But it was not only conservatives who resisted the radical portrait of Bonhoeffer disseminated by the secularizers. In 1966 David E. Jenkins, later Bishop of Durham and popular spokesman for prophetic Christianity in Great Britain, wrote that "to the day of his death Bonhoeffer remained a convinced Lutheran, [and] . . . that this faith was in Jesus Christ who is sufficiently and historically (and *not* mythically) shown to us in the gospels and that behind Jesus and in Jesus stood God." Whatever Bonhoeffer meant by his call to live "without religion," Jenkins wrote, it was not a call to live "without God."[55] The same year Paul Lehmann—a leading representative of liberal Protestantism and one of the few American theologians who had actually known Bonhoeffer—registered his disappointment with the direction Bonhoeffer scholarship had taken. "Seldom has an author, living or dead," he wrote, "been so misrepresented by his commentators and translators." The most conspicuous offenders, according to Lehmann, were the so-called death-of-God theologians who had interpreted certain phrases in Bonhoeffer's later writings "as a kind of quintessential 'new essence of Christianity.'"[56]

The effect of these complaints is difficult to gauge. But by the end of the 1960s Anglo-American radical theology had run its course and Bonhoeffer was once again firmly anchored within the broad parameters of Christian orthodoxy. In 1969 John A. Phillips expressed the frustration that Bonhoeffer's re-domestication had created among his radical interpreters. "Since the radicals had not read Bonhoeffer's letters in the light of his earlier works," Phillips observed, "Bonhoeffer scholarship could now enter the field, capitalize on the interest and set the record straight." In the process it had established a defensive Bonhoeffer who warns us that "we cannot move in this or that direction, or that we must take a little more orthodoxy with us as we go." Phillips had hoped, he wrote, to provide a Bonhoeffer clear enough for contemporary theology to move beyond, not the curriculum for a Bonhoeffer "school." But by 1969 the school had taken over "with its morning devotionals and lectures and concern for disciplining unruly students," and Phillips wanted no part of it.[57]

The Radical Bonhoeffer's "Impressive Unity"

In the previous chapter it was claimed that Bonhoeffer's reception has always been conditioned by the "impressive unity" between his life and thought. Does this observation apply to the radical Bonhoeffer as well? Did secularizing appropriations of Bonhoeffer rely on his "witness" as well as his radical ideas? On one hand, the death-of-God thinkers tended to focus on concepts in Bonhoeffer's writings that were fruitful for their own theological projects. On the other hand, as John Macquarrie wrote at the time, the secularizing theologians invoked Bonhoeffer's ideas "together with the glamour of their author's martyrdom."[58] In subtle ways they capitalized on his authority as an opponent of Nazism, a prisoner of conscience, and a victim of totalitarianism, highlighting his writings from prison at a time when thoughtful Americans were shaken by King's "Letter from Birmingham Jail."

The radicals also traded on Bonhoeffer's credibility outside the church and academy. For, as they loved to point out, radical theology was gaining a hearing among those who were deaf to the voice of the religious establishment. Robinson claimed in *Honest to God* that "Bonhoeffer is talked of where 'religion' does not penetrate." Hamilton added that Bonhoeffer was very much alive "where men are struggling with new forms of the congregation; where the problem of the Protestant and the city is being faced; where Negro and white students are trying to discern the ethical and theological implications of the radical forms of the civil rights movement."[59] Thus Bonhoeffer was a darling of radicals in part due to his credibility "on the street." Like the appropriations of Bonhoeffer surveyed elsewhere in this book, radical theology sought to capitalize on Bonhoeffer's moral authority as a way of buttressing its claims to legitimacy.

The Legacy of the Radical Bonhoeffer

The image of a radical Bonhoeffer is naturally associated with the secularizers of the 1960s who invoked him as both inspiration and authority. But the significance of Bonhoeffer the radical is not exhausted by his contested role in the death-of-God movement. We encounter Bonhoeffer the radical, in fact, whenever he is cast as a transitional figure or perceived as a prescient mind who glimpsed the lineaments of a new era—be it the age of the death of God, the time "after Christendom," or the postmodern. These perceptions derive credibility from Bonhoeffer's own awareness of living between the times on the brink of a "world come of age."[60]

Bonhoeffer after Christendom

Seeking to discredit the Constantinian model of the church's relationship to empire, Douglas John Hall identifies Bonhoeffer's ecclesiastical reflection as an aid in the "necessary transition from cultural Christianity to new forms of Christian life and witness."[61] But the desire to make Bonhoeffer a spokesman for post-Constantinian Christianity is most prominent among those who regard him as presaging postmodern theology. For scholars such as Ronald Thiemann, Walter Lowe, Wayne Whitson Floyd Jr., Barry Harvey, and Hans D. van Hoogstraten, Bonhoeffer's writings reveal remarkable parallels with contemporary postmodernism.

Van Hoogstraten compares Bonhoeffer's antimetaphysical pronouncements in *Letters and Papers from Prison* with the postmodern critique of metaphysics by Richard Rorty and Gianni Vattimo.[62] Harvey asserts that Bonhoeffer's "deconstruction of religion" provides a point of departure for developing a postcritical theological critique of a rationalized society.[63] Lowe attempts to establish a conversation between Bonhoeffer and deconstruction, noting that the postmodern vision—with its dissolution of any unitary, "metaphysical" world picture, and the "deconstruction" of the human subject—bears a similarity to Bonhoeffer's account of "a world which would have outgrown the temporary crutches of metaphysics and inwardness."[64]

Floyd claims that Bonhoeffer's thought resists foundationalism and that from the time of *Act and Being* Bonhoeffer pursued a nonmetaphysical, antisystematic approach to theology. It is surprising, Floyd writes, to find postmodernism's subversion of the subject already described by Bonhoeffer in just such terms in his *Habilitationsscrhift* of 1931.[65] Floyd proposes that the future of Bonhoeffer's theology may lie in a critical appreciation of the *style* of his thought and its expression in fragmentary *form*, for in the fragmentariness of the letter Bonhoeffer "comes closest to being able to let the future speak in the present . . ."[66]

Thiemann observes that Bonhoeffer's work is "remarkably prescient" of the situation at the beginning of the third millennium. Indeed, the thoughts published in *Letters and Papers from Prison* provocatively foreshadow contemporary postmodernism, as Bonhoeffer not only "describes the fundamental character of our postmodern condition but also provides us with the basic outlines of a Christian theology appropriate to these times."[67] Those of us living in a postmodern age can learn from figures such as Bonhoeffer, George Orwell, and Anna Akmatova, Thiemann claims, as we "struggle to recapture a sense of the morally and spiritually motivated public intellectual."

Like other radical interpreters of Bonhoeffer, Thiemann is drawn to the prison writings, particularly Bonhoeffer's letter of April 30, 1944, in which he admits being bothered by the question "who Christ really is, for us today." Thiemann recognizes in Bonhoeffer's musings on this question important hints for the development of a Christian theology that is "genuinely Christocentric yet fundamentally connected to those who do not confess the name of Christ." "In a manner strikingly akin to postmodern thinkers," Thiemann maintains, Bonhoeffer sketches a theology that is "non-metaphysical and non-foundational, in solidarity with the powerless and suffering, and committed to righteous action in perilous and uncertain situations."[68]

Thiemann concludes that Bonhoeffer "did not respond to the challenges of the modern period by seeking transcendental, metaphysical, or foundational arguments to shore up the Christian claims to revelation." Rather, like postmodern philosophers, he eschewed "totalizing and universalizing schemes" to develop a theology and an ethics that are non-foundational and situational.[69] Thiemann is particularly taken by Bonhoeffer's affirmation of solidarity with the other, which he finds "reminiscent of Derrida's deconstructive philosophy." This theology of solidarity is resolutely Christocentric, Thiemann observes, despite remaining vigorously connected to the non-Christian "Other."

According to Thiemann, the spiritually motivated public intellectual must find in Bonhoeffer a model of the "connected critic" who is part of communities of commitment and engagement.[70] Like Bonhoeffer, such critics help us negotiate life "between the times" in a postmodern age.

The Marxist Bonhoeffer

In 1964 Harvey Cox remarked that the reader of Bonhoeffer who is familiar with Marx cannot help noticing "certain remarkable areas of similarity."[71] But while intellectuals in the capitalist West took note of such resemblances, some in Eastern Europe used them to fashion a portrait of Bonhoeffer the harbinger of postwar socialism. As Hanfried Müller, the leading East German exponent of the Marxist Bonhoeffer, wrote in 1961,

anyone who has anything to do with Dietrich Bonhoeffer today realizes again and again the amazing extent to which he provides answers to questions that only now, some twenty years later, begin to raise their heads. He anticipated solutions for problems we are only now beginning to recognize as our problems. When I speak here of "us" and "we," I mean those among us who see the necessity of thinking in the light of the revolutionary upheaval of our time, during the course of which central Europe has seen the socialization of society.[72]

During the 1960s and 1970s, Müller and other regime-friendly theologians in the German Democratic Republic capitalized on Bonhoeffer's antifascist identity by interpreting selections from his writings as legitimations of Marxist-Leninist ideology. Of course, casting Bonhoeffer as "all but a Marxist" strained credulity for anyone familiar with his life.[73] But the desire to portray the anti-Nazi crusader as a "champion of proletarian liberation" was driven by fears that he might become, as he eventually did, a focus for political opposition in the GDR.

Naturally, postwar European communists were attracted by Bonhoeffer's heroic struggle against fascism in its political and ecclesiastical forms. But GDR party strategists went further, gleaning from Bonhoeffer's writings values that resonated with communist propaganda, including humanism, commitment to world peace, and support for the labor movement. Further, because Bonhoeffer had waged "a consistent struggle against bourgeois nationalism" in the ecumenical movement, communists invoked his memory "to persuade the contemporary international ecumenical movement to make common cause with them against the warmongering West."[74]

Like other radical interpreters of Bonhoeffer, Marxists argued for an intellectual break after which he was drawn in a distinctly "nonreligious" direction.[75] Müller, for instance, carefully traced Bonhoeffer's "movement" toward Marxism by drawing an evolutionary picture dominated by images of "development" and "process." Because Bonhoeffer so clearly evolved in the direction of Marxist understanding, Müller argued, he legitimately belongs to those who recognize "the historical and objective significance" of a "stable and complete" development toward socialism.[76] In other words, we cannot carry forward Bonhoeffer's thought by fixing on a "transitory stage of his life as a key to understanding him," particularly if we are devoted to "the restoration of a Christian world whose collapse Bonhoeffer freely anticipated . . ."[77]

Far from being fragmentary and contradictory, in Müller's view the prison writings clarify Bonhoeffer's ideas and reveal "the final and highest stage" of his thought. This is especially clear when the prison writings are contrasted with *Ethics*, where we encounter a restorationist Bonhoeffer concerned with rescuing "the grand heritage of the Christian West in the face of Nazism" and unaware that fascism is bourgeois society's "last stage of decay." What happened to Bonhoeffer between the writing of *Ethics* and the end of his life? During the war years he took the step from conservative opposition to Hitler to an antifascism based not in a restoration of the past but in boldly grasping what was to come.[78]

According to Müller, the "breakthrough" occurred in 1944 when Bonhoeffer "progressed to an advanced bourgeois anti-fascism." While he never used the term "revolution," Bonhoeffer did perceive the contradictions in the bourgeois revolution that animated the Enlightenment and recognized the counterrevolutionary character of Nazism. These insights enabled him to confront fascism with the "revolutionary heritage of the Reformation" and recognize the sufferings of God in the world. He who does so, Müller writes, "is set free to see the world *etsi deus non daretur,* as though God were not given, freed for an atheistic world view."[79] Yet Müller stresses that Bonhoeffer's "religionlessness" does not mean what "intellectual sceptics with nihilistic overtones" claim, but a "healthy, common, socially active, strong, optimistic, world mastering atheism." For Marxist atheism is "not intellectual but positive, productive, and progressive."[80]

It is important to place Müller's radical reading of Bonhoeffer in political context, for one of its goals was to convince the East German pastorate to accept the rule of so-called real existing socialism as "perfectly consistent with the essence of the gospel."[81] From his post at Humboldt University, and with the help of his wife Rosemarie Müller-Streisandt and other members of the Weissensee Circle, Müller promoted a pro-communist, "refunctioned" Bonhoeffer theology of church and state.[82] While the Marxist Bonhoeffer is easily dismissed as a product of political necessity, he ought to be viewed in tandem with the Bonhoeffer who inspired the religio-political opposition that led to the East German government's downfall (reviewed in the next chapter).

Assessing the Radical Bonhoeffer

We must ask whether it makes sense to speak of the radical Bonhoeffer apart from the liberal Bonhoeffer described in the following chapter. After all, attempts to establish Christian faith's relevance for contemporary culture have long been associated with the liberal impulse in Christian theology. Don't Robinson, Hamilton, Altizer, van Buren, and Müller, then, belong in the broad category of liberal interpretations of Bonhoeffer's legacy? The key to distinguishing radical and liberal portraits of Bonhoeffer is to be found in radicals' desire to lift Bonhoeffer out of his own age by demonstrating that he saw beyond it; liberals, meanwhile, are more concerned with Bonhoeffer's time and place and its connections with our own.[83]

For radicals Bonhoeffer is a "seer"—a man born out of time who perceived the future with uncanny prescience. Some radical interpreters are quite explicit about Bonhoeffer's putative break with the past. On the epoch-making significance of Bonhoeffer's prison writings, Vahanian reminds us that "it is not the first time that an age has come to an end":

> Did not the Judaeo-Christians of Antioch experience something comparable when the apostle Paul insisted that the gospel must be de-Judaicized in order both to preserve its integrity and make it accessible to pagans (Gal. 2:1-21)? . . . Indeed, the gulf that separates Christianity from the modern world is infinitely greater than the gap between nascent Christianity and the pre-Christian world.

We stand today, Vahanian claims, at another "decisive crossroads of Christianity."[84] Similarly, Harvey Cox describes Bonhoeffer as one who foresaw "the transition today from the age of Christendom to the new era of urban secularity." Standing on the border between church and the world, he perceived "frontier issues" that continue to perplex us. "His uncanny capacity to uncover the hidden skeletons in the closets of theology and to see issues coming around the corner," Cox writes, means that we cannot move beyond him.[85] The conviction that Bonhoeffer was the harbinger of a historical turning point contributes to radicals' eagerness to liberate him from the confines of the Christian tradition, a desire particularly evident among the death-of-God theologians.[86]

Assuming that the radical Bonhoeffer does in fact represent a distinct contribution to his overall reception, how should its significance be assessed? First, it must be acknowledged that the images of Bonhoeffer fashioned by his radical interpreters reflect the time and place in which they came into vogue. We have already observed how the Marxist Bonhoeffer is inscribed with the vicissitudes of the East German experience. It is also helpful to view the radical Bonhoeffer of Anglo-American theology as one manifestation of a particular social milieu. As Keith Clements writes, Bonhoeffer's role in the radical theology movements of the 1960s was psychological as much as intellectual, his appeal being greatest among those who were coming of age at the time, "who felt the need to submit Christian faith and practice to ordeal by questioning, and yet to remain identified with the Christian tradition."[87]

Just how well Bonhoeffer's radical portrait conformed to the ethos of the 1960s is suggested by those who were alienated from the institutions and creeds associated with traditional religion, but were admirers of Bonhoeffer nevertheless. Writing in 1969, Robert E. Huldschiner related the comments of a group of Japanese TV producers: "Religion just doesn't interest us. But we have read Bonhoeffer, and there is a man we understand, a true humanist who rejected religion just as we have." Huldshiner comments: "It is the unhappy genius of Dietrich Bonhoeffer to have coined a few easily translatable terms (religionless Christianity, man for others, world come of age) that could be cheerfully misunderstood by all those around the globe in search of respectable support for their rejection of a religious dimension for life."[88]

Another aspect of the intellectual milieu in which the radical Bonhoeffer emerged should not be overlooked. This chapter began by noting that Bonhoeffer's initial reception in America (and to a lesser extent in Europe) cast him as a dialectical theologian in the Barthian mold. We are now prepared to understand how this image of Bonhoeffer determined his role in radical theology. Just as dialectical theology can be understood as a sustained assault on the patriarchs of "liberalism" by the World War I generation, it is useful to see radical theology as an attack on the neoorthodox parent by its rebellious children. As Langdon Gilkey made clear at the time, the death-of-God movement represented "an explicit and potent rejection of the dominant neoorthodox 'establishment' in theology that preceded it."[89] Neoorthodoxy's comfortable position in the seminaries, its pessimism regarding human nature, its existentialist turn to the inner life, and its avoidance of the problems associated with religious language all came under attack by theologians who fashioned themselves "real radicals."

In a withering critique, William Hamilton wrote: "it is ironical that neoorthodoxy, born as a radical protest against liberal conformism, became one of the fashionable ideologies for the Eisenhower period in American intellectual life—that time when men sagely advised us that the real battle was not bohemia or radical politics or ideology, but the mystery of the inner life."[90] To this social quietism Hamilton juxtaposed the "new optimism" to which he and other radical theologians were attuned, an optimism resonating with the "move from alienation to politics, from blues to the freedom song." It is no coincidence that the radical theologians portrayed themselves as being "with the Negro community in its struggle." For they conceived of their relationship to the religious establishment as analogous to that of Martin Luther King Jr., who had revealed the deep-seated conservatism of white "moderates."

Significantly, Hamilton used that very term to describe the "Honest-to-God, ecclesiastical school" of radical theology, as well as to criticize the neoorthodoxy that had become socially irrelevant. In contrast, the true radicals boasted of being "nonmoderate" in matters sexual and political.[91] The death-of-God movement, then, responded not only to the church's perceived irrelevance in a "world come of age," but to crisis theology's steady loss of social radicalism over the course of the twentieth century. Since the radical interpreters of Bonhoeffer tended to be former Barthians, they took discernible glee in attacking the theological father with tools fashioned by one of his own sons.

Second, it must be conceded that radical theology was insufficiently attentive to many of Bonhoeffer's own concerns. Some death-of-God thinkers claimed that their optimism was rooted in Bonhoeffer's own perceptions of the movement of history. But there are significant problems with this linkage. Not only did Bonhoeffer's recognition of "the world come of age" not entail the sort of optimism evinced by the 60s radicals,[92] but these theologians never came to terms with personal suffering—or solidarity with those who suffer—in the way Bonhoeffer did. In a 1996 symposium at which some of the death-of-Goders were asked to reflect on their early encounter with the Holocaust, it became clear that this encounter had occurred largely in retrospect.[93]

Indeed, it is ironic that during the 1960s scrutiny of Bonhoeffer's theological legacy focused so narrowly on aphoristic pronouncements from his last writings; this at a time when his legacy vis-à-vis the "Jewish question" and racial issues more generally might have spoken prophetically to American culture. Radical theologians in America, particularly William Hamilton, boasted that they were more politically involved and more invested in the "Negro question" than the neoorthodox theologians under whom they had trained. However, despite their fascination with Bonhoeffer, there is little evidence that these theologians imagined how his commitments with regard to race might be fleshed out in an era of social turmoil.

Another area in which Bonhoeffer's radical interpreters failed to gauge the man is evident in their un-Bonhoefferian perceptions of the church and the practices that sustain it. Jackson Ice and John Carey have observed that the American death-of-God movement aroused such strong reactions in part because most churchmen perceived the radical theologians as "strongly antichurch [and] opposed to personal piety." The work of these supertheologians—"often nonchurch in orientation and outlook"—became the source of numerous "diatribes against ministers, institutions, and policies."[94] To be fair, the radicals were at home in the world of academic theology and were thus largely uninterested in demonstrating how Bonhoeffer could be used to invigorate the American church. Still, the antiecclesiastical orientation of Anglo-American radical theology makes it difficult to understand the movement's claim on Bonhoeffer.

Whatever Bonhoeffer meant by "religionless Christianity," he certainly did not think it eclipsed the need for prayer, worship, or sacrament. As Larry Rasmussen reminds us, even when he was decrying "religion" from prison, Bonhoeffer continued to practice regular prayer and meditation. Rasmussen claims, in fact, that to the extent that secularizing appropriations of Bonhoeffer overlooked worship and tradition, they missed Bonhoeffer "almost entirely."[95] Yet with the exception of Bishop Robinson, the Anglo-American radical theologians were notorious for their irreligion, including their repudiation of all forms of communication with (or on behalf of) a personal God. In the words of John Macquarrie, the secularizers' disregard for spiritual practices meant that their "religionless" Christianity was actually "instant" Christianity. Unlike Bonhoeffer, they failed to understand that spiritual maturity is something attained only through discipline and training.[96]

While insisting that they remained Christians who were firmly grounded in the "essentials" of the biblical tradition, the radicals explicitly repudiated traditional forms of Christian spiritual practice. Altizer wrote that the theologian "must exist outside of the church: he can neither proclaim the Word, celebrate the sacraments, nor rejoice in the presence of the Holy Spirit." And Hamilton: "If prayer is defined as a religious form of address to a personalized being called God, then we can make nothing of it at all."[97] Bonhoeffer—even the Bonhoeffer of the prison writings—seems as far removed from such attitudes as the Christian fundamentalist.

Noting these distortions in the portrait of the radical Bonhoeffer, as well as the ways they are rooted in the ethos the 1960s, leads us to wonder about its enduring impact. For some, the radical Bonhoeffer represents a false start in Bonhoeffer interpretation. Others have regarded radical theology's embrace of Bonhoeffer as little more than a nuisance. In 1967 Jaroslav Pelikan lamented that "a couple of pages from [Bonhoeffer's] *Letters and Papers from Prison* have become, quite distortedly, the program of those who announce 'the death of God.'"[98] Pelikan placed these secularizers on the same intellectual level as chapel-shy undergraduates. Yet the death-of-God movement had the ironic effect of establishing Bonhoeffer as a seminal theologian in his own right, as an inspiration for professional theologians as well as a hero for disaffected youth.

Nevertheless, because radical theology was so short-lived and widely excoriated, if the radical Bonhoeffer's significance is tied up with the fate of death-of-God movement, its legacy would seem to be quite meager. In 1967 Jackson Lee Ice and John J. Carey wrote that death-of-God theology was "here to stay, whether we like it or not."[99] Yet by 1970 radical theology had been eclipsed by a host of emerging liberationist approaches that made this erstwhile religious vanguard look like another movement dominated by white male professors in elite divinity schools. In the meantime, the radical Bonhoeffer had been discredited by prominent scholars who viewed his use by the death-of-God group as a grievous misinterpretation.

Still, the influence of the radical Bonhoeffer can be detected today in ongoing debates over whether particular readings of his work are compatible with the "real Bonhoeffer." This question, which emerged with urgency in the wake of radical readings of Bonhoeffer's legacy by Müller, Robinson, van Buren, and Hamilton, implies another: How are the parameters of this authentic Bonhoeffer to be determined? Should we defer in all things to those who knew him? With particular reference to Bonhoeffer's letters and papers from prison, most of which were addressed to Eberhard Bethge, should Bethge's construals be regarded as authoritative? If so, then does his conclusion that the death-of-God theologians "misinterpreted and misunderstood" Bonhoeffer, indeed "tampered with his thought, and with an insufficient knowledge of his work, did violence to or destroyed his dialectical way of expressing himself," obligate us to regard the radical Bonhoeffer as a fabrication?[100]

It seems that a balanced response to these questions must acknowledge the problem in trusting any interpreter—including Bethge—to communicate what Bonhoeffer meant by words he himself did not have time to elaborate, terms he did not clearly define ("religion"), or thoughts he never fully developed ("the religionless interpretation of biblical concepts"). As J. Sperna Weiland reminded us in 1968, in attempting to comprehend the texts on which the radical Bonhoeffer rests, "we have very little material at our disposal—only eight or ten letters, written within a period of less than four months, a total of about forty to fifty pages of text."[101] Filling such textual gaps requires imagination as well as exegesis. Thus, the hermeneutical question raised by radical appropriations of Bonhoeffer's writings—to wit, what are the parameters of valid interpretation?—remains quite relevant.

There was evidence of enduring interest in this hermeneutical question at the 1996 International Bonhoeffer Congress, where Ralf K. Wüstenberg revisited "Bonhoeffer's Tegel Theology" with the aim of correcting long-standing misunderstandings of "what Bonhoeffer actually meant."[102] Readings of Bonhoeffer's letters from prison that cast him as an "atheist," "secularist," or the "father of death-of-God theology" reflect the perspectives of the interpreters rather than the assumptions of Bonhoeffer himself, Wüstenberg argued. This conclusion was no doubt justified, as were Wüstenberg's claims that the interpreters in question had neither plumbed the sources for Bonhoeffer's views of "religion" and "nonreligiousness" in Barth and Dilthey nor taken into account "how profoundly his theology was informed by his Christology."[103] But their rehearsal thirty years after the influence of death-of-God theology had peaked is indicative of the way the radical Bonhoeffer continues to provoke controversy and resistance.

The prophets still walk among us, and I believe that I have traversed a certain distance with a prophetically gifted man, Dietrich Bonhoeffer.

—GAETANO LATMIRAL

Following the admonition of Bonhoeffer that the church must be the church for others and that Christians must be people for others, the churches in every time and place must stand in solidarity with those who are hated, objectified, oppressed, denied fundamental human and civil rights, victimized by alienating stereotypes, or otherwise isolated and treated unjustly by any institution of society or government.

—DOUGLAS A. HUNEKE

Not surprisingly, Bonhoeffer the conspirator is an attractive figure for theologians of Latin America and other regions burdened by neocolonial legacies, where options for democratic struggles and reform have been foreclosed by police-state repression.

—G. CLARKE CHAPMAN

PROPHET

THE LIBERAL BONHOEFFER

Was Bonhoeffer a liberal? Many assume that he was. After all, he possessed immense respect for his teacher Adolf von Harnack, the quintessential liberal theologian of his generation,[1] was indebted intellectually to theological liberalism, and shared its vital concern "that the world be taken seriously and that an effort be made to understand modern man without resort to the use of Christian euphemisms or clichés."[2] Bonhoeffer even exemplified liberalism's attitude toward tradition by adapting the Christian message to changes in his social and intellectual environment. But the purpose of this chapter is not to clarify Bonhoeffer's relationship to theological liberalism but to plot his reception by religious and secular liberals in the years since his death. As we shall see, Bonhoeffer's liberal portrait is constructed from images of a prophetic figure who, because he was committed to following Christ in his own time, is a model for us as well.

Tracking the Liberal Bonhoeffer

It is not surprising that Bonhoeffer's role in the German Church Struggle and his active opposition to Hitler have made him something of a hero for liberal Protestants, or that this heroic image is reflected in periodicals such as *Christianity and Crisis* and the *Christian Century*. *Christianity and Crisis* was actually the first magazine to bring Bonhoeffer to the attention of American Protestants, a fact not unrelated to the editorial role of Bonhoeffer's friend Reinhold Niebuhr. In 1945 *C & C* noted Bonhoeffer's "martyrdom," and in the 1960s published articles on various aspects of his legacy. Attention to the German theologian in the magazine's pages waned after 1970, however, and *Christianity and Crisis* ceased publication in 1993.[3]

Serious considerations of Bonhoeffer have been a staple of the *Christian Century* since 1959, and their frequency has increased over the years. Between 1945 and 1975, thirteen *Century* pieces dealt substantially with Bonhoeffer and his legacy, while nineteen Bonhoeffer-related items appeared in the relatively brief period between 1995 and 2003.[4] What dimensions of Bonhoeffer's life and thought are appealing to the liberal Protestant constituencies served by these publications? How are these dimensions of Bonhoeffer's liberal portrait understood and communicated? These questions will guide us through the remainder of this chapter.

Bonhoeffer and the Church's Public Vocation

Concern for the church's role in society is a dimension of Bonhoeffer's legacy that interests a broad array of interpreters, but has received particular attention from liberals. As Geffrey B. Kelly argues, Bonhoeffer was convinced that the church was the church only when it existed for others, even if this meant "unflinchingly to accept the 'death' of its present forms and the denial of some of its less-than-central aims." Kelly notes that Bonhoeffer's 1932 lectures on ecclesiology were deeply critical of the German church's tendency to occupy "the privileged places . . . among the bourgeois" and that its course during the ensuing years only heightened Bonhoeffer's sense that the church could not "take a forthright stand on any issue other than its own survival."[5] Kelly regards Bonhoeffer's confession of the German church's guilt for its failure to exercise "responsible action" and "to suffer for what is known to be right" as a charge directed at the contemporary church for its "flight from the world into the safe haven of religiosity and sacramentality."[6] For Kelly, Bonhoeffer's theology represents a profound challenge to the churches, as does his participation in the conspiracy to overthrow Hitler: "Bonhoeffer's imprisonment and execution were a lonely witness to where the church ought to have been: the 20th century's Golgotha of Nazi prisons and scaffolds."[7]

In discussing the church's public vocation, Larry Rasmussen links Bonhoeffer and Reinhold Niebuhr, both of whom regarded public engagement as a proper activity of the theologian. Decrying Reagan-Bush America's co-optation of "Judeo-Christian values" to legitimate itself as "a righteous empire in a world read largely in Manichean terms,"[8] Rasmussen looks to Bonhoeffer and Niebuhr in developing a "permanent eschatology" in which a non-triumphalist community of the cross assumes the sort of public posture that relativizes all authorities and "breaks the hold of controlling ideologies." The public role of an eschatological community of the cross, Rasmussen contends, includes "ministry centered in the flawed faces of human life as this is manifest in suffering of all kinds."[9]

In comparing Bonhoeffer with theologians Douglas John Hall and Stanley Hauerwas, Rasmussen explores his Lutheran theology of the cross.[10] There is no *theologia crucis* in North America, Rasmussen observes; rather, the working theology of North American culture and Christianity is a "theology of glory" that is, in Bonhoeffer's words, "the religious rounding off of an [essentially] profane conception of the universe."[11] Bonhoeffer's contribution to North American Christianity, then, "is to envision and embody a community of the cross with an ethic of imitation, or participation, as the church's societal vocation and presence."[12]

Just as Rasmussen looked to Bonhoeffer to illuminate the serious demands of discipleship during the Reagan years, Geffrey B. Kelly utilized Bonhoefferian insights to expose the "idolatries" behind the so-called Republican revolution of 1994. Among these Kelly includes the worship of material prosperity, consumerism and its callous disregard for the less fortunate, and the cult of violence associated with national security. Bonhoeffer's theology offers a "prophetic critique" of such idolatrous behavior precisely because America in the mid-1990s had so much in common with Hitlerian Germany. One of the reasons so many Germans paid homage to Hitler during the 1930s, Kelly writes, was that he had delivered them from economic deprivation and the ravages of depression. "Hitler had promised the German people a 'new world order'; the Republican Congress has made a similar promise through its 'Contract with America.'"[13] Kelly reminds us that in *The Cost of Discipleship* Bonhoeffer wrote that Christians must have "an irresistible love for the downtrodden, the sick, the wretched, the wronged, the outcast and all who are tortured with anxiety." In stark contrast, Kelly notes, the American religious right supports policies that "single out the poorest, weakest citizens to bear the brunt of the suffering inevitable in any budget-slashing legislation."[14]

As we shall see when we encounter Daniel Berrigan's 1970 review of Eberhard Bethge's biography of Bonhoeffer, the practice of utilizing the German theologian in sustained criticisms of the American government is over thirty years old. In 1971 theologian Robert M. Brown offered a systematic application of Bonhoeffer's experience to the situation of the American church in a time of war. For Brown, Bonhoeffer's story took on increased meaning as he came to believe that churchmen today must be willing to oppose evil policies of evil governments and that the evil policy of the American government in Southeast Asia made it an evil government. "I have tried to resist making facile comparisons between nazi Germany and the United States," Brown wrote, "but as the Vietnam war has mounted in intensity, the Bonhoeffer experience has seemed more and more relevant to the American experience."[15]

Bonhoeffer and Critical Patriotism

Related to the liberal project of applying Bonhoeffer's prophetic vision to conceptions of the church's role in society are attempts to problematize reigning assumptions about the Christian meaning of patriotism. Liberal commentators stress that Bonhoeffer's religious convictions led him to eschew uncritical obedience to his nation and reject theologies that affirmed the state as a direct expression of God's will. They also place before us two uncomfortable aspects of Bonhoeffer's legacy—that he held pacifist views, worked avidly for peace, and sought to avoid military conscription; and that he became actively involved in treason against his government. Counterintuitive though it may seem, liberals argue that it is precisely in his tortured relationship with the German nation that Bonhoeffer became the patriot par excellence. In recent decades Bonhoeffer's critical patriotism has been applied to crises as diverse as the Vietnam War, the Falklands conflict, nuclear deterrence, American involvement in the Arab world, and the use of revolutionary violence.

The most substantial consideration of Bonhoeffer's relevance for a Christian understanding of patriotism and civil religion is Keith W. Clements's *A Patriotism for Today: Love of Country in Dialogue with the Witness of Dietrich Bonhoeffer*. In the wake of the Falklands War and the resurgence of British nationalism it evoked, Clements was concerned with what "patriotism" meant for contemporary Britain. Insisting that being British and loving Britain should not be left to the political right, Clements claimed that "there is much in Bonhoeffer that calls us in Britain, too, to re-examine the ways in which we relate to our country."[16]

Clements observed that Bonhoeffer's life was charged with a tension between being Christian and being German, a tension captured in Eberhard Bethge's description of Bonhoeffer's relationship with his homeland in terms of "exile and martyrdom." As loyalty to Christ and loyalty to country became increasingly incompatible, Bonhoeffer had to face the question whether "one could maintain one's Christian identity other than by distancing oneself form the rest of the people and indeed much of the church."[17] According to Clements, we are aided in addressing this question not only by Bonhoeffer's life, but by his notion of "orders of preservation," which he elaborated in 1932 in response to nationalist and racist applications of the traditional "orders of creation." In Clements's view, Bonhoeffer's understanding of people and nation as orders of preservation "prevents a falsely exalted view of country and a pathological form of patriotism."[18]

Clements also found contemporary salience in Bonhoeffer's insistence that Christians accept guilt—personally and corporately—for the crimes of Nazis and Germans more generally. One of Bonhoeffer's most significant contributions, Clements insisted, is the way he "transposed the traditional Lutheran theme of guilt and forgiveness into a key other than that of purely individual salvation."[19] Bonhoeffer's message is not that patriotism always ends in idolatry, but that loyalty to country must include "recognition and acceptance of one's country's guilt, and intercession and action for its expiation." In any case, following Bonhoeffer patriotism can never again carry the traditional sense.[20]

In another elaboration of the liberal Bonhoeffer, Donald W. Shriver brings his legacy to bear on the task of distinguishing authentic Christianity from American civil religion.[21] Americans have no trouble believing, Shriver observes, that Adolf Hitler's assassination was God's

will, or that Bonhoeffer was a saint partly because he died in that political cause. Yet they fail to realize that most members of the Confessing
Church were far from convinced of these things. More crucially, there
is hardly a politician or political institution that they would consent to
destroying on theological grounds. This is because, seen from inside,
almost nothing about the nation is unambiguously good or evil. For
this reason Bonhoeffer is "the theological tutor most needed by the
American pietist, the American churches, and the refugee people of
American civil religion."[22]

Larry Rasmussen is another liberal thinker who perceives in Bonhoeffer a "stimulus for reflection on our own reality." The reality to
which Rasmussen refers is American society at the end of the 1980s,
the Reagan-Bush years in which patriotism was accompanied by a
surge of religious vitality. But is American "religious patriotism" true
patriotism? Rasmussen asks. And what can Bonhoeffer teach us here?
There is no doubt but that the Bonhoeffers resisted Hitler precisely
because they were Germans; yet since most Germans did not resist in
this way, we must ask what made them different. In Dietrich's case, it
was experience abroad, his habit of trekking to "what were for him the
margins in order to see the center from the edges and, if need be, to
relocate his viewpoint."[23]

The price Bonhoeffer paid for this transnational perspective was the
lingering suspicion—even among members of the Confessing
Church—that he was anti-German, soft on communism, an enemy of
the state. But Bonhoeffer revealed the depth of his "ecumenical
patriot[ism]" by returning to his homeland in 1939 as war loomed.
"The privilege of ecumenical refuge had to be set aside for the sake of
being an authentically Christian German," Rasmussen remarks.[24]
What can Bonhoeffer's "patriotism of conspiracy" teach us about the
substance of Christian patriotism in contemporary America? Among
other things, a patriotism in the spirit of Bonhoeffer will be faithful to
the "cosmopolitanism of the body of Christ" and view its own nation
from "external and marginal points of view."[25]

In order to elucidate Bonhoeffer's lessons for North Americans, Rasmussen compares him with indigenous religious figures including
Daniel Berrigan. Since Father Berrigan was engaged in active political
resistance during the Vietnam era, there is a natural affinity here. In
fact, when Berrigan went underground to elude the FBI in 1970, he

took with him Bethge's biography of Bonhoeffer. In a published "review" of the book, Berrigan made it plain that he viewed his activism through the lens of Bonhoeffer's life:

> I begin these notes on 9 April 1970. Two hours ago, at 8:30 A.M.,
>   I became a fugitive from injustice, having disobeyed
>   a federal court order to begin
> a three-year sentence for destruction of draft files two years ago.
> It is the twenty-fifth anniversary of the death of Dietrich Bonhoeffer
>   in Flossenbürg prison, for resistance to Hitler.[26]

"I think I know the direction of Bonhoeffer's life—even from here," Berrigan wrote. Indeed, as Rasmussen observes, parallels between the two men extend beyond the decision to undertake "some drastic action of resistance" and include a strong theology of the cross, a love/hate relationship with the church, an intense sense of national and ecclesiastical guilt (related to accusations of war crimes against their governments), and an affinity for Gandhi. Ultimately, their decisions with regard to revolutionary violence differed; still, Berrigan could cite Bonhoeffer as a model for his moral resistance to the Vietnam War, which he regarded as "a parable in its genocidal character to Hitler's war and his near extinction of the German Jews . . ."[27]

"I am responsible," Berrigan reminded his readers, "not to the warmakers and purveyors of violence but to the community of peacemaking resistance."[28] In the post-Vietnam era those who claimed to speak for this community tried to stake out a Bonhofferian position on Cold War deterrence. In Great Britain, Keith Clements cautiously applied Bonhoeffer's legacy to debates over the morality of nuclear armament, writing that "it is difficult to believe that, had Bonhoeffer survived, he would have done other than regard [nuclear weapons] as signs of the ultimate human apostasy, in face of the divine command to preserve life and not to kill."[29] American G. Clarke Chapman reached a similar conclusion. Concerned that the image of Bonhoeffer the political conspirator might be "contorted to one of Bonhoeffer the reluctant Cold Warrior," Chapman denied that the Cold War presented a credible parallel with Nazi Germany. In fact, Chapman asserted, America's "brew of Messianic nationalism, injured innocence, and crusading confidence," far more resembles the ideology Bonhoeffer opposed.

The segment of Bonhoeffer's life that most nearly matches "our situation" in 1988, Chapman wrote, is the "peacemaking" Bonhoeffer of the early 1930s, whose energy was focused on the "supreme totalism" that threatened peace. What would Bonhoeffer say to Christian peacemakers today?

> He would, I believe, denounce once again the totalism that endangers peace. That is, he would brush aside the tactical, political, and perhaps even the moral arguments about the Bomb which are common today. Instead he would push decisively to the theological core of the matter: the idolatry that befuddles minds, the new form of totalism which displaces Christ. For us, in this time and place, it is not fascism that is the issue. Nor, arguably, is it even Communism. Instead the totalism we confront is "nuclearism."[30]

In Chapman's view our world is connected to Bonhoeffer's not by our resistance to "godless communism" but by nuclearism—an idolatry rivaling that of Nazism.

More recently, the relevance of Bonhoeffer's critical patriotism for American politics has been emphasized by Geffrey B. Kelly and F. Burton Nelson. In the wake of Gulf War I, the "9/11" terrorist attacks, and the war in Afghanistan, Kelly and Nelson noted that American audiences with an interest in Bonhoeffer assumed that he would have supported recent U.S. military activities:

> Because so many Americans have turned Bonhoeffer into a folk hero and modern martyr, they seem to expect that Bonhoeffer would have been proud of the way in which the United States has been a force for peace in the world ever since the allied victory in World War II. If they would examine Bonhoeffer's writings more carefully, however, they might find a withering condemnation of any political system, including that of the United States, that engages in ideological, domineering, manipulative attitudes toward vulnerable peoples and nations.[31]

Bonhoeffer's spirituality, Kelly and Nelson continued, "stands as a bracing reminder to America's gung-ho 'patriots' that war, however well orchestrated by skilled politicians, brilliant military strategies, and smooth spinners of presidential policies, is still a denial of the gospel teachings of Jesus Christ."[32] These words were published just as America prepared to invade Iraq in 2003.

Bonhoeffer and Christian Ecumenism

Larry Rasmussen contends that through his involvement in the international ecumenical movement Bonhoeffer "subordinated his national citizenship to membership in the transnational church."[33] As this gloss on Bonhoeffer reveals, the German theologian's relevance for contemporary liberalism is often tied up with his role as an ecumenical peace activist. Bonhoeffer's period of ecumenical activity, like his life, was relatively brief; yet its effects on him and ecumenism generally were lasting.

Bonhoeffer dated his first experience of "ecumenical Christianity" to his sojourn in Spain (1928–29), when he made his first real contact with Roman Catholicism.[34] This was followed by a series of encounters with the wider church during the 1930s. In 1931 Bonhoeffer was named youth secretary of the World Alliance for Promoting Friendship through the Churches. In 1934, at the age of twenty-eight, he became a member of the governing council of the World Alliance, and during his ministry to German congregations in London from 1933 to 1935 he worked closely with the British churches. Even though Bonhoeffer was absent from some major ecumenical meetings during the 1930s, his impact was felt.[35]

Particularly important was the role Bonhoeffer played in preparation for the 1934 meeting in Fanö, Denmark, which has been described as a "one-man campaign to mobilize the ecumenical movement for action" with regard to the German Church Struggle.[36] Bonhoeffer was relentless in trying to convince the movement's leadership (most of whom were a generation older than him) that if the movement did not pass judgment on the German situation it would become a useless association in which nice speeches are delivered: "For the sake of Jesus Christ and the ecumenical cause it is necessary to speak quite honestly, especially concerning our attitude to the state. It must become clear—however terrible this is—that we are approaching the choice: either national socialist or Christian."[37]

Bonhoeffer's influence on the ecumenical movement in the crucial decade of the 1930s can be gauged in other ways, including publications such as "The Confessing Church and the Ecumenical Movement," in which he offered a theology of the movement in line with his vision of the church as a fraternity of mutual correction and forgiveness; and "The Church and Its Function in Society," a document that echoed Bonhoeffer in stressing that the ecumenical movement was not a utilitarian association but an embodiment of the Church of Christ. W. A. Visser 't Hooft, author of that volume, concludes that Bonhoeffer's thought "made a very real contribution to the creation of that theological climate in which it became possible to propose the formation of a World Council of Churches . . ."[38]

In addition to the challenge to nationalism he represents, Bonhoeffer is often cited when the ecumenical community is called to stand with churches and peoples struggling for justice. Bonhoeffer's spirit was evident at the World Council of Churches Sixth Assembly in Vancouver in 1983 (which saw the establishment of the Conciliar Process on Justice, Peace and the Integrity of Creation) and at the European Ecumenical Assembly at Basle in 1989.[39] Bonhoeffer's ecumenical vision, in which all frontiers are transcended in a universal church, continues to influence the international ecumenical movement and is "one of its great sources of continuing inspiration."[40]

Bonhoeffer and Liberation

For three decades Bonhoeffer's reception among religious and social liberals has foregrounded his identity as the grandfather of liberation theology. Many note an adumbration of political and liberation theologies in Bonhoeffer's late affirmation (Christmas, 1942) that "we [in the Resistance] have for once learnt to see the great events of world history from below, from the perspective of the outcast, the suspects, the maltreated, the powerless, the oppressed, the reviled—in short, from the perspective of those who suffer."[41] But Bonhoeffer's connection with liberation is organic as well as thematic. For in the

1950s and 1960s some of liberation theology's pioneers came under the sway of the man, his writings, and his students. Since that time Bonhoeffer's influence on liberation movements has spread through Europe and Latin America to parts of the "third world"—including West Africa, Cuba, Japan, India, and South Korea.[42]

Confirming our earlier contention that Bonhoeffer's reception is determined to a large extent by the unity of his life and thought, it is noteworthy that liberation-minded Christians have been taken both by his theology and "his courage in the face of death, his opposition to totalitarianism, his radical *imitatio Christi*, his concern for renewal of both church and society . . ."[43]

Latin America

Among those who have reflected upon Bonhoeffer's role in the emergence of liberation thought among Protestant theologians in Latin America are Julio de Santa Ana and Beatriz Melano. Melano, who refers to Bonhoeffer as the greatest theologian of the twentieth century as well as a prophet and saint, seeks to explain "why Bonhoeffer made such an impact on my generation as young Latin American theologians in the decade of 1950 to 1960."[44] She demonstrates that this impact was transmitted through Richard Shaull—a professor at the Presbyterian Seminary in Campinas, Brazil, in the 1950s—and Paul Lehmann, who taught young Latin Americans at Princeton Theological Seminary.[45]

Both Santa Ana and Melano emphasize Bonhoeffer's impact on ISAL ("Church and Society in Latin America"), the emergence of which cannot be explained apart from Bonhoeffer's stimulus. Melano credits Bonhoeffer with informing ISAL's journal *Christianismo y Sociedad*, which "assumed a responsibility for promoting ecumenism, Latin American unity, and Christian education—themes distinctly Bonhoefferan."[46] According to Santa Ana, ISAL members' encounter with Bonhoeffer's writings (particularly *Letters and Papers from Prison*, *The Cost of Discipleship*, and *Ethics*) allowed them to overcome church/world dualism and appreciate the significance of secularization, to negotiate the relationship between faith and ideologies, and to follow Christ in situations of social and political crisis.[47]

Of course, it was not always easy to discern the implications of Bonhoeffer's thought for the specific demands of discipleship in the Latin

American context. Yet it was natural for ISAL members to apply Bonhoeffer's thinking as they considered the ethics of violence in the liberation struggle.[48] If some confused Bonhoeffer's legacy for Latin America with justifications for guerrilla warfare, those who had studied his theology gained from Bonhoeffer "faith and courage when the police interrogated us in or homes and in the jails, inventoried our personal libraries and falsely accused many of us of being 'subversives' and 'communists.'"[49]

Apart from shaping the development of Latin American liberation theology in the Protestant sphere, Melano credits Bonhoeffer with providing the fundamental insight at the heart of the liberationist paradigm—that theology and ethics must be contextual. From Paul Lehmann she and others learned "an ethic based on the life and thinking of Bonhoeffer—not only how to do theology in one's particular context, but also to follow an ethic that was contextual, not normative, an ethic related to the changing reality in the world."[50] Given her understanding of Bonhoeffer as the intellectual progenitor of liberation theology, it is not surprising that Melano's account of his life illuminates an acute social consciousness. In Melano's portrait of Bonhoeffer, in fact, concern with the poor and their oppression is one of the theologian's strongest instincts. Walking the streets of Berlin,

> the young theologian saw the unemployed workers, young men, and the proletariat, and he observed the Nazi storm troopers as they attacked political opponents and striking workers. It was in the street, not behind a desk, that Bonhoeffer began to see the necessity for a contextualized theology to renew the church—a reformation of the church in the midst of the social, political, and economic problems that the country faced.[51]

According to Melano, Bonhoeffer's education in contextualized theology continued at Union Theological Seminary, where fellow student Frank Fisher took Bonhoeffer to Harlem and introduced him to "the outcasts, the marginalized and pariahs of American society." Professor C. C. Webber's course "Church and Community" familiarized Bonhoeffer with the church's role in confronting "the problems of labor, civil rights, and juvenile criminality."[52] Harry F. Ward, whose "untraditional approach to Christian Ethics was tinged with socialism," also left his mark. In New York, in other words, Bonhoeffer learned to see the world "from below." Melano notes that upon returning to Germany Bonhoeffer taught a confirmation class among a "restless proletariat" in the working-class district of Wedding, keeping "direct contact with the people, including the communists and the socialists."[53] These experiences provided the raw material that would be refined in Bonhoeffer's theological writings.[54]

In Melano's account of Bonhoeffer's theological development, his affinity for the poor and oppressed leads him to do "'theology from below,' from the historical context" long before the phrase "liberation theology" came into vogue.

South Africa

The first to offer a detailed assessment of Bonhoeffer's significance for the South African apartheid crisis was John W. de Gruchy, who in 1984 published *Bonhoeffer and South Africa: Theology in Dialogue.*[55] As de Gruchy pointed out, Bonhoeffer's legacy had been a matter of discussion among South African Christians since the Sharpeville massacre in 1960. In the wake of Sharpeville the Barmen Declaration and the German Church Struggle attained symbolic power for Christian opponents of apartheid, some of whom called for a confessing movement in South Africa.[56] Thus while Europeans and Americans were struggling to comprehend Bonhoeffer's prison writings, South Africans were concerned with his contribution to the church struggle and his "ethical reflections on Christian witness in boundary situations."[57]

De Gruchy emphasizes that in addition to his symbolic importance, several aspects of Bonhoeffer's witness made him an ideal dialogue partner for those engaged in the antiapartheid struggle. First, he swam against the stream—within Germany, within the ecumenical movement, and even within the Confessing Church. Second, his theology became increasingly inseparable from praxis. Third, a growing number of South Africans, in part because of the churches' support of apartheid, could no longer regard God as a "working hypothesis." For these secular persons, Bonhoeffer's theology of "the Christ who is persecuted and who suffers" represented a valuable point of contact. Fourth, Bonhoeffer's condemnation of pietism's private spirituality illuminated the "white escapist syndrome" in South Africa. De Gruchy regards this as a particularly fruitful aspect of Bonhoeffer's

legacy, since his story reveals the "liberation of the privileged" that is
so difficult for those of fortunate birth. Because Bonhoeffer was able to
transcend the limitations of his heritage, de Gruchy regards his life as
a resource for constructing a white theology of liberation.

According to de Gruchy, Bonhoeffer is also a paradigm for Christian
civil disobedience. Given Bonhoeffer's background, the influence of
Luther and Hegel on his understanding of the state, and his reserva-
tions regarding liberal democracy, there is irony in this claim. But Bonhoeffer's life bears eloquent testimony to the ability of Christians to
overcome an innate conservatism and glimpse God's will in active
resistance to the state. De Gruchy does not take the matter of resistance lightly, for he is aware that many would invoke Bonhoeffer's
authority on the side of revolutionary violence. But he argues that Bonhoeffer's theology of the cross links the timid tradition of Barmen with
"contemporary theologies that undergird the Christian participation in
the struggle for human rights, justice, and peace in the world."[58]

The legitimacy of applying Bonhoeffer's witness to the apartheid
struggle was confirmed in the early 1970s by Eberhard and Renate
Bethge, who while visiting South Africa were struck by aspects of the
situation that reminded them of Germany during the 1930s and 1940s.
"An observer from Germany," Eberhard wrote, "can hardly fail to be
impressed by the striking parallels with the Hitler period."[59] But de
Gruchy himself is careful not to overstate these parallels. On one hand,
he cites prominent South Africans—including Desmond Tutu and Alex
Boraine (an opposition member of parliament during the 1970s)—who
reflexively compare apartheid South Africa and Hitler's Germany. On
the other hand, he never loses sight of the differences and reminds us
that "the Holocaust and apartheid cannot be equated."[60]

In 1988, South African activist and theologian Alan Boesak
addressed the Fifth International Bonhoeffer Congress in a moving
address titled "What Dietrich Bonhoeffer Has Meant to Me." Boesak
related that while imprisoned by the South African regime he
requested that his wife send him Bethge's biography of Bonhoeffer.
Boesak recalled letting Bonhoeffer "speak to me, no longer in the academic background in Kampen, but in the silence of my cell for the one
day that I was allowed to read."[61] Boesak then challenged his listeners
to hear for themselves this theologian who made it impossible for anyone to do theology without understanding "the meaning of struggle,

the meaning of identification with those who are voiceless, the meaning of participating in the battles of this world that seek to establish justice and peace and humanity." Can one be a theologian, Boesak asked,
and not do this?[62]

When the Seventh International Bonhoeffer Congress met in Cape
Town in 1996, a number of presenters linked Bonhoeffer's legacy to
recent events in South Africa. "Is Bonhoeffer Still of Any Use in South
Africa?" one presenter queried. "Is an interest in Bonhoeffer today anything more than nostalgic loyalty to a remarkable person?" asked
another. Considering these questions, participants applied Bonhoeffer's "ethics of responsibility" in the South African context and con-
templated the significance of Bonhoeffer and Levinas for "ethics in
Africa." Updating his earlier reflections, John de Gruchy noted Bonhoeffer's part in recent debates over conscientious objection and the
legitimacy of armed struggle, in considerations of the church's role in
a post-Constantinian age, and in "putting a spoke in the wheel" of government.[63]

Asia

Bonhoeffer's influence on liberationist thought is evident throughout
Asia—particularly India, Japan, and Korea. His impact in South Korea
is described by theologian Chung Hyun Kyung, who credits Bonhoeffer with the "blooming of political theology, the theology of secularization, and Minjung theology." Kyung points out that Bonhoeffer was
"the major theological mentor" for the Korean Student Christian
movement, "not because we understood the details and nuances of
[his] theology but because we were inspired by [his] life story."[64]

At International Bonhoeffer Conferences during the 1980s and
1990s Asian scholars brought Bonhoeffer's insights to bear on the task
of contextualizing theology in their situations. Poulose Mar Poulose
identified six criteria for "doing theology in the Indian context in view
of Bonhoeffer's theology," including understanding faith as a demand
to live radically in the midst of the world, and living dialogically and
pluralistically in a community that "transcends the boundaries of
Christian religion and of religion as a whole."[65] The extent to which
Poulose viewed Bonhoeffer as a theologian of liberation came to light
in his claim that "responsible involvement in the world means active
political participation, identifying with the oppressed and exploited,

fighting for the cause of civil liberty and human rights and joining those who struggle for their freedom."[66]

In reflections on Bonhoeffer's influence on the church in Japan, Hiroshi Murakami proudly noted that the first biography of Bonhoeffer by a Japanese appeared in 1964 and that the Japanese section of the International Bonhoeffer Society was founded in 1978. As in other Asian countries, Bonhoeffer's role in Japan is related to his "open[ing] the way to the 'view from below' and thus prepar[ing] the soil for new theologies such as 'liberation theology' and 'Minjung Theology.'" Yet, according to Murakami, Japanese identification with Bonhoeffer's theology is rooted in guilt. Responding to Bonhoeffer's assertion in *Ethics* that the church must recognize, confess, and take upon itself the nation's sins, in 1985 the Japan Bonhoeffer Society confessed the sins of the Japanese church in a formal "Declaration of the Guilt."[67] Keeping with Bonhoeffer's concern for human rights, Murakami charged Japanese Christians to recognize that "behind the prosperity which Japan enjoys today there is much discrimination and oppression." The Japanese church cannot sing Gregorian chants, Murakami asserted, with eyes closed to the plight of minority groups within Japan, neo-colonial structures, pollution, or sex tourism.[68]

Eastern Europe

Bonhoeffer is often counted as a representative of "political theology," a European strain of liberation thought whose leading figures include Dorothee Sölle, Jürgen Moltmann, and J. B. Metz. Yet Western European political theology has treated Bonhoeffer more as inspiration than as guide, his writings more as a collection of *testimonia* reinforcing already-held convictions than as a starting point for constructive theology. There is no doubt that Moltmann and Sölle reflect Bonhoeffer's influence.[69] Yet it is telling that Rebecca Chopp's study of European political theology does not contain a single index entry on Bonhoeffer.[70]

The story is much different in Eastern Europe. Anna Morawska, a Polish Roman Catholic who authored a biography of Bonhoeffer and a collection of his writings, writes that "he has dared to anticipate in thought our problem of how to meet Christ in a religionless world." Bonhoeffer assists Polish Christians, Morawska observes, in asking who they are in the midst of atheism, "we [who] . . . do not wish to understand ourselves as agnostics, but feel veneration for Christ; how may we interpret our relation to Jesus?"[71] In Czechoslovakia as well Bonhoeffer was a dialogue partner for Christians living under socialism. Czech theologian Josef Smolik notes that Bonhoeffer's notion of the "Church without privileges" (based on his "outline for a book," as well as his 1932 course on the "nature of the Church") is an especially rich concept for Protestants in Eastern Europe.[72]

Similarly, Bonhoeffer was signally important in discussions of the church's relationship with the socialist government in the former German Democratic Republic. Among the Bonhoeffer themes that influenced the Protestant Church in East Germany, according to Gregory Baum, were the primacy of practice, refusal to regard institutional survival as an end in itself, and recognition of God's presence with the victims of history.[73] John A. Moses goes further, arguing that one can understand neither the GDR's collapse nor the East German church's self-perception without taking into account Bonhoeffer's influence.

Moses stresses that due to the church's peculiar status as the single agency outside the regime's direct control, theological reflection in the GDR necessarily took on political significance. Particularly after 1954 (and the formation of the Task Force for Church Questions in the Central Committee of the Socialist Unity Party) the East German church was forced to decide whether it would accept the state's claim to embody "total truth." Was it legitimate to oppose a state that wanted to marginalize the church, Christians asked, or was it one's duty to submit?[74] Bonhoeffer's example was a critical factor in the thinking of those who chose opposition. Bishops and other high-profile churchmen drew inspiration from Bonhoeffer (and Barth) "in their struggle to maintain loyal witness to the gospel" against the state's strenuous efforts to keep the church on the margins of East German society.[75]

When the Federation of Protestant Churches was founded in 1969 the Bonhoefferian phrase "church for others" was a rallying point. Heino Falcke's 1972 "freedom speech" drew heavily on Bonhoeffer's *Ethics*, and by the late 1970s committees dedicated to Bonhoeffer studies and the history of the Confessing Church were springing up around the country. As the East German church increasingly became a site for critical public discourse, Bonhoeffer's official role as apologist for communism was challenged. By the time of the fourth International Bonhoeffer Congress in Berlin in 1984, Bonhoeffer's official East German reception had been counterweighted by the image of

Bonhoeffer as inspiration for those suffering under an oppressive socialist government.

Describing Bonhoeffer's influence on the "Protestant Revolution" of April 1989, Moses identifies an "undeniable line of continuity between the witness of the persecuted Bonhoeffer in the Third Reich and the opposition movement which contributed so much to the overthrow of communism in the GDR."[76] Still, some criticized the church for not being consistent in its emulation of Bonhoeffer. Following the communist regime's demise, Ernst Feil wondered why church leaders in the GDR had not followed Bonhoeffer's radical path of opposition until the end. "It is necessary to consider why," Feil writes, "instead of unconditional opposition, conditional cooperation was practiced."[77]

North America

Religious rationales for political liberation are generally associated with indigenous theologians of the third world. However, many of the scholars who have been most persistent in exploring liberation themes in Bonhoeffer's writings are white North Americans.[78]

Probably the first North American writer to note Bonhoeffer's relevance for understanding liberation theology was Robert M. Brown, whose *Theology in a New Key: Responding to Liberation Themes* appeared in 1978. In that book Brown interpreted Bonhoeffer's statement from "After Ten Years" ("we have learnt to see the events of world history from below . . .") as evidence that it is sometimes possible for the products of mainline Christianity to "put cherished presuppositions on the line, and begin to see things in a new way." Brown argued that, like Camilo Torres, the well-to-do Colombian who joined an armed resistance movement and experienced a violent death, Bonhoeffer teaches us that those in positions of privilege *can* be changed.[79]

In 1981 G. Clarke Chapman identified in Bonhoeffer the seed of what would become a very fruitful insight of liberationist thought: that as a class the victimized and marginalized may develop "a privileged insight into the reality of God and the world." Chapman elucidated parallels between Bonhoeffer and Latin American liberationists Paulo Freire, Gustavo Gutiérrez, José Miguez Bonino, and Juan Luis Segundo, and compared Bonhoeffer's conception of *Nachfolge* (discipleship) with what liberationists call "praxis" and "cheap grace" with the "banking" concept of education.[80] He also noted that in the German resistance community Bonhoeffer had faced the Christian liberationists' dilemma of how far one should collaborate with non-Christians in the quest for liberation. Is Bonhoeffer to be counted among the liberationists? Chapman asked. Yes, inasmuch as he possessed remarkable insight into "issues of human liberation" and offers the careful reader "significant beginnings for a new liberation ethic."[81]

In several publications during the 1990s, Geffrey Kelly asserted not only that Bonhoeffer had influenced Latin American liberationists such as Gutiérrez and Jon Sobrino, but that he had been a liberation theologian *avant la lettre*. Kelly elaborated four facets of Bonhoeffer's "theology of liberation"—his solidarity with the oppressed, his appeal to a suffering God whose power is revealed in human weakness, his call for a this-worldly Christianity, and his demand that the church live up to its promise to represent Christ to the world.[82] Like previous writers, Kelly noted the liberationist spirit in Bonhoeffer's reference to viewing "the great events of world history from below"; but he contended that these words did not represent a sudden shift in Bonhoeffer's vision. For his initial transformative encounter with human oppression had come during his vicarage in Barcelona in 1928, while in America two years later he learned how poverty was tied to racism and classism. Upon his return to Germany, Bonhoeffer connected American racism with the rising tide of European anti-Semitism and demonstrated his solidarity with the oppressed by entering into "a fellowship of rejection and adversity" on behalf of the Jewish "underclass."[83]

Linking Bonhoeffer's social context with contemporary liberation movements, Kelly calls third-world totalitarianism "Nazism . . . metastasized" and writes that Bonhoeffer's gadfly role in the German church has its counterpart in liberationists' charge that "the problems of the poor in Latin America have been exacerbated by church officialdom's having become too long identified with the rich and powerful . . ."[84] Indeed, for Kelley Bonhoeffer is liberation personified; his legacy is "prophetic outrage and practical action"; his prescription "prayer . . . conjoined to concrete action on behalf of social justice."[85]

Yet this image of Bonhoeffer the proto-liberationist is tempered by Gustavo Gutiérrez's critical assessment of the German theologian's contributions to the movement. In "The Limitations of Modern Theology: On a Letter of Dietrich Bonhoeffer,"[86] Gutiérrez contends that while Bonhoeffer was an exemplar of what is most progressive in bourgeois

Christian theology, it is necessary to acknowledge the "historical limitations of his undertaking."[87] Although Bonhoeffer moved toward the perspective liberation theologians call "theology from the underside of history," at no time did Bonhoeffer point out that the historical agent of modern society and ideology is the bourgeois class. Neither the protest movements of the poor nor the contemporary labor movement find a place in Bonhoeffer's historical focus. In fact, Gutiérrez writes, "it is remarkable that the phenomenon of Nazism, against which he struggled so courageously, did not lead Bonhoeffer to a deeper analysis of the 'crisis in today's society.'"[88]

The Limits of the Liberal Bonhoeffer

Gutiérrez concludes that while Bonhoeffer's testimony is charged with liberative potential, he never escaped the frontiers of the modern bourgeois world. This assessment leads us to consider the ironies involved in casting Bonhoeffer as the grandfather of liberation. It is an odd fact that, despite his celebrated role as harbinger and inspiration of liberationist thought, Bonhoeffer's influence continues to be greatest among first-world men. Indeed, while feminism is probably the most influential mode of thought in the liberationist paradigm, it has proceeded with few approving references to Bonhoeffer. Mary Daly, Elisabeth Moltmann-Wendel, and Maria de Groot explicitly criticize Bonhoeffer's writings, while leading feminist theologians such as Elisabeth Schüssler Fiorenza and Rosemary Radford Ruether ignore him altogether.

How do we explain the meager impact of Bonhoeffer the proto-liberationist upon feminist religious discourse? Perhaps women find off-putting the preponderance of graying white men (including this one) who attend Bonhoeffer conferences and publish books and articles about him. Or maybe Bonhoeffer's place in the pantheon of modern Christian heroes has earned him something of a free ride from feminists. René van Eyden indicates this may be the case when she confesses "a conflict of loyalty in [her] commitment both to Bonhoeffer studies and to critical reflections from the viewpoint of theological women's studies."[89] The source of this conflict is the paradox between

Bonhoeffer's celebrity status among liberals and his solidly traditional understanding of gender roles and overall androcentrism.

In references to the "order of marriage" in sermons and lectures from the 1930s, Bonhoeffer taught that the man "is lord while loving his wife and the wife is subservient to her man while likewise loving her husband." "The glory of women is not to be sought in the public sphere," he declared, but "rather in modesty and in propriety, i.e., clothed in the secret mantle of unostentatiousness. So has God given to woman her vocation in her subordination under her husband." In *Ethics*, Bonhoeffer lent religious sanction to the patriarchal structure of bourgeois marriage and family and this hierarchical view was reiterated in his "Wedding Sermon from the Cell" (May 1943):

> God establishes an order which enables you to live together in marriage . . . In setting up your household you are completely free, but in one thing you are subjected to a law: the wife should be subordinate to her husband, and the husband should love his wife . . . As the head he is responsible for his wife, for his marriage and for his house. The place where the wife was put by God, is her husband's house . . .[90]

While it is unfair to judge Bonhoeffer by cultural standards that reign sixty years after his death, the truth is that his descriptions of the "biblical order" for relations between men and women were conservative even for his own time, in which the biblical basis of male domination was beginning to be questioned.[91]

But it is not only his traditional view of marriage that presents a barrier for feminists who would embrace Bonhoeffer. Korean scholar Chung Hyun Kyung laments that by the mid-1970s she and other Christians involved in political resistance found Bonhoeffer's theology "too embedded in traditional western doctrines of Christ," and his ethics insufficiently concrete. Thus, while appreciative of Bonhoeffer's "confession of the core of costly discipleship" in the phrase "men for others," Kyung concludes that updating Bonhoeffer's image of discipleship by framing it in terms of "women for others" is problematic:

> "Women for others" doesn't give me any new theological imperative or inspiration. Why? Because that is what we women have

been for the last five thousand years of patriarchal history. Remember our mothers', grandmothers', and great-grandmothers' lives? They sacrificed their life for others: their husbands, their children, their communities . . . For some of us who were colonized in our body, mind, and spirit by the oppressive forces of sexism, racism, classism, and cultural imperialism, it seems we have to unlearn "Women for others" for a while and relearn "women for herself first, then for others and for her community by choice."[92]

Indeed, Kyung finds questionable the very concept of "others," since as Simone de Beauvoir, Edward Said, and others have argued, Western male concepts of "the other" lie at the root of the urge to control and dominate "less powerful men, women, children, and even the natural world."[93]

It may be that, had Bonhoeffer survived to experience the feminist revolution, he would have welcomed these criticisms of his thought and of the patriarchal biases of Western theology. Support for this view is found not only in his willingness to make theological adjustments in the light of new experience, but in some of his early readings of the biblical creation story, in his ordination of a female candidate in 1936, and in his relationships with women in which subordination played no part.[94] But if we conclude, as some have, that "the man Bonhoeffer is better than the theologian Bonhoeffer,"[95] we prevent his thought from being subjected to illuminating feminist critique. We will encounter a similar problem when considering Bonhoeffer's relevance for post-Holocaust theology in a subsequent volume.

Assessing the Liberal Bonhoeffer

Liberals have a decided advantage in interpreting Bonhoeffer, for he was a product of liberal teachers (Harnack, Seeberg, Niebuhr, Lehmann) and institutions (Tübingen, Berlin, and Union Theological Seminary),[96] and he reflected these influences throughout his life. In fact, because he moved so comfortably in the world of liberal Protestantism, it is natural to portray Bonhoeffer as a progressive spirit who possessed a "truly prophetic vision for the Universal Church" and whose theology was "centered on human questions, and completely committed to dialogue."[97]

Enhancing Bonhoeffer's relevance for contemporary liberals is the intimate connection he maintained between thought and life. Prior to the advent of the liberationist paradigm, theologians eschewed consciously autobiographical writing and interpreters were unlikely to suppose that a thinker's personal circumstances possessed explanatory value. But this has changed with the advent of liberation theology and the widespread influence of postmodernism. Thus today the early essays on Bonhoeffer that "tended to be person-centered, largely biographical works, intrigued by the heroic dimensions of his life and death" do not seem strange at all.[98]

However, significant ironies are involved in making Bonhoeffer the sort of religious liberal familiar to twenty-first-century Christians. First, while it is not surprising that North American liberals want to cast him as an exemplar of progressive religiosity, Bonhoeffer's own experience made him severely critical of American theology. Bonhoeffer was immersed in American liberal Protestantism during his yearlong sojourn in New York, and he was unimpressed. The humanistic language, the privileging of the social gospel, the "philosophical and organizational secularization of Christianity," the lack of concern for doctrine, and the "unbearable" sermons built around quotes from William James all contributed to Bonhoeffer's dismissal of liberal Protestantism as vapid humanism.[99] Thomas W. Ogletree reminds us, in fact, that Bonhoeffer's attitude changed little through his life:

It is important to note that Bonhoeffer has explicitly rejected one role of the church which has been considered quite important in America, at least since the time of Walter Rauschenbusch. This is the task of promoting programs for making the world itself a better, more "Christian" place to live. For Bonhoeffer . . . this is nothing other than the enthusiasm of the hard-headed "do-gooder" who has forgotten that the kingdom is wholly God's kingdom. Bonhoeffer holds fast to this position throughout his writings. In *Ethics* he continues to warn against any relapse into "that programme-planning for the ethical or religious shaping of the world." He even suggests that the unsolved state of some of the world's problems may be of more importance to God than their solution, "for it may serve to call attention to the fall of man and to the divine redemption."[100]

Second, as G. Clarke Chapman points out, although Bonhoeffer's assessment of revolutionary violence in his own context "has parallels if not also some influence on liberation theology," Bonhoeffer expressed horror at the idea of rebellion, offered no systemic social analyses (least of all economic ones), "and not a glimmer of revolutionary thought."[101] More specifically, the confinement of Bonhoeffer's ethical thinking to the personal and interpersonal spheres meant that his perception of sociality was fundamentally apolitical. And despite the hint of class consciousness in his famous phrase *"der Blick von unten"* (the view from below), Bonhoeffer maintained a "general disdain" for Marxism and never fully questioned his own privilege.[102]

Third, portraying Bonhoeffer as a "liberal" familiarizes his religious experience in a way that may distort it. An excellent example is found in liberal glosses on Bonhoeffer's "conversion" of 1931/32. As we shall see in the next chapter, conservatives tend to read this experience as a second birth. But liberals prefer to think of it as part of an ongoing "process" of spiritual development. Reminding us of Bonhoeffer's antipathy for "stories of conversion told by pietists for purposes of edification," John de Gruchy declares that Bonhoeffer's "great liberation" should not be understood in the revivalistic sense. Rather, it liberated him "from a powerful and rather self-centered ego to a concern for others in and through the service of the church."[103] According to Josiah Ulysses Young, Bonhoeffer's "change in personal faith" was part of a reorientation toward the world that took place in Harlem, a turn from cerebral to spiritual faith forged in the black church and its engagement with oppression.[104] Donald Shriver contends that Bonhoeffer's "1932 experience of becoming a Christian" was in fact a great turn towards the church.[105] And Geffrey Kelly writes that "if there was a radical shift or 'conversion' in [Bonhoeffer's] life, it was in that period when he rediscovered the Sermon on the Mount and realized that there were things, such as peace and social justice, for which an uncompromising stand is worthwhile."[106]

Other scholars have construed Bonhoeffer's "conversion" in psychological rather than religious categories. Clifford J. Green speaks of a late-adolescent "identity crisis" fueled by Bonhoeffer's competitive drive

"to excel like the other men of the family and at the same time to secure an identity quite distinct from them." With Erik Ericksen's psychohistorical treatment of Martin Luther as his model, Green describes a gradual resolution to Bonhoeffer's identity crisis (which he defines as narcissism based in "disordered ego functions"). Green argues that *The Cost of Discipleship* is the "direct theological expression of Bonhoeffer's personal liberation" from lingering theological and personal conflicts, and that these were only fully resolved in the *Letters*.[107]

Similarly, Robin W. Lovin and Jonathan P. Gosser view Bonhoeffer's crisis in light of a transition from "stage three" to "stage four" faith, as described in James Fowler's theory of faith development. This transition brought a "heightened ability to view his world in terms of polarities and to draw sharp and unbending lines separating divergent points of view . . ."[108] Is there validity in these liberal interpretations of the "something [which] happened" to Bonhoeffer that "transformed [his] life"? Or does their appeal lie mainly in their capacity to rescue Bonhoeffer's narrative from pietistic renderings that make liberals uncomfortable?

Fourth, it is not clear whether liberal interpreters of Bonhoeffer are willing to hear his prophetic voice in a world where the imperative for peace must be articulated amid echoes of "9/11." Recognizing Bonhoeffer's legacy as a powerful tool in opposing the idol of "national security" that links our world to his, liberal interpreters have long wielded Bonhoeffer's commitments to peace and pacifism as a battering ram against conservative ideologies and their uncritical Christian supporters. Geffrey Kelly writes that his church presentations in the wake of the first Gulf War served as a forum for correcting a faulty image of Bonhoeffer as the patriot par excellence:

Because so many Americans have turned Bonhoeffer into a folk hero and modern martyr in a just cause, they seemed to expect me to associate Bonhoeffer's opposition to Hitler with the newfound cause, getting rid of the "Hitler-like" tyrant, Saddam Hussein. My audiences were for the most part surprised to find that the writings of Bonhoeffer and his actions leading up to his eventual arrest and execution at the hands of the Gestapo could just as well be directed against the American overkill of Iraqis and the massive destruction, unrelated to the liberation of Kuwait, that took the lives of countless civilians, including an estimated 49,000 children. Indeed, Bonhoeffer's legacy to the churches stands as a bracing reminder to pretentious "patriots" that war, however well orchestrated by self-serving politicians and military propaganda teams, is still a denial of the gospel teachings of Jesus Christ.[109]

At this writing, it remains unclear how far liberal commentators are willing to lean toward Bonhoeffer's brand of patriotism when the lives at stake include "ours," or how far they are willing to go in daring peace when they are targets of terrorists with weapons of mass destruction.[110]

On Bonhoeffer's relevance for informing theological attitudes toward violence, it should be acknowledged that while liberals by and large are attracted to Bonhoeffer's privileging of peace, he determined that in his own situation peace could be achieved only by means of revolutionary violence. Because Bonhoeffer did not resort to violence in self-defense, it is difficult to regard him as the innocent victim of an oppressive system as King and Gandhi were. Further, despite his refusal to justify tryanni-cide as a theological principle, is not this dimension of Bonhoeffer's legacy inseparable from his conscientious objection to military service and his peace activism? The question is particularly salient in assessing liberationist readings of Bonhoeffer emanating from the third world. Beatriz Melano pinpoints the problem when she writes that

> those who considered resorting to armed violence in the process of liberating Latin America—in my judgment—did not under-stand that Bonhoeffer would have never defended a guerrilla group. This option to use violence, however, seduced many Latin American Christians, and unfortunately some chose to see the death of Dietrich Bonhoeffer at the hands of the Nazi scourge, and his earlier participation in a plot to assassinate Hitler, as a kind of inspiration and legitimation of violence as a possible Christian recourse. They did not know about Bonhoef-fer's earlier writings on peace or that his decision to be involved in the assassination conspiracy was a choice he knew was not Christian . . .[111]

Nevertheless, it seems reasonable to assume that Bonhoeffer would recognize the necessity of violence in some situations, and that he would not deny this option to oppressed persons, even if it could not be defended as Christian per se. In any case, not all third-world interpreters have been as reluctant as Melano to invoke Bonhoeffer in support of revolutionary struggle. In a sermon delivered at Westminster Abbey in 1975, Desmond Tutu inquired pointedly why Europeans regarded Bonhoeffer as a saint for joining a plot to assassinate Hitler while Africans resorting to similar methods were condemned as violent terrorists.[112] Indeed, it would seem that if first-world liberals wish to make Bonhoeffer's legacy synonymous with political activism and the willingness to resist evil, they also cede the right to object when third-world Christians are inspired by Bonhoeffer's story to engage in responsible action of their own.

As we watch Bonhoeffer in prison and then moving to the gallows, we cannot help seeing other heroes of the faith—people like Paul—who went before him, who dwelt in such places, and whose lives ended the same way.

—DAVID P. GUSHEE

Many saints have been prepared to die for their faith. Dietrich Bonhoeffer was arrested for something even more difficult for a true saint—he was prepared to kill.

—THE CHRISTIAN READER

Bonhoeffer led a life that is an example to all fellow believers in the Crucified . . . He lived and acted the works of a Christ-like individual.

—LANDON LESTER

APOSTLE

THE CONSERVATIVE BONHOEFFER

The Other Bonhoeffer

Over the years many commentators have noted the conservative elements in Bonhoeffer's background, many of which are reflected in his mature theology.[1] Even champions of the liberal Bonhoeffer concede that he was essentially an aristocratic man who could be shocked by the smallest offense against order.[2] Bonhoeffer's views on marriage, one writes, "reek with cozy, upper-class, Prussian and Lutheran patriarchalism."[3] Even *Ethics* contains "passage after passage where Bonhoeffer seems to advocate a highly stratified, patriarchal society as most nearly conforming to 'Christian' order."[4] Similarly, interpreters of a conservative theological bent have asserted that, despite his ill-fated foray into political resistance, Bonhoeffer remained an orthodox Christian.[5] Until the appearance of Georg Huntemann's *The Other Bonhoeffer* in 1989, however, few had argued that Bonhoeffer's contemporary relevance was tied up with his social and theological conservatism.[6]

Concerned that European evangelicals have tended to regard Bonhoeffer as a heterodox theologian under the spell of modernism, Huntemann seeks to set the record straight. Not surprisingly, he laments the domination of Bonhoeffer scholarship by liberal academics and overzealous popularizers who perpetuate an image of the German theologian as "the church father of modernist, socialist theology."[7] The conservative Bonhoeffer portrayed by Huntemann is "an enemy of liberal theology and thereby of modernism" and thus an opponent of revolution in all its forms. First and foremost, Bonhoeffer stands against the "revolution against fatherhood and order" that reached its apotheosis in Nazism.[8] Bonhoeffer did not mistake the Nazi revolution for a reactionary movement, Huntemann assures us; rather, he recognized it as a revolt against the patriarchal world, an uprising of the masses that threatened all order and "God-ordained values."

In fact, Huntemann inverts the image of a liberationist Bonhoeffer who identified God's activity in "the view from below," making him a defender of law and order *against* the revolution from below. Indeed, images of a demonic uprising boiling up from the depths of the human collective permeate Huntemann's descriptions of Bonhoeffer's thought. "The aristocratic Bonhoeffer saw in National Socialist ideology a creature from the deep, an uprising of the masses, of the collective, of the ordinary, of rampant disorder," Huntemann writes.[9] He also discredits Bonhoeffer's reception as a "liberation theologian" by highlighting the "socialist" component in National Socialism. For Huntemann, any attempt to privilege the collective above the individual is a recapitulation of Nazi ideology.

Feminism is another form of revolutionary modernism that Huntemann views as utterly incompatible with Bonhoeffer's thought. He charges that feminist theology has "perverted Bonhoeffer's statements about the powerlessness and suffering of God for its own ends,"[10] yielding a needy, tender, and feminized god that reeks of both fascism and New Age religion. Huntemann contends, in fact, that "a high point of the feminization of God was reached precisely where modern theologians search for it least of all, namely in the 'faith of Adolf Hitler,'" where nature, *Volk* and race were idolized.[11]

If Bonhoeffer opposed both revolution and modernism, what was he *for*? In a word, order. Standing squarely within the Prussian tradition, Bonhoeffer was a "conservative, Christian Occidental ethicist of order," his *Ethics* a "living testimony against the nihilism and terror of the cultural and moral revolution that is also taking place right now."[12] Contra Hanfried Müller, Huntemann asserts that Bonhoeffer's concern with preserving the Occident through the restoration of law, order, and peace persisted to the very end of his life. "Bonhoeffer is not a church father of the progressives, the feminists, or the emancipators." He can only be claimed as a political leftist in "the theater of the absurd characteristic of modern contemporary theology."[13]

Huntemann's book is a thorough refashioning of Bonhoeffer to suit the theological and social tastes of conservatives. As we shall see, however, the figure who intrigues evangelical Christians is not dependent on arguments regarding the social outlook of the historical Bonhoeffer.

A Chance Encounter

Perhaps the best way to introduce the Bonhoeffer who enthralls conservative Christians is to describe a chance encounter with a devotee. On a recent commercial airline flight from Phoenix to Memphis, I stood in the aisle talking to a colleague about medieval hagiography and its relation to Bonhoeffer. After a few moments, the passenger sitting in front of my colleague turned around. "I'm sorry to interrupt," he said, "but are you talking about Dietrich Bonhoeffer?" I responded that we were and asked if he had heard of him. "Yes . . . he's one of my heroes," the young man said.

Aware there might be data for my project here, I engaged him in conversation. "I'm writing a book on Bonhoeffer," I said. "Can you tell me something about what he means to you." "He's just awesome," the young man replied. "The things he did, the commitment he had. How intense he was." And which of Bonhoeffer's works had he read? I inquired. He paused before admitting that although he once started *The Cost of Discipleship*, he found Bonhoeffer's work difficult going. Then how had Bonhoeffer become one of his heroes? I wondered aloud. My young friend responded that he learned of Bonhoeffer in college. And where was that? "I attended a Bible college in Phoenix called Master's Commission," he said. I was not familiar with the institution, but from his description I gathered it was an evangelical Protestant school.

When I arrived home, I looked up "Master's Commission" on the Web, where it is described as a "Christian leadership training program for young adults between the ages of 18 and 25," an intensive discipleship school where students commit a full year. "The vision of The Master's Commission," I learned, "is to train these future leaders to overcome the pressures and influences of the world, shake off the bonds of dead religion, and walk as true sons and daughters of the Kingdom." The institution sponsors the "Christian Life School of Theology," a distance learning curriculum administered through local churches and taught by "some of the finest pastors and Bible teachers in America today."[14]

What had this young "pastor" (that is how he described himself, though he did not mention seminary) learned of Bonhoeffer at Master's Commission? We did not have time to discuss this question, but a look at the Christian Life School of Theology curriculum reveals no courses dealing with Bonhoeffer or any other figure of modern theology. The practical approach at Master's Commission is evident in course titles such as A Theology of Power, A Theology of Success, Advanced Deliverance I ("topics include the origin of Satan, how to recognize demons, seven steps to deliverance, how to minister deliverance and the aftercare of those delivered"), Biblical Prosperity, Let There Be Light: Creationism, Spiritual Warfare, End Times: A Pre-Tribulation Approach, and Understanding Dreams and Visions. It is possible that my friend encountered Bonhoeffer in classes like Biblical Discipleship or Christology, concerns close to Bonhoeffer's own. But course descriptions suggest otherwise.

In any case, it was clear based on our conversation that Bonhoeffer had had a considerable impact on this young Christian's imagination, that Bonhoeffer's life rather than his theology was the focus of his admiration, and that such attitudes were likely shared by many graduates of Master's Commission.[15] I relate this chance conversation because it serves as a fitting introduction to the conservative Bonhoeffer as he functions within the subculture of American evangelicalism. Despite its size and influence (over 130 "campuses" nationwide, according to its Web site), the Master's Commission is not the sort of institution that is taken seriously among scholars of religion. But if young and enthusiastic graduates of such places are embracing Bonhoeffer as a hero of faith whose commitment to Christ is exemplary for twenty-first-century living, then Bonhoeffer scholarship should take note of this fact.

Bonhoeffer's Conservative Reception

Bonhoeffer's reputation among conservative Christians is perhaps the clearest marker of his unique stature in the world of modern theology. Despite his respect for and debt to Nietzsche and Kierkegaard, despite his ongoing dialogue with the thought of Feuerbach, despite the theological experimentation that made him the doyen of radical theology, Bonhoeffer is something of a cult hero among evangelicals. The significance of evangelicals' favorable, if cautious attention to Bonhoeffer can only be appreciated when it is contrasted with the evangelical reaction to Continental theology more generally. The major figures of twentieth-century European theology—Bonhoeffer's rough contemporaries Paul Tillich, Rudolf Bultmann, and Karl Barth—are typically regarded by American evangelicals as something less than "true" believers whose theologies are all the more danger-ous for their apparent orthodoxy. Yet today, when it is difficult to find a positive mention of any of these men in evangelical publications,[16] Bonhoeffer (who had much in common with them and was a product of the same church and university systems) is honored by a broad array of evangelical authors, publications, and institutions.

The most scientific evidence for Bonhoeffer's warm reception among evangelicals comes from surveys of evangelical opinion. At the end of the last decade, the editors of *Christian History* magazine (pub-lished by Christianity Today, Inc.) asked readers and historians to list the five most influential Christians of the twentieth century, as well as the five well-known Christians who had been most influential for them per-sonally. When the results were published in the magazine's winter 2000 edition, Bonhoeffer ranked tenth among both scholars and readers on the "most influential" list, and fifth on the most "personally influential" lists of both groups. Bonhoeffer was not only the highest-ranked theolo-gian, but was one of only six figures who finished in the top ten in all four categories (the others being Billy Graham, C. S. Lewis, Mother Teresa, Martin Luther King Jr., and Francis Schaeffer—all preachers, activists, or apologists).[17]

Evangelical Publications

A longitudinal measure of evangelical attitudes toward Bonhoeffer may be gained from examining *Christianity Today*, the weekly periodical that serves as the evangelical counterpart to the *Christian Century*. Bonhoeffer appeared on the magazine's radar in 1966, and the image was not a welcome one.

In "Religionless Christianity: Is It a New Form of Gnosticism?" Mil-ton D. Hunnex charged that since "religionless" Christianity laid claim to a new revelation, it was not "greatly different in spirit from the

Gnostic reinterpretations of the first few centuries."[18] As for Bonhoeffer, Hunnex doubted that he had anything to say that had not already said by "historical orthodox Christianity," compared his theology unfavorably with that of Paul Tillich (!), and complained that what Bonhoeffer "wrote under the understandable stresses of life in a Nazi prison has become the rallying cry for a wholesale defection from New Testament fundamentals in ecclesiastical high places where the interest has become not so much the interpretation of the Gospel as its reinterpretation."[19] Later that year, in a *CT* editorial titled "The Old 'New Worldliness,'" Harold B. Kuhn strenuously resisted the Bonhoeffer who was being extolled by secularizing theologians. "Evangelical Christianity has something to say that natural man does not especially wish to hear— a call to repentance and to vital faith in the Redeemer," Kuhn wrote. For the urban man needs to learn of Jesus Christ, "who is not merely the 'Man for others' but the crucified and risen Lord of life." The times do not call for secularizing the church, Kuhn concluded, but for a new affirmation of Christian supernaturalism.[20]

By 1972 the magazine's tone with regard to Bonhoeffer was more curious, if still cautious. In an article titled "But Which Bonhoeffer?" Kuhn noted the growing popularity of the German theologian in "current religious thought" and observed wryly that "it is an exceptionally courageous writer of theology who does not today sprinkle his pages generously with quotations from Dietrich Bonhoeffer."[21] Kuhn's ambivalence reflected Bonhoeffer's changing status in the evangelical world. On one hand, Kuhn questioned whether Bonhoeffer's conduct during the last years of his life entitled him to the hearing he enjoyed, and he denied Bonhoeffer's claim that Christianity preached a "God of the gaps." In this sense, Kuhn charged, Bonhoeffer probably misunderstood historic Christianity, or at least saw it through distorting lenses.[22] On the other hand, Kuhn accused Bonhoeffer's radical interpreters of ignoring his work's *Sitz im Leben* and exercising "an authoritarian use of proof-texts." In concluding, Kuhn counseled evangelicals to "cast a continuing discerning eye" in Bonhoeffer's direction. Most conservative publications sounded a similarly cautious tune during these years, tending to describe Bonhoeffer, like Barth, as an orthodox-sounding modernist.

When we revisit the pages of *Christianity Today* twenty years later, the mood in relation to Bonhoeffer is notably different. A 1991 review of a recently published edition of Bonhoeffer's writings praised the text under consideration as a faithful guide to "a life that still rings with Christian authenticity" and encouraged Christians to "sit at Bonhoeffer's feet."[23] A CT essay by David P. Gushee commemorating the fiftieth anniversary of Bonhoeffer's death in 1995 documented his relevance for the concerns of contemporary evangelicals. It opened with a quotation from Flossenbürg's prison doctor, who described Bonhoeffer on the last morning of his life "praying fervently" and remaining "entirely submissive to the will of God."[24] And Gushee applauded Bonhoeffer's parents, "nominal" Christians though they were, for instilling "family values" in the young Dietrich.[25]

Much in Gushee's portrait of Bonhoeffer is designed to appeal to evangelical readers: Bonhoeffer recognized that German Protestantism was "nearly bankrupt." He pursued a revolution in theological education that demanded "profound spiritual discipline, pure biblical theology." His return to Germany in 1939 was an act of "incarnational discipleship and authentic Christian patriotism." The death of this modern apostle proves that "the blood of the martyrs is the seed of the church."[26] Yet Gushee does not downplay Bonhoeffer's "Christ-centered commitments to social and racial justice":

One of the besetting sins of certain strands of American evangelicalism is precisely our tendency to acculturate Christian faith to the "American way of life." How frequently we have confused being Christian with being American, loving nation with loving God. How often we have mixed unjust and oppressive cultural norms like racism and indifference to injustice into this distasteful stew, calling it Christian. Bonhoeffer bears witness to the fact that authentic Christianity sometimes leads one into principled opposition to nation and culture—even to a gallows, or a cross.[27]

With whom does Bonhoeffer call American Christians to stand in solidarity? Gushee asks. Immigrants? Poor mothers and their children? Prisoners? The unborn? Gushee observes that Bonhoeffer's involvement in the anti-Hitler conspiracy has been invoked by those who defend the killing of abortion doctors: "He conspired to kill in order to prevent evil; why can't we?" But Gushee declares "our situation" significantly different from Bonhoeffer's, since it presents a number of options for responsible action that do not entail violence.

Since 1995, attention to Bonhoeffer in the pages of *Christianity Today* has notably increased: Between 1995 and 2002, there were fifteen pieces dealing in some way with the German theologian. These included articles on the evangelical doctrine of the church and the Christian importance of the Old Testament,[28] a reference to Bonhoeffer's *Life Together* as a model for evangelical prison ministry,[29] evidence of the remarkable popularity of Bonhoeffer among members of the millennial generation, an article by Focus on the Family president James Dobson, and reviews of *Bonhoeffer: Agent of Grace*, *Love Letters from Cell 92*, and a book by a former homosexual.

During the same period, other popular evangelical publications carried items dealing with Bonhoeffer. A feature in the *Christian Reader* listing the best devotional books of all time (*The Cost of Discipleship* came in at #9, just behind *The Book of Common Prayer*) described Bonhoeffer as "a pastor and trainer of pastors."[30] *Books and Culture* published a review of two biographical novels—Mary Glazener's *The Cup of Wrath* and Denise Giardina's *Saints and Villains*—and an essay titled "The Church, the Nazis and the Holocaust," in which Bonhoeffer was identified as being virtually alone in recognizing the importance of the "Jewish Question" in Nazi Germany.[31] *Leadership Journal* included an article by Gordon Macdonald titled "Speaking into Crisis" which extolled Bonhoeffer and Helmut Thielicke, German pastors "who stood to speak for God" during the Third Reich.[32] Finally, the Christian History Institute prepared an issue of "Glimpses" (church bulletin inserts on notable figures in church history) devoted to Bonhoeffer, whose writings were said to provide "valuable insight for Christians seeking to live faithfully to the Gospel in a culture dominated by hostile ideologies."[33]

While more conservative Christian publications such as *Eternity* and *Moody Monthly* have been less enthusiastic in their response to Bonhoeffer,[34] the German theologian has generated considerable interest on the left wing of American evangelicalism. *Sojourners* published sixteen items mentioning Bonhoeffer between 1995 and 2000, among them an article advocating Bonhoeffer's "incarnational discipleship," a description of the Servant Leadership School at Washington, D.C.'s Church of the Saviour as modeled after Bonhoeffer's underground seminary, an article commemorating the fiftieth anniversary of Bonhoeffer's death arguing that he "deserves to be remembered and studied as a 20th-century martyr in the same breath with Rev. Martin Luther King, Jr. and Archbishop Oscar Romero," a piece by Walter Wink questioning the use of Bonhoeffer in support of just-war thinking after "9/11," and reviews of Denise Giardina's *Saints and Villains* (named one of the "best books of the year" for 1999), Mary Glazener's *The Cup of Wrath*, and the film *Hanged on a Twisted Cross.* [35]

Evangelical Authors

Bonhoeffer's stature within evangelicalism can also be gauged by noting the number of leading evangelical authors who refer favorably to him. Some of these references occur in passing. For instance, Promise Keepers founder Bill McCartney notes that while Hitler, Stalin, and Madalyn Murray O'Hair had abusive fathers, Bonhoeffer, "the German theologian who stood up to Hitler, and paid for it with his life, grew up with a father who treated his children with respect and affection." [36] But many evangelical authors utilize Bonhoeffer not only to garnish their arguments, but to inject them with political and theological substance. Charles Colson, for example, portrays Bonhoeffer as a model for evangelical activism. Asking how Christians should live under a government "whose policies we sharply disagree with—even one whose positions we find morally offensive?" Colson responds that "civil disobedience must be chosen whenever civil magistrates frustrate our ability to obey God" and cites Bonhoeffer as a model in this regard. [37]

The most influential evangelical leader to identify Bonhoeffer as a paradigm for Christian cultural engagement is James C. Dobson, founder and president of Focus on the Family. In a series of articles published between 1999 and 2002, Dobson offered Bonhoeffer's life as a case study in Christian activism at a time when the evangelical obligation to shape society was being called into question. In a *Christianity Today* article titled "The New Cost of Discipleship," Dobson responded to the charge that Christians have wasted their time opposing abortion, homosexual marriage, pornography, and the assault on traditional values. Citing Bonhoeffer's failed activism, Dobson asked: "Since when did being outnumbered and under powered justify silence in response to evil?" Bonhoeffer took a stand against the Nazi regime and paid with his life. Would those endorsing Christian isolationism suggest that he should have accommodated Hitler's henchmen because he had no chance of winning?[38]

In the May 2000 edition of his *Focus on the Family Newsletter*, Dobson cited Bonhoeffer again, this time in reference to God's role in history during the Second World War:

> Relating our present situation to the past, we have to ask whether Christian people have the courage to stand firm when the odds against us seem overwhelming. Or will we be like Lord Halifax and Prime Minister Neville Chamberlain, groveling and accommodating those who are plotting evil? These fearful men were not the only men who compromised under pressure, of course. The German Lutheran Church was also dancing to Hitler's tune in 1940. Jews were disappearing and their synagogues burned. The murder of innocent women and children was commonplace. Yet the church offered little resistance.[39]

Following a long quote from *Ethics*, written "before he was hanged, naked, from a piano wire in 1945," Dobson updates Bonhoeffer's confession of guilt on behalf of the church: "Thirty-nine million babies have been killed by abortionists since 1973, to which many of our church leaders remained passive." Assessing the church's culpability in this tragedy, Dobson quotes Bonhoeffer: "By her own silence, she has rendered herself guilty because of her unwillingness to suffer for what she knows is right."[40]

Evangelical Education

A further measure of Bonhoeffer's penetration into American evangelical life is his role in the curriculum of evangelical institutions. At Fuller Theological Seminary, America's flagship evangelical seminary, Bonhoeffer's texts are required reading in a number of courses. These include Introduction to Theological Study (selected readings); Spirituality & Discipleship in College and Young Adult Settings (*Life Together*); Classics of Christian Ethics, Method for Concreteness in Christian Ethics, and The Ethics of Bonhoeffer (all of which require *Ethics*); Christian Discipleship in a Secular Society (*The Cost of Discipleship*);

and Bonhoeffer: Life and Thought (*The Cost of Discipleship*, *Ethics*, *Christ the Center*, and *Letters and Papers from Prison*).[41]

Themes in the Evangelical Portrait

As will become clearer in the next chapter, those who wish to universalize Bonhoeffer's legacy are tempted to downplay those aspects of his biography that tie him to historic Christianity. Conversely, the evangelical portrayal of Bonhoeffer accentuates these distinctively Christian elements of his portrait. If the liberal Bonhoeffer teaches us to adapt tradition in order to ensure its cultural relevance, the evangelical Bonhoeffer encourages us to remain steadfast in the faith handed down by church fathers and reformers. While he may be compared with Gandhi, this Bonhoeffer is ecclesiastically anchored, Scripture-guided, and Christ-centered, his legacy inseparable from his faithfulness to God unto death.

Familiar Values

Bonhoeffer attracts evangelicals, in fact, because his experiences and values appear to be so much like their own. He hails from a close family and a privileged environment, one that seems quite familiar in the suburban, upper-middle-class world in which many evangelicals live. Furthermore, Bonhoeffer speaks a language evangelicals understand. Richard Weikart warns that evangelicals often do not realize that words which mean one thing to Bonhoeffer mean something quite different to them.[42] But if evangelical admiration for Bonhoeffer skates on the surface of his theology, it is in part due to his familiar-sounding phraseology.

Bonhoeffer was a theologian of deep complexity who displayed an impressive grasp of the religious and philosophical traditions he inherited. Nevertheless, because much of his prose lends itself to excerpting and memorization, his words often become sermon seasoning or fodder for daily devotions. I mentioned in the preface my collegiate affinity for Bonhoeffer's gnomic statement, "when Christ calls a man he bids him come and die." In fact, *The Cost of Discipleship* is replete with such spiritual apothegms. The student of theology is likely to regard the sentence "only he who believes is obedient, and only he who is obedient believes" as a reflection of Bonhoeffer's dialectical sensibility. More to the point, however, such phrases "preach," and it is this homiletical quality that appeals to evangelical Christians.

Evangelicals also feel at home with Bonhoeffer's presumed philosemitism, a fact not surprising given the pro-Israel trajectory in American evangelicalism since the late 1960s. Ralph Reed, former head of the Christian Coalition, confirms the link between Christian support for Israel and "a proud tradition" that includes Corrie ten Boom and Dietrich Bonhoeffer, "who sacrificed their own lives while resisting Nazi tyranny and protecting Jews from the Holocaust."[43] As David Gushee reminded evangelical readers on the fiftieth anniversary of his death, Bonhoeffer "stood with the Jews" and grieved over their abandonment by the church.[44]

Bonhoeffer's story also reverberates with an ambivalence toward religious institutions that is quite common among conservative Christians. Many evangelicals point out that Bonhoeffer's faithfulness to Christ brought him into conflict with the church hierarchy in Germany. Indeed, among Christians who are themselves often alienated from mainline churches, Bonhoeffer represents a valuing of Christian community coupled with a familiar suspicion of ecclesiastical authority. Yet beyond the comforting language, the pro-Jewish outlook, and the conflicted relationship with his church, evangelicals are heartened by Bonhoeffer's attention to familiar Christian practices—especially Bible reading, prayer, devotion to Christ, obedience, discipleship, and life in community.

Interest in Bonhoeffer's piety is reflected in the evangelical love affair with *The Cost of Discipleship* and *Life Together*. Eberhard Bethge notes that neither book has earned the theological reception enjoyed by his academic treatises. "Their language and style are considered to be not sober enough and too didactic, and their form of piety is regarded as out of date," Bethge observes.[45] Among evangelicals, however, it is not uncommon to identify Bonhoeffer's literary legacy exclusively with these "classics of modern Christian literature."[46] As Richard Weikart notes, these books address enduring evangelical dilemmas. "Just as *The Cost of Discipleship* has stirred the interest of evangelicals concerned with spiritual impoverishment of individual Christians, who settle for cheap grace instead of the costly grace of real discipleship, *Life Together* has appealed to those concerned with the spiritual destitution of the church as a community."[47]

Confirming its honored place in annals of evangelical literature, *The Cost of Discipleship* was named one of the ten "best devotional books of all time" in 1997 by *The Christian Reader* (which also honored such timeless classics as *Pilgrim's Progress*, *The Screwtape Letters*, *The Practice of the Presence of God*, *The Imitation of Christ*, *The Book of Common Prayer*, and Augustine's *Confessions*),[48] and was second (behind C. S. Lewis's *Mere Christianity*) on *Christianity Today*'s list of "100 books that had a significant effect on Christians" in the twentieth century.[49] The role of this book in evangelical culture is reflected in the following story, which introduces InterVarsity Press's six-part study titled *Dietrich Bonhoeffer: Costly Grace*:

> The garage sale was at the home of a leader in the local Christian community. On a table among a collection of books, we spotted a hardback copy of Dietrich Bonhoeffer's classic work *The Cost of Discipleship*. It was in good condition, though its pages were heavily marked with notes and underlining. We wondered why anybody, let alone someone in Christian ministry, would so casually let it go for a quarter.
>
> Not long afterward, the news came out that this person was involved in immorality. A ministry was gone, a church fellowship was hurt and confused, two families were deeply-wounded—and *The Cost of Discipleship* was on someone else's bookshelf.
>
> Perhaps there was no connection between the two incidents. Perhaps this person had bought a newer edition of the book and didn't have space for both copies. Or perhaps appearances told the truth: this Christian leader had weighed "the cost of discipleship" against other desires and found the price was too high.[50]

It would be a mistake to suggest that *The Cost of Discipleship* is not held in high regard by non-evangelicals;[51] but its special appeal among conservative Christians is related to the familiar ring of the word "discipleship" in evangelical ears.[52] For evangelicals, discipleship has both transitive and intransitive properties. One *becomes a disciple* or follower of Christ (as all Christians are expected to do); and one *disciples others* by preaching the good news in obedience to Christ's Great Commission and by nurturing young believers in the faith.[53] Thus, discipleship and evangelism are frequently linked in evangelical discourse, one reason mainline Christians shy from the term.

For evangelicals, discipleship also connotes the countercultural demands of Christian faith, which beckon believers to choose the narrow path of authentic Christian living over the broad way of participation in culture-defining institutions. This view of discipleship is reflected in evangelical concerns with persecution and martyrdom, phenomena which confirm their expectation that genuine faith will always engender resistance in "the world." Thus, to the extent that Bonhoeffer emphasized "the cost of discipleship," his book and his life are apt metaphors for Christian existence.

Discipleship is a theme in Bonhoeffer's thought that evinces a "personal relationship" with Christ. Most evangelicals consider this relationship the sine qua non of authentic faith and assume that it has proceeded from an experience of rebirth. Thus Bonhoeffer's "conversion," typically overlooked or discounted by non-evangelical interpreters, takes on monumental importance in evangelical recountings of his life. In 1931 Bonhoeffer apparently experienced "a change" as he was beginning work in the university, the church, and the ecumenical movement.[54] Bonhoeffer wrote of the experience in 1936:

> I plunged into work in a very unchristian way. An . . . ambition that many noticed in me made my life difficult . . . Then something happened, something that has changed and transformed my life to the present day . . . I had often preached, I had seen a great deal of the church, and talked and preached about it—but I had not yet become a Christian . . . I know that at that time I turned the doctrine of Jesus Christ into something of personal advantage for myself . . . I pray to God that that will never happen again. Also I had never prayed, or prayed only very little. For all my loneliness, I was quite pleased with myself. Then the Bible, and in particular the Sermon on the Mount, freed me from that. Since then everything has changed. I have felt this plainly, and so have other people about me. It was a great liberation. It became clear to me that the life of a servant of Jesus Christ must belong to the Church, and step by step it became plainer to me how far that must go . . . My calling is quite clear to me. What God will make of it I do not know . . . I must follow the path.[55]

Without doubt something profound occurred in Bonhoeffer's life around 1931. But what weight it should receive in interpreting his subsequent life and work is less definite. Ironically, Eberhard Bethge supplies impetus for an evangelical reading of this experience by describing it under the heading "the theologian becomes a Christian." Bethge employs this phrase to indicate a shift in Bonhoeffer's focus from academy to church, a growing certainty in his vocation that "certainly took months and years to reach maturity."[56] Yet despite this disclaimer and Bethge's reminder that Bonhoeffer disliked the term "conversion," conservative biographers do not hesitate to speak of a "conversion experience . . . as deep as St. Augustine's or Charles Wesley's."[57]

In part, this is because Bethge's image of the transition from theologian to believer corresponds to the evangelical dichotomy between "head knowledge" and "heart knowledge" that informs perceptions of the proper relation between academic and spiritual life. Unlike fundamentalists, evangelicals do not oppose secular education per se. But they do regard it as spiritually corrosive if not sustained and guided by a personal commitment to Christ. While the study of theology is a legitimate endeavor for any Christian, experience teaches that the institutions and methods of the mainstream often lead students away from authentic faith. Thus, when interpreted as a "transition from theologian to Christian," Bonhoeffer's conversion confirms the evangelical maxim that studying theology does not always nurture belief. The fact that Bonhoeffer's change occurred *after* his ordination substantiates the conviction that institutional endorsement is not evidence of genuine faith.[58]

In these ways the evangelical version of Bonhoeffer's "great liberation" resounds with the ambivalence many conservative Christians feel toward theological education. On one hand, Bonhoeffer ennobles the vocation of professional theology. As a Baptist scholar observed in the 1960s, Bonhoeffer's testimony "rebukes those churches who are suspicious of theological education. For we must not forget that Bonhoeffer's voice, the voice that helped save the German church from silent acquiescence to Hitler, was the voice of a seminarian."[59] On the other hand, Bonhoeffer reminds us "that becoming a theologian doesn't necessitate one being a Christian — it is just the same today. Indeed there is plausible evidence that Bonhoeffer wasn't a Christian until after he had studied theology and written his dissertation."[60] Behind such warnings lurk legends of academically gifted believers who went off to graduate school only to lose their faith, or just as disturbingly, become "liberals."

Drawing Lessons from Nazism

Just as in the mainstream, conservative Christians exemplify an enduring fascination with Nazism and the fate of the church under Hitler. Often this sad chapter in history is mined for religious lessons—including the politicization of the church, the corrosive effects of theological liberalism, and the failure to recognize Jews' continuing election—that are valued in the evangelical world.

Evangelical explorations of the church's failed resistance to Nazism honor Bonhoeffer as one of a handful of German Protestants who maintained "a biblical witness against fascism."[61] Representative of works in this genre is Erwin W. Lutzer's *Hitler's Cross*, which relates the dramatic struggle "between two saviors and two crosses." Lutzer repeats well-worn conservative verities—that homosexuality was rampant in Hitler's inner circle, that the Führer dabbled in the occult, that Nazism resembles New Age thought, and that America is perpetrating a "silent 'holocaust' in which five thousand tiny victims lose their lives every day."[62] According to Lutzer, drawing lessons from the church's confrontation with the swastika not only aids in distinguishing the "true church" from the "false church"; it offers a foretaste of the persecution that will attend the Fourth Reich, which the Bible predicts will precede Jesus' return. The connection is established through identifying Hitler as "a prototype of the Antichrist" whose magnetic power over the German people was due to his "personal acquaintance with satanic powers."[63]

If Hitler and his treatment of Jews offer a preview of the "final holocaust," then the Christians who opposed him naturally assume angelic stature. Chief among these seraphic heroes is Bonhoeffer, who called his church back to "fidelity to the gospel of God." In doing so, he witnessed to the indispensable truth that the German church's contest with Nazism was essentially spiritual rather than political, and that Christians must continue to "proclaim a Christ who stands above politics, above the sacred and the secular." Indeed, Lutzer believes, today's societal ills reflect a loss of confidence in the power of the gospel to change people from the inside out.[64] Bonhoeffer also witnesses through his resistance to the "liberal scholarship that stripped Christianity of its uniqueness" and fueled the ovens of Auschwitz.[65] Lutzer stresses that while Bonhoeffer was initially "impressed" by liberalism, he never accepted the conclusions of his liberal professors.

> Bonhoeffer's exposure to liberalism both in Germany and later at Union Seminary has often made evangelicals in America skeptical of his theology. The fact that he did not condemn liberalism outright, and his own references to "a religionless Christianity," have left some evangelicals doubting his genuine commitment to the Christ of the New Testament. However—and this is important—Bonhoeffer went out of his way to insist that the Bible is the revelation from God, even though he was unable to answer all of the arguments of those who objected to such evangelical theology.[66]

Bonhoeffer's essential "evangelicalism" is basic to his contemporary relevance, since today's "social libertarians" and "liberated social planners" represent the same threat to the church's survival as did "liberalism" in Bonhoeffer's day.

Finally, Lutzer argues, Bonhoeffer keeps us in mind of the fact that "many of our Christian heroes were lawbreakers." Because the current assault on traditional values by liberal elites is so "reminiscent of Hitler's Germany," because the growing power of the secular state confronts us with "the American version of Hitler's 'positive Christianity,'" Bonhoeffer's radical example calls every Christian to activism:

> If Christians are silent at our universities for fear of being disgraced; if believers are intimidated at work because of new laws that might keep religion out of the workplace; if a Christian nurse is silent about abortion because to speak out would put her job in jeopardy; in short, *if we keep Christ to ourselves out of fear of reprisals, are we not taking our stand with those pastors in Germany who chose to close ranks with Hitler?* Is not our sin even greater since the consequences of our obedience to Christ are so minimal in comparison with what they faced? Are we qualified

to sit in judgment of the church in Germany if we ourselves have never lost a job or failed a course because we are Christians?[67]

Lutzer's Bonhoeffer stands before us as "a constant reminder that the church must always remain the church, even at great personal cost."[68]

A similar perception of Bonhoeffer's position in the twenty-first-century culture wars animates Georg Huntemann's portrait of the German theologian. Huntemann insists that since "liberalism" was the root of the church's seduction by Nazism, contemporary liberalism must be eschewed at all costs. Bonhoeffer's struggle against National Socialism "can be readily carried over to our day," Huntemann writes, since "all of the anti-Christian elements of the Nazi period continue to be at work precisely among those who count themselves, often with such careless disregard of history, part of the progressive or left-wing scene."[69]

Indeed, Huntemann's "other Bonhoeffer" is fashioned to appeal to Christians who feel alienated by shifting cultural mores. As Bonhoeffer opposed shamelessness and hedonism in his own time, Huntemann contends, he encourages us to stand against the "present-day revolution as a rejection of parental authority, the weakening of sexual taboos and the denial of all biblical ordinances for sexual life."[70] "If it were to follow Bonhoeffer's intention," Huntemann concludes, "theology's task today would be to oppose decisively the cultural and moral revolution of our time."[71]

Bonhoeffer Meets Christian Biography

A further indication of Bonhoeffer's high standing in the evangelical community is his penetration into the various forms of inspirational literature that are marketed to conservative Christians. For instance, Bonhoeffer appears in several of the biography series distributed by evangelical publishers. These include *Dietrich Bonhoeffer: Opponent of the Nazi Regime* in Barbour's Heroes of the Faith Series (which heroes include John Bunyan, Charles Finney, Francis and Edith Schaeffer, Billy Sunday, and Corrie ten Boom) and *Dietrich Bonhoeffer* in Bethany

House's Men of Faith Series (which contains volumes on Billy Graham, C. S. Lewis, D. L. Moody, Jim Elliot, John Wesley, and Oswald Chambers). The back cover of one of these texts captures the essence of the genre: Bonhoeffer "was never truly alone in his concrete cell, because the Lord was with him . . . He had written 'the cost of discipleship'—and paid that cost with his life. His investment, though, continues to pay dividends for those who follow his example."

Dietrich Bonhoeffer: Opponent of the Nazi Regime by Michael van Dyke dramatizes Bonhoeffer's life by using description and dialogue to enhance the major episodes in his biography. Van Dyke's treatment of this "hero of the faith" is remarkably balanced: He does not downplay Bonhoeffer's debts to liberalism, crisis theology, the social gospel, pacifism, ecumenism, Gandhi, or Catholicism. Yet he does underscore aspects of Bonhoeffer's life that are of particular interest to evangelical readers. Among these are his preaching and pastoral work,[72] the "conversion" through which Dietrich "sought and found a deeper place in his relationship with God,"[73] and the completion of his intellect in genuine faith. Missing from Dietrich's life during his years of intense theological and philosophical study was "a warm heart of true faith. He was learning everything that had ever been said about God, and yet he never spoke to God himself. He never prayed or read the Bible in order to hear what God was saying to him personally."[74]

Another aspect of Bonhoeffer's evangelical portrait highlighted by van Dyke is concern for Jews. While a student at Union Seminary, van Dyke's Bonhoeffer seeks to sensitize Americans to the "irrational prejudice against Jews in [his] country" and soon recognizes through his encounters with Negro America the striking parallels to the Jewish situation in Germany—"the segregation, discrimination, and political persecution."[75] Van Dyke describes the Confessing Church as an "emerging resistance movement" and the Barmen Declaration as "one of the most important documents in the history of Christendom," similar to the American Declaration of Independence.[76]

Not content simply to tell Bonhoeffer's story, such books communicate the implications of his life for evangelical readers. Van Dyke attempts to do so with the purposely vague statement that Bonhoeffer's ecclesiastical home was "the evangelical Church" and with claims that he was "a man who knew that he could only achieve true manhood by allowing himself to be inwardly transformed into the image of the incarnate Christ . . . ," one whose "daily life was anchored in the simple disciplines of Bible study and prayer . . ." "Dietrich Bonhoeffer's life can serve as a model," van Dyke concludes, "for twenty-first-century Christians who are faced with the prospect of newly emerging paganisms and overweening rulers."[77]

In her contribution to Bethany House's "Men of Faith" series, Susan Martins Miller elucidates Bonhoeffer's "lasting legacy" and in the process further illuminates the lineaments of his evangelical portrait. Here we learn that although Bonhoeffer was a student of liberal theology, he also "rooted himself very deeply in historic Christianity" and "acted on his simple but genuine conviction that the Bible is the Word of God."[78] From his example we learn the importance of an "unfailing discipline of reading the Bible, meditating on its words, and praying for others" and are reminded of the church's duty to "stand apart from the flow of culture."[79] Bonhoeffer's salience for post-"9/11" America is implied in the book's emphasis on his "faith lived out in action in a time of personal and national crisis."

In 1991, *Christian History*—an occasional publication of Christianity Today, Inc.—devoted an entire issue to Bonhoeffer. Previous issues of the magazine had profiled Augustine, Calvin, Luther, the Puritans, John Wesley, George Whitefield, Charles Finney, Dwight Moody, and Columbus (!), but only one had been devoted to a twentieth-century figure (C. S. Lewis).[80] While featuring articles by non-evangelical scholars such as Geffrey Kelly, John Godsey, and Eberhard Bethge, the Bonhoeffer issue of *Christian History* portrayed a man quite compatible with evangelical sensibilities. For instance, the longest excerpt from Bonhoeffer's writings is from *The Cost of Discipleship*, F. Burton Nelson's contribution is titled "Pastor Bonhoeffer," and a list of "questions for today" includes a reference to abortion.[81]

Another example of Christian biography designed to increase awareness of Bonhoeffer's life among evangelicals is Focus on the Family Radio Theatre's 1997 production of *Bonhoeffer: The Cost of Freedom*.[82] This Peabody Award-winning drama is remarkable for its quality and accuracy; yet it depicts Bonhoeffer in shades that blend into the American evangelical landscape.[83] The peculiarly American idiom in this rendition of Bonhoeffer's story is the language of freedom. "Faith. Freedom. Individual liberties. We often take them for granted . . . until they're taken away from us," reads the play's promotional literature.[84]

As we have seen, the evangelical Bonhoeffer is twice-born; thus this production clarifies Bonhoeffer's cryptic statement that he went from being a theologian to being a Christian: "I became a believer, not a minister or theologian, but a believer in Jesus Christ." Evangelical themes also figure in the production's treatment of Bonhoeffer the seminary professor. Previous experience, we are told, had robbed the Finkenwalde students of the ability to experience Christianity in a heartfelt way. Yet rather than the "cool, academic detachment" they had learned to expect, those under Bonhoeffer's tutelage enjoyed a "full spiritual life."

"Bonhoeffer: The Cost of Freedom" presents a figure whose witness and martyrdom challenge us to reconsider the dividing line between personal faith and civic duty, a guiding theme in attempts to utilize Bonhoeffer on the part of Focus on the Family. Yet overall, "Bonhoeffer: The Cost of Freedom" fits the established evangelical pattern. Attention to Bonhoeffer's writings is limited almost exclusively to *The Cost of Discipleship, evangelische* is rendered "evangelical" without clarification of the German word's nuances, and dimensions of Bonhoeffer's life that challenge evangelical stereotypes are downplayed. For instance, Bonhoeffer's theological education at Tübingen and Berlin is completely overlooked and Union Theological Seminary is barely mentioned.

In the early 1990s Bonhoeffer finally entered the genre of "Christian fiction," which is sold primarily at Christian bookstores and read almost exclusively by evangelicals. Michael Phillips, whose books have sold over five million copies, incorporated Bonhoeffer as a secondary character in *The Eleventh Hour*, the first volume in his "The Secret of the Rose" series. Unlike mainstream novels such as Mary Glazener's *The Cup of Wrath* and Denise Giardina's *Saints and Villains, The Eleventh Hour* is not a recounting of Bonhoeffer's life. Yet the theologian does play an increasingly prominent supporting role as the story unfolds. At the book's end, Phillips appends a "note on Dietrich Bonhoeffer" which explains his decision to include him. Phillips writes:

The further along I got in the story and research, the more I found, as described in the introduction, that Bonhoeffer himself was turning out to be the unexpected personality who—unknown even to me as the author!—was proceeding to intrude himself onto the pages at every turn. Indeed, I came to feel, and feel such more strongly than ever, that the saga of brave and committed evangelical believers in Germany during the Second World War cannot in an accurate way be told without the large, looming presence of Dietrich Bonhoeffer playing a pivotal role. I knew about him but scantly when undertaking this project. I find the admiration and honor I feel toward him now to be equal to what I feel toward any other single man of God. It is my conviction we all owe him a tremendous debt for his example, and I have been changed by my encounter in the spirit with this brother who gave his life rather than water down or relinquish what he knew was true.[85]

Phillips states that his intent in including Bonhoeffer in the novel is "to honor him and give him what I consider his rightful stature in the history of European evangelicalism in this century."[86] These words make explicit what is evident throughout the book itself: that Phillips regards Dietrich Bonhoeffer as an exemplary evangelical Christian.

Bonhoeffer enters the novel on page 119. It is 1937, and Baron Heinrich von Dortmann has just returned to his Pomeranian country estate from a visit to Finkenwalde, where he has been auditing Bonhoeffer's lectures on Jesus' Sermon on the Mount. In a conversation with his wife, von Dortmann expresses both admiration and concern for Bonhoeffer, who seems unafraid of death: "He has been flying in the Nazis' face for years, making enemies with his bold pro-Jewish sentiments and his pronouncements to the church to awaken from its complacency."[87] What is it you told me he said to you recently? his wife asks. "When Christ calls a man, he bids him come and die," is the baron's response. This reference to *Nachfolge*, the published version Bonhoeffer's Finkenwalde lectures, foreshadows the role Bonhoeffer will play in the novel.

We learn that Bonhoeffer came to von Dortmann's attention in early 1933, when he heard an anti-Hitler lecture broadcast over Berlin radio, and "found his heart immediately in tune with this one who was courageous enough to address the nation so boldly."[88] Von Dortmann made Bonhoeffer's acquaintance at Ulm the following year and between that meeting and 1937 the two have become "deep friends of the spirit" who spend time alone together during the baron's visits to

Finkenwalde. When Gestapo agents close the seminary, Bonhoeffer calls his friend and asks for refuge at *Lebenshaus*, the von Dortmann country estate.

When Bonhoeffer next appears in the novel it is February, 1938. While supervising "collective pastorates" in the region, Bonhoeffer visits *Lebenshaus* and confides to the baron that he has made contact with the German resistance. "I have prayed and prayed for years about what should be our response as Christians to the Nazi evil . . . My conscience tells me that the Nazi evil against the Jews is of such magnitude that bringing force against it may be necessary," Bonhoeffer says. As for the baron, he is unable to reconcile such activity with the example of Jesus: "I feel God may give me to speak to men's spiritual needs in the midst of the darkness, rather than to try to eliminate the cause of that darkness . . ."[89]

Yet despite differing views of the political implications of Christian faith in Nazi Germany, the two men agree on the necessity of taking personal risks to aid persecuted Jews. "The ministry of *Lebenshaus* may be to give life and retreat and seclusion in new ways than we have seen before," the baron tells Bonhoeffer in one of their conversations. This colloquium presages the unfolding of the novel's plot, for later we learn that the baron's own wife is Jewish, and that he will be called to act on behalf of "her people." By the end of the war, von Dortmann has become a crucial link in an underground rescue network "meshing Christians and Jews in a loose federation of dangerous compassion." Following Bonhoeffer's arrest, the baron naturally assumes his place "as the leader of [this] subversive Christian network."[90]

Like his mentor, von Dortmann resists Nazi anti-Semitism by emphasizing Jewish-Christian solidarity. Indeed, the baron's admiration for God's people continues to grow until he can not "look upon these descendants of Abraham and not sense a kinship and affinity with them deep within his being."[91] His theological understanding of this alliance is revealed in his discussions with a rabbi who takes refuge in his home. In one of their extended conversations, the rabbi comments that his host's views on religion are quite "Jewish," to which the baron responds, "I have always considered myself a Jew—in the spiritual sense."[92] But their rapport does not preclude the baron from witnessing to the rabbi about Jesus. He explains that Judaism is not wrong, "only incomplete. Jesus didn't bring a *new* system of belief; he brought completion to

Judaism." The two men can be "cousins," he says, although not siblings. This term is reserved for the relationship between the baron and his wife, "Jew and Gentile joined in that wonderful bond of *Christian* brother and sister."[93]

Ideal evangelical that he is, von Dortmann combines a love for God's people with a zeal for proselytizing them. "Make me especially their servant," he prays, "that I might reveal to them the life and character of your Son, Jesus." This prayer begins to be answered when a Jewish rescuee marvels at her Christian hosts, who treat Jews "like fellows of belief, speaking of their worship of the same God." She does not understand why they call her sister, and her husband brother. "But she could feel it changing her. She would never be the same."

The Eleventh Hour ends with Baron von Dortmann facing Emil Korsch, the Gestapo agent who is pursuing the Jews hidden on his estate. "By the authority of Jesus Christ, I command your men to hold your fire and to allow those people to go to safety," he shouts at an incredulous Korsch while the Jews make their escape. The meaning of von Dortmann's action is not lost on the grateful Jews who witness it: "The profundity of the man's Christian faith spoke louder and more forcefully to each with every passing day." The rabbi, in particular, was never able to forget the baron's words about Christianity bringing to fulfillment what the law of Judaism had only begun.[94]

Phillips does several things designed to transform the historical Bonhoeffer into a credible character in this work of evangelical fiction. First, he inserts Bonhoeffer into an evangelical narrative world where he functions as the hero's mentor and soul mate.[95] Second, he makes Baron von Dortmann a sort of conservative lay Bonhoeffer—an unsophisticated man of the country with no clear church affiliation, but possessing a profound devotion to God that is expressed in prayer, Scripture reading, and hospitality.[96] In the process the baron is shorn of those Bonhoefferian qualities with which many evangelicals are uncomfortable. While inspired by the theologian's courage and sacrifice, von Dortmann's loyalties are with "the people of God" rather than the institutional church; he is suspicious of the ecumenical movement and ignorant of non-Christian religions; he remains uneasy with Bonhoeffer's active political resistance, and is incapable of lying to the Gestapo.[97] In these ways Baron von Dortmann personifies evangelical ambivalence toward the historical Bonhoeffer.

Third, Phillips makes Bonhoeffer the purveyor of a message to which evangelicals are naturally receptive: German Christians—especially those who counted "themselves among those who love the people of God"—were also to become victims of the Nazis. "Judaism was not to be the only religion trampled under Nazi boots," the narrator reminds us. This Nazi antipathy for Christianity is embodied in Gestapo agent Emil Korsch, whom Himmler has appointed as his "special assistant to deal with the Christian problem." As far as Korsch is concerned, the Jews can stay. "If he had his way, they would get rid of the Christians instead." Thus the Jewish-Christian bond is forged in the suffering that inevitably befalls God's people, "Jews and Christians alike."[98]

What about *Letters and Papers from Prison?*

It is no surprise that Bonhoeffer's prison writings are rarely featured in evangelical portrayals of the German theologian. Indeed, conservative Christians have found much of what Bonhoeffer says in these letters to be "disturbing when considered in the light of Scripture."[99] However, once Bonhoeffer has been judged theologically orthodox, there are ways of dealing with the otherwise unattractive aspects of his legacy. For instance, one may emphasize Bonhoeffer's continuing reliance on the tradition. "Everything he wrote, even personal letters in the last weeks of his life," writes one evangelical author, "was infused with his comprehensive knowledge of the Bible."[100] Another assures us that Bonhoeffer's conclusions regarding World War II "were the direct result of a personal relationship with Christ."[101]

Alternatively, conservative interpreters can co-opt aspects of Bonhoeffer's theology that may at first glance appear foreign to evangelical sensibilities. Even Bonhoeffer's enigmatic talk of "religionless-less," which for more radical interpreters resembles atheism, can be recast in familiar evangelical language. In 1965 an article in *Eternity* characterized Bonhoeffer's view of secularity as "the God-willed deliverance of Christianity from the bondage of false religiosity" and his late theology as the product of "a man of faith facing the facts of life and at the same time burning with the desire to claim the 'religionless' man and 'adult' world of today for Jesus Christ."[102] Thirty years later David Gushee noted in *Christianity Today* that while many evangelicals mistrust the "prison Bonhoeffer," in fact he eschewed Christian "religion" in order to "follow Jesus Christ the living Lord in the midst of a collapsing culture and faithless church."[103] Michael van Dyke adds that Bonhoeffer understood religion as a social construction opposed to faith itself.[104] For American evangelicals who have embraced Bonhoeffer as one of their own, such renderings of his prison theology fit the image of the man they have come to love.

The manner in which Bonhoeffer's late theology may be rescued for Christian orthodoxy was demonstrated beautifully in the late 1960s by Kenneth Hamilton.[105] This response to faddish interpretation of the German theologian cast *Letters* in light of Bonhoeffer's earlier writings on Christian discipleship and some of his lesser-known prison letters. When considering the controversial themes in *Letters and Papers from Prison*, Hamilton wrote, if we make the focus of inquiry the nature of Christian discipleship, "the inner cohesion of Bonhoeffer's thinking may reveal itself."[106] Hamilton finds the "heart of his message" in Bonhoeffer's letter of July 21, 1944, where he asks that "God in his mercy lead us through these times. But above all may he lead us to himself." Bonhoeffer has much to teach us, Hamilton concludes, "because he fixed his faith, beyond all religion, on the God who has revealed Himself."[107]

But Is He Really Evangelical?

As Bonhoeffer's popularity among conservative Christians continues to bloom, some are questioning whether he belongs in the evangelical fold. Evangelical readers are often cautioned to judge Bonhoeffer's writings "in the light of God's word," and a few authors have cast doubt on the orthodoxy of his views.[108] But not until Richard Weikart's *The Myth of Dietrich Bonhoeffer: Is His Theology Evangelical?* (1997) had an evangelical scholar sought to revoke Bonhoeffer's conservative credentials. Weikart attacks the "uncritical endorsement" of Bonhoeffer rooted in the myth that he was an orthodox theologian whose commitments match those of contemporary evangelicals. In fact, he sets out to demonstrate the fundamental incompatibility of Bonhoeffer's thought with Christian orthodoxy. The problems are legion.

For one, Bonhoeffer embraced a coherence theory of truth that is at odds with the "rational communication" view of revelation espoused by Carl F. H. Henry, the founder of modern evangelicalism. Another difficulty is Bonhoeffer's view of Scripture, which Weikart regards as sub-orthodox. "Nothing about Bonhoeffer appeals to evangelicals," Weikart acknowledges, "more than his emphasis on the authority of the Scriptures." But evangelicals fail to realize that Bonhoeffer stressed Scriptural authority while accepting the validity of "liberal biblical criticism."[109] Furthermore, Bonhoeffer did not view Bible interpretation as an individual enterprise; rather, in an authoritarian tone repugnant to most evangelicals, he "directed people to listen to the church rather than to seek personal revelation through studying the Scriptures."[110]

According to Weikart, Bonhoeffer also was deeply influenced by both liberal and neoorthodox theology.[111] He never completely forsook Barthianism, an influence that led him to adopt a neo-Kantian division of knowledge into two independent realms (*Historie* and *Heilsgeschichte*). Bonhoeffer's conception of self-contained biblical history is evident, Weikart claims, in his description of the gospel accounts of Jesus' life as "overgrown with legends." To accentuate Bonhoeffer's distance from evangelical views of the Bible, Weikart observes that he "welcomed the works of Bultmann," expressing "great joy" at the appearance of *The New Testament and Mythology*.[112]

Furthermore, Bonhoeffer adopted an irrationalism (Weikart also calls it "existentialism" and "decisionism") for which he was indebted to both Nietzsche and Dilthey. Indeed, it is the "striking affinity" between Nietzsche and Bonhoeffer's remarks on "religionless Christianity" that led radical theologians to claim him as a founding father of death-of-God theology. Weikart does not think this movement fairly represented Bonhoeffer's thought ("Bonhoeffer the death of God theologian is almost as mythical as Bonhoeffer the evangelical").[113] Nevertheless, his comments in *Letters and Papers from Prison* questioning God's eternal immutability and omnipotence and denying the metaphysical reality of Sheol, Hades, and redemption constitute a "forthright rejection of orthodox Christianity" that is indebted to Nietzsche and Heidegger and anticipates process theology.[114] Nothing in Weikart's book is more damning than his linkage of Bonhoeffer with Nietzsche, the "demonic, Promethean anti-Christ." In a passage calculated to chill evangelical ardor, Weikart declares that *The Cost of*

Discipleship clearly demonstrates Bonhoeffer's agreement with "Niet-zsche's ideas."[115]

Weikart also charges that, like Barth, Bonhoeffer was a universalist. To read *The Cost of Discipleship* as if Bonhoeffer equates discipleship with salvation is "an egregious misinterpretation," Weikart insists.[116] God extends the call to discipleship and the offer of salvation to all, Bonhoeffer believed, and he did not consider those who refused the path of discipleship as being damned or eternally separated from God. In fact, while attracted to his "religionless" fellow prisoners, Bonhoef-fer denied any intent to evangelize them. According to Weikart, Bon-hoeffer rarely refers to Jesus Christ as "savior" and shows a total lack of concern for Jesus' sacrificial work on the cross.

Neither did Bonhoeffer undergo the sort of personal conversion familiar to evangelicals. As for the "great liberation" celebrated by con-servative commentators, Weikart writes that Bonhoeffer rarely men-tioned this experience and "later considered continuity, not conversion, a more apt description of the course of his own spiritual life." In fact, Bonhoeffer had no sympathy for the evangelical concep-tion of conversion "as an experience of regeneration and salvation."[117]

Finally, Weikart maintains that Bonhoeffer was an ethical relativist whose existentialist approach reveals the influence of Kierkegaard, Dostoevsky, Dilthey, and Nietzsche. "It is remarkable," in fact, "how much of Nietzsche's ethical thought he as a Christian theologian did swallow."[118] Although conservatives delight in the pro-life stance espoused in *Ethics*, Weikart reminds them that Bonhoeffer's positions on euthanasia, abortion, and suicide "must be seen as concrete com-mands for the present situation, not as objective norms that can be applied universally."[119] In this way, Weikart drives a wedge between Bonhoeffer's ethics and the political resistance that has made him a Christian hero. Since "his opposition to Nazism and racism was rooted in his family's political and social views . . . opposing viewpoints could be built on the same shaky foundation that Bonhoeffer erected."[120] While Bonhoeffer's death is commonly viewed as an outgrowth of the theology he articulated in *The Cost of Discipleship*, in fact his partici-pation in the plot to murder Hitler was as much a repudiation as an extension of these ideas.[121]

Thus, evangelicals' tacit assumption that Bonhoeffer shared their deepest commitments is a dangerous misconception. His distance from contemporary evangelicalism is not a matter of style, but of theological substance. As a result, Weikart does not even recommend Bonhoeffer's books for edification, since his theology shares "elements of deception common in the main currents of twentieth-century theology."[122]

Other attacks on Bonhoeffer's orthodoxy proceed at the grassroots level. Biblical Discernment Ministries warns evangelicals who are "taken in by his warm-hearted piety and his high sounding devotion to Christ and call to suffer for His sake" that Bonhoeffer was "in reality a practical atheist and a religious humanist who denied virtually every cardinal doctrine of the historic Christian faith." According to BDM, Bonhoeffer proclaimed a situational ethics, developed an existentialist theology, espoused pantheism, universalism, sacramentalism, and evolution, and questioned Christ's Virgin birth, deity, and physical resurrection. He saw value in higher criticism, denied the inerrancy and authority of the Bible, and influenced Marxist-inspired liberation theology.[123] The authors of this broadside leave no doubt about their wish to counteract Bonhoeffer's reputation among prominent evangelical figures and institutions, including Charles Colson, *Christianity Today*, and Grand Rapids Baptist College (which in 1991 scheduled a play extolling Bonhoeffer's memory).

Assessing the Conservative Bonhoeffer

The surest indication of Bonhoeffer's place in the pantheon of evangelical heroes are these kinds of warnings about his insidious influence in conservative circles.[124] But just as evangelical admiration for Bonhoeffer does not depend on the arguments of authors such as Georg Huntemann or Erwin Lutzer, these sorts of diatribes are not likely to have much effect on the evangelical rank and file. Indeed, the conservative Bonhoeffer is probably impervious to scholarly critique, even that of concerned evangelicals.

However, critics on the right do point to dimensions of Bonhoeffer's legacy that, if truly countenanced by evangelicals, are sure to give pause. On this list must be included Bonhoeffer's enthusiasm for Bultmann's "demythologizing" project, his call for a reexamination of antiquated statements in the Apostle's Creed, his training at flagship liberal institutions such as Berlin and Union, his self-identification as a "modern theologian" who took part in the Barthian revolution while bearing the heritage of liberal theology, his view of apologetics as a futile attempt to convince people they cannot live without "religion," and his advice that the postwar church disinvest itself.

Also potentially problematic for conservatives (and many other interpreters) are Bonhoeffer's complex attitudes regarding violence. Most evangelicals are aware of Bonhoeffer's participation in a violent coup against Hitler. Although they may find this decision troubling, they view it as one made in a situation of extreme duress by a man engaged in mortal conflict with the epitome of human evil. More unsettling for contemporary evangelicals is Bonhoeffer's persistent engagement in the ecumenical and peace movements of his day. Bonhoeffer's ecumenism, which made him highly suspect in his own day, is probably no more acceptable among today's conservatives.[125] Certainly conservative Christians are no less likely to honor national and ethnic identity over what they view as "universalist" sentiments.

"Nowadays it can hardly be imagined," writes Eberhard Bethge, "that ecumenism at that time concerned only a minority, and that it was practically outlawed, as something to do with 'decadent internationally-minded democrats'—an effective, powerful word of insult describing the alleged enemies of national pride."[126] But anyone familiar with evangelical culture really has no difficulty imagining these attitudes. For evangelicals retain a great deal of ambivalence toward ecumenism and the denominational bodies that support it. In fact, the coup de grace in Biblical Discernment Ministries' attack on Bonhoeffer's orthodoxy is a declaration of his role in the World Alliance for International Friendship—"a forerunner of the apostate World Council of Churches."[127]

As for Bonhoeffer's peace activism, it is important to recall that it was not based exclusively in his opposition to idolatrous Hitler-worship and aggressive war. Long before Nazism revealed its genocidal character Bonhoeffer had decided he could not serve in the German military. Aware that his students at Finkenwalde saw the impending "call-up" as an opportunity to demonstrate their patriotism, Bonhoeffer made sure they "went in with a bad conscience."[128] This influence did not go unnoticed. In 1936 Bonhoeffer's church superior wrote that due to "the reproach that can be raised against [Bonhoeffer] that he is a pacifist and an enemy of the State, it might be advisable for the Provincial Church Committee to disassociate itself from him and take measures to ensure that German theologians no longer be trained by him."[129]

Significantly, Bonhoeffer's position did not soften as war loomed. Before his voyage to America in 1939, he informed Bishop George Bell that he was leaving Germany to avoid military call-up: "He had said he could not damage his weakened and defeated Confessing Church by another disastrous case, the case of Bonhoeffer the conscientious objector . . ."[130] As Larry Rasmussen notes, when Bonhoeffer sounded pacifist themes, he did so almost wholly alone, even within the Confessing Church. At the war's outset, there were a grand total of two conscientious objectors among active Protestants; both were executed without support from the church.[131]

These facts carry considerable freight in a post-"9/11" world in which the vast majority of Americans cannot imagine withholding military service from their nation. Even if they dissent from specific government policies, most Americans feel that in an emergency doing one's part is a patriotic—perhaps even a religious—duty. But during the 1930s Bonhoeffer came to the well-considered conclusion that as a Christian he could not participate in waging war. While the "war on terrorism" may tempt us to seek in Bonhoeffer a theological sanction for just war, that search is doomed to failure.[132]

Thus Bonhoeffer raises penetrating questions for conservative Christians who are wont to blur the lines between "God and country": Can they acknowledge Bonhoeffer's claim that peace is the opposite of security? Are they willing to pray for the defeat of their nation, as Bonhoeffer did? Can they affirm espionage as a legitimate activity for a Christian, let alone a pastor or theologian? In general, can they embrace Bonhoeffer's brand of critical patriotism?

Another aspect of Bonhoeffer's legacy that is off-putting for evangelicals is his respect for Roman Catholicism. Reflecting the evangelical discomfort with things Catholic, Richard Weikart accuses Bonhoeffer of becoming enamored of the Catholic church and letting this fact negatively influence his ecclesiology. It is ironic, in fact, that evangelicals show a special affinity for the writings of Bonhoeffer's Finkenwalde period (i.e., *The Cost of Discipleship* and *Life Together*), for this experiment in clergy training was animated by Bonhoeffer's vision of a classical *vita communis* in the monastic mold. He even referred to his use of the Sermon on the Mount at the seminary as "spiritual exercises." At the time, Finkenwalde attracted visitors from the Oxford Movement (an Anglo-Catholic renewal effort within the Church of England) and was viewed by some German Protestants as a "sinister re-Catholicization" of the tradition.[133]

Similarly, if conservatives are determined to give a pietistic cast to Bonhoeffer's "conversion" they should remember Bonhoeffer's negative reaction to Finkenwalde visitors whom he believed substituted "the testimony of personal change" for the testimony of Scripture.[134] They should also keep in mind that the "momentous" experience of 1931 was accompanied not only by increased church attendance, an interest in oral confession, systematic meditation on the Bible, and a "community life of obedience and prayer," but also by the beginning of Bonhoeffer's involvement in the ecumenical movement and his enduring interest in Gandhian pacifism.[135]

Despite all this, there are aspects of Bonhoeffer's legacy that his evangelical admirers challenge us to recall. One is the extent to which "pastor Bonhoeffer" appears to have struggled with honoring both his gifts as a theologian and his call to ministry. In the 1930s he wrote, "at present I am faced with a pretty momentous decision, whether to take a pastorate at Friedrichshain in East Berlin at Easter. It is strange how hard it is to decide . . . The problem is how to combine the ministry with university teaching."[136] Related to this vocational struggle was Bonhoeffer's determination to maintain a regimen of spiritual discipline through the changing circumstances of his life. The image of a professional theologian who actually prayed, read the Bible, and admitted doing both is one that evangelicals understandably celebrate.[137]

It is tempting for Bonhoeffer scholars and non-evangelical Christians to dismiss the evangelical Bonhoeffer as a figment of the conservative religious imagination. And to a large extent it may be so; but it is a powerful figment nonetheless. In the United States alone there are somewhere between fourteen and fifty million evangelical Christians, and American organizations such as Focus on the Family exercise worldwide influence. According to the group's Web site, James Dobson's internationally syndicated radio programs are heard daily by more than two hundred million people around the world. And despite his dubious image of Bonhoeffer as a guide for Christian opposition to abortion, a recent "feedback" survey in *Focus on the Family Newsletter* revealed that nearly 90 percent of readers agree with Dobson that men such as Dietrich Bonhoeffer are "admirable role models because their faith motivated them to practical action that subsequently made a positive impact on society."[138] We dismiss such appropriations of Bonhoeffer at our own risk.

In resistance against dictatorship and terror they gave their lives for freedom, justice and human dignity.

—PLAQUE AT FLOSSENBÜRG COMMEMORATING BONHOEFFER AND OTHER RESISTERS

Bonhoeffer was a universal man, at least an international man, at home in the whole world. He gloried in his freedom to identify with everyone everywhere.

—THEODORE A. GILL

So many now claim his support . . . that [Bonhoeffer] seems to have become all things to all men.

—WILLIAM BLAIR GOULD

[Bonhoeffer] stands for all in our time who act according to their conscience, who go against the stream, who will not submit to wrong.

—RONALD GREGOR SMITH

All over the world people who are trying to find meaning and joy in life, despite the disorder of the world, are listening attentively to what [Bonhoeffer] says, because he was granted the great opportunity of confirming his message through his life and his death.

—W. A. VISSER 'T HOOFT

BRIDGE

THE UNIVERSAL BONHOEFFER

In the years since his death, Dietrich Bonhoeffer has come to be revered as an exemplary Christian and human being. At a London memorial service held in July 1945, Bishop George Bell declared that Bonhoeffer represented "both the resistance of the believing soul, in the name of God, to the assault of evil, and also the moral and political revolt of the human conscience against injustice and cruelty."[1] Bell's words were not only commemorative, but prophetic as well. For during the next sixty years Bonhoeffer's legacy would increasingly be construed in ecumenical, interfaith, and universal terms. In exploring the parameters of the universal Bonhoeffer, we will revisit some of the themes elaborated in the preceding chapters. Identifying regions where the radical, liberal, and conservative portraits overlap will aid us in discerning Bonhoeffer's place in the religious imagination broadly conceived.

Prisoner of Conscience and Modern Martyr

Without doubt, Bonhoeffer the opponent of Nazism is the commanding image in his universal portrait. The appeal of this image is enhanced by popular fascination with the Third Reich, as well as by the view that Bonhoeffer was imprisoned for "his beliefs."[2] This perception of Bonhoeffer as a prisoner of conscience places him in a line of heroic figures stretching from Boethius to Sir Thomas More to Nelson Mandela. And while referring to Bonhoeffer with a religiously charged term like "martyr" may appear to limit his influence, in the age of totalitarianism the word is applied to many forms of sacrificial resistance. Depending on one's theological or political proclivities, Nazism may be understood as a movement of the far right supported by conservative elites or a neopagan rebellion against Western, Christian values. In either case, Nazi victims are portrayed as having sacrificed their lives in defense of their ideals.[3]

Among the very first to use the epithet "martyr" in describing the late German theologian was Reinhold Niebuhr, who in June 1945 informed readers of *Christianity and Crisis* of Bonhoeffer's demise under the headline "The Death of a Martyr."[4] The following month, in a London memorial service broadcast by the BBC, Bishop Bell referred to Bonhoeffer as "one of a noble company of martyrs . . ."[5] As Keith Clements notes, after the war the Bonhoeffer-as-martyr image held broad appeal:

> In the immediate postwar years, with Hitler and Nazism synonymous with evil, there was an instinctive response to any figure who represented resistance—as the case of the imprisoned Martin Niemöller before and during the war had shown. Perhaps the life and death of Bonhoeffer even offered some further psychological assurance that the war against Nazi Germany had been justified, if any further justification was needed. There had even been Germans, good Germans, who had opposed Hitler to the point of ultimate sacrifice. And of course the martyr-figure has a powerful appeal. As yet, the political and ethical complications of the conspiracy against Hitler still lay hidden under the simple, heroic concept of "resistance."[6]

In the English-speaking world Bonhoeffer's stature as a martyr was enhanced with the publication of *The Cost of Discipleship* in 1948. "The book was read as a commentary on the martyrdom," Clements writes, "and Bonhoeffer's death was seen as a straightforward fulfillment of the theme of the book."[7] Within two decades, Bonhoeffer's legacy had become synonymous with sacrificial witness to the faith. "There can be no doubt," wrote John Gibbs in 1964, "about Bonhoeffer's place in the annals of church history as a Christian martyr."[8] Around the same time, Charles E. Lange opined that "the suffering of Dietrich Bonhoeffer and the suffering of the first-century martyrs were rooted in remarkably similar circumstances." Like them, Bonhoeffer was a "man of faith and integrity who refused to sell his soul in order to live in dishonorable peace under the Nazi regime."[9] Over the past four decades, scholarly works, church periodicals, and the popular press have persisted in classifying Bonhoeffer as a "martyr." Even when the details of his life are muddled, his martyrdom is professed.[10]

In Germany, memories of Bonhoeffer's sacrifice have been conflicted. Initially, it was commonplace to think of Bonhoeffer as a martyr, as Christians in postwar Germany were eager to draw parallels between the Nazi era and earlier seasons of persecution. The religious ethos that animated recollection of the German resistance in the immediate aftermath of liberation is indicated by Fabian von Schlabrendorff, who was imprisoned with Bonhoeffer: "Surely never since the days when the Christians were persecuted in ancient Rome did such an abundance of noble, truly Christian men and women populate the prisons and dungeons of such barbarians as the SS and the Gestapo."[11] Such thinking nourished the assumption that those who opposed Nazism on religious grounds died as religious martyrs.

However, concerns over Bonhoeffer's putative martyrdom materialized fairly quickly in Germany. The publication of *Letters and Papers from Prison* and increasing awareness of Bonhoeffer's political activities led some to question the authenticity of his "martyrdom," particularly in relation to Paul Schneider, a clergy victim whose image was unsullied by political intrigue.[12] In the 1950s, Bishop Hans Meiser of Munich refused to attend a Flossenbürg memorial service because he regarded Bonhoeffer's death as a political rather than a religious act. As recently as 1986, an article in a German magazine argued that "from a biblical point of view Bonhoeffer is not an ecclesiastical, but a political-secular martyr."[13] Many Germans have had difficulty in coming to terms with Bonhoeffer's "treason," in part because his witness constitutes a "standing reproach" to those who did not actively oppose National Socialism.[14]

Eberhard Bethge argues that such disagreements over the meaning of Bonhoeffer's sacrifice indicate the need for a clear concept of martyrdom in the modern world. "Contemporary martyrdom," Bethge maintains, is an expression of solidarity with the oppressed. "Whereas formerly martyrdom was the result of bearing testimony to the name of Jesus Christ in a hostile world," Bethge writes, "now martyrdom . . . has become a sacrifice for the sake of humanity."[15] According to this model, Bonhoeffer's martyrdom does not rely on "synodical decisions and official authorization," but "expresses itself completely in the power of humiliation."[16]

Still, not everyone has been willing to concede the issue. In 1972 Alistair Kee challenged popular interpretations of Bonhoeffer's death in an article published in the *Christian Century*. "Martyr" is an inappropriate designation for Bonhoeffer, Kee wrote, since "there was no question of his being arrested and executed because of his beliefs—and that by definition is what 'martyr' means."[17] Kee's cranky resentment of Bonhoeffer's popularity notwithstanding, he was technically correct. Although *martus* originally referred to one who "witnessed," early on the term acquired a more ominous and specific meaning. "Within the lifetime of the Apostles," *The Catholic Encyclopedia* instructs us, the term "came to be used in the sense of a witness who at any time might be called upon to deny what he testified to, under penalty of death . . ." Thus a martyr or witness of Christ is one who gladly suffers death rather than deny the truths of the Christian faith.[18]

If "martyr" is used in the traditional sense of describing one who is executed for refusing to recant faith in Christ, we must acknowledge that Bonhoeffer never faced this choice, and thus calling him a Christian martyr is misleading. Had Bonhoeffer made peace with National Socialism, as many Christians in Germany did, he most likely would have escaped the attention of state authorities. When Bonhoeffer did arouse the regime's suspicions, his religious convictions per se were not in question. The Nazis censored him, placed him under surveillance, made it increasingly difficult for him to preach, write, or travel, and eventually arrested and imprisoned him; but they never demanded that he denounce Christ. He was hanged for "political high treason," for decisions that, while arrived at through a process of theological reflection, he did not regard as incumbent on all Christians.

None of this means that Bonhoeffer should be denied the appellation "martyr," as long as it is recognized that the title is primarily honorific. Otherwise we risk obscuring the witness of committed believers who *did* die for their stubborn refusal to recognize Nazi authority, a phenomenon of which Paul Schneider (the "witness of Buchenwald") and Jehovah's Witnesses are better examples. But such considerations will not deter the guardians of Bonhoeffer's legacy from referring to his "martyrdom by the Nazis," or church historians from including him

among the ranks of "modern martyrs."[19] In fact, as suffering for the faith
increasingly comes to the attention of Western Christians, Bonhoeffer
will remain an emblem of the martyred, whose ranks grew by 45 million
during the twentieth century.

Spiritual Mentor

From Eberhard Bethge to the authors of InterVarsity Press's Christian
Classics Bible Study, there is broad agreement that Bonhoeffer was one
of the great inspirational writers of the twentieth century.[20] But the
image of Bonhoeffer the spiritual mentor is of recent vintage. While
early commentators recognized his message for "the individual,"[21] the
term "spirituality" did not appear in classic studies of Bonhoeffer's life
and work (including Bethge's biography). But in the past decade this
topic has begun to make an impact on Bonhoeffer studies as scholars
capitalize on the growing openness to spirituality among otherwise secular persons.[22]

Mary Glazener finds a model for contemporary Christian existence
in Bonhoeffer's "personal faith," a term she uses to describe Bonhoeffer's reverence for the Bible, his emphasis on discipleship and commitment to preaching, his focus on "relationship" with God and others,
and his "quiet meditation on the life, sayings, deeds, sufferings, and
death of Jesus."[23] Gregory Baum credits Bonhoeffer with "a new development in the history of Christian spirituality," the spiritual message
that God cares for "the suffering of others, especially the hungry, the
exploited, and the persecuted."[24] Foregrounding Bonhoeffer's role as
spiritual guide, John D. Godsey imagines Bonhoeffer giving us this
advice:

> In your private life, be disciplined in your reading and medita-
> tion on the word of God in Scripture, in prayer and intercession.
>
> In your church life, join in the life of the community, being
> attentive to the preached word and the administered sacraments,
> being active in its mission of loving service to the world, and
> building up the fellowship through the ministries of listening,
> active helpfulness, bearing and forbearing, and, when it seems
> called for, speaking the word of God to another.

In your public life, be an everyday disciple of Christ by entering into the sufferings of God at the hands of a godless world,
courageously existing for others and thereby exhibiting in the
ordinary affairs of secular life God's will for righteousness.[25]

In 2003 Geffrey B. Kelly and F. Burton Nelson published the first
book-length study of Bonhoeffer's spirituality. According to the authors,
The Cost of Moral Leadership: The Spirituality of Dietrich Bonhoeffer
represents their response to the popular hunger for models of Christian
faith, discipleship, and community. Particularly interesting is the way
Kelly and Nelson illuminate the contours of Bonhoeffer's religious
experience while addressing the concerns of contemporary believers
and seekers. Like other writers who emphasize Bonhoeffer's "spiritual"
dimension, they highlight his "critique of religion" in a bid to reach
those who "are asking how they can hold onto a faith in the God of the
Old and New Testaments without binding themselves to a structure of
institutional forms and doctrines that simply make no sense in an
increasingly complex and chaotic world."[26]

With these disaffected souls in mind, the authors remind us that
Bonhoeffer believed "Jesus could set his word even above that of the
religious leaders of his day," that his catechesis emphasized community
spirit rather than doctrine, that he never equated "religion with all its
institutional structures and laws" with faith as God's gift, that he had
more in common with Jesus and the prophets than with the church,
and that he had a habit of annoying the German ecclesiastical establishment. In the same vein, they quote Bonhoeffer's statement from
The Cost of Discipleship that "it is not ultimately important to us what
this or that church leader wants. Rather, we want to know what Jesus
wants."[27] It is significant that this depiction of Bonhoeffer's spirituality
by two devout Christians is quite similar to the portrait drawn by the
agnostic Robert Coles, who compares Bonhoeffer's faith during the last
decade of his life to that of the earthly Jesus who was "a considerable
thorn in the side of all established religious and political authority."[28]

A reliable gauge of Bonhoeffer's contemporary role as a spiritual
mentor is the frequency with which his writings appear on lists of inspirational classics. In 1997 *The Christian Reader* named *The Cost of Discipleship* one of the top ten "best devotional books of all time," along
with such timeless classics as *Pilgrim's Progress, The Screwtape Letters,*

The Practice of the Presence of God, The Imitation of Christ, The Book of Common Prayer, and Augustine's *Confessions*.[29] In late 1999, when HarperCollins honored the "100 best spiritual books of the century," *The Cost of Discipleship* and *Letters and Papers from Prison* made the list (the latter was included in the top ten), along with selections by Black Elk, Martin Buber, Abraham Joshua Heschel, T. S. Eliot, Simone Weil, and Pierre Teilhard de Chardin.[30] In April 2000, when *Christianity Today* noted "100 books that had a significant effect on Christians" in the twentieth century, Bonhoeffer's *Cost of Discipleship* was number two, just behind C. S. Lewis's *Mere Christianity*.[31]

As Bonhoeffer's recognition by these diverse publications suggests, his spirituality may be cast in traditional categories familiar to orthodox Christians (e.g., commitment to prayer, Bible reading, preaching),[32] in more progressive terms that appeal to mainline liberals (e.g., discipleship that emphasizes peace and justice), or in quasi-secular terms suited to a pluralistic, post-Christian culture (integrity between his convictions and behavior, advocacy for human rights). In the latter case, the character of Bonhoeffer's spiritual legacy must be expressed in somewhat vague terms. A Web site announcing a one-man play on Bonhoeffer's life describes the German theologian as a "spiritual writer" who gave his fellow prison inmates "guidance and spiritual inspiration." Bonhoeffer, James C. Howell tells us, "went into prison with a profound grasp on things of the spirit."[33] And an article in the *Saturday Evening Post* claims that Bonhoeffer represents the importance of embracing "a set of core beliefs."[34] Such generic language is calculated to expose Bonhoeffer to audiences that, while perhaps alienated from traditional religion, are open to the language of "spirituality."

As with other masters of spirituality, Bonhoeffer's works have been edited with religious inspiration in mind. The first such collection of Bonhoeffer's spiritual wisdom was Otto Dudzus's *Bonhoeffer Brevier* (1963), which has been reprinted in several German editions and appeared in English in 1986 as *Bonhoeffer for a New Generation*.[35] Over the past fifteen years, Bonhoeffer's words have been collected in an anthology of "devotional classics"[36] and in several bedside table-sized volumes edited for devotional consumption. These include *Seize the Day with Dietrich Bonhoeffer, My Soul Finds Rest: Reflections on the Psalms by Dietrich Bonhoeffer, Voices in the Night: The*

Prison Poems of Dietrich Bonhoeffer, Meditations on the Cross, and
The Wisdom and Witness of Dietrich Bonhoeffer.[37]

Bonhoeffer's active and profound spiritual life is no doubt one of the
things that distinguishes him from most academic theologians. But the
image of Bonhoeffer as a spiritual guide is more than a reflection of his
"enlightened pietism."[38] It also mirrors the "impressive unity" of life
and thought mentioned in the preceding chapters. Godsey claims that
"the witness of his life and the power of his writings" are what have
made Bonhoeffer an influential theologian and spiritual leader.[39] Kelly
and Nelson write that in living what he wrote, Bonhoeffer "challenges
the dichotomy between faith and daily life in all its complexities."[40]
And Robert Coles affirms that "the heart of Bonhoeffer's spiritual
legacy to us is not to be found in his words, his books, but in the way he
spent his time on this earth . . ."[41] In the end, Coles writes, "his spiritual
gift to us, especially, is his life. The principles he avowed and discussed
in his writings gain their authority from the manner in which he con-
ducted that life."[42]

Soul Healer

A number of authors have sought to use Bonhoeffer as a bridge
between the insular territories of theology and psychology. In 1966,
Thomas C. Oden borrowed from Bonhoeffer's mature writings—particularly *Ethics* and *Letters and Papers from Prison*—to enliven the
stagnated "theology-therapy dialogue." He noted, for instance, that
many aspects of Bonhoeffer's view of God's participation in this broken
world are "surprisingly analogous" to Carl Rogers's notion of client-
centered participation in the troubled person's frame of reference.
Oden also maintained that "religion of the sort Bonhoeffer describes
and protests" must be rejected by Christian faith and psychotherapy
alike. "Let us then pursue the dialogue between therapy and theology
on the assumption that we are discussing the relationship between a
religionless psychotherapy and a religionless Christianity, and see
where this takes us," Oden wrote hopefully.[43]

But by far the most ambitious effort to apply Bonhoeffer's legacy to
psychological growth and healing is Uwe Siemon-Netto's *The Acquittal
of God: A Theology for Vietnam Veterans.*[44] The author is a seminary

graduate and former Vietnam War correspondent with experience as a chaplain at a Veterans Administration hospital. Observing that "Vietnam veterans often express the conviction that the almighty deserted them in the jungles and rice paddies of Indochina" and has stayed away ever since, Siemon-Netto's goal is to acquit God of the charge of desertion.[45] Why turn to Bonhoeffer for help in this endeavor? Because, Siemon-Netto argues, Bonhoeffer possessed deeper insights into the phenomenon of suffering than any theologian of the twentieth century. Noting that as many veterans have "committed suicide or lost their lives in other than natural circumstances" as died in Vietnam, Siemon-Netto decided to take Bonhoeffer's theology of suffering into therapy with veterans.

At the suggestion of Eberhard Bethge, Siemon-Netto introduced "After Ten Years" to a veterans rap group in Brainerd, Minnesota. The results were astounding:

> The discussion lasted almost three hours and turned out to be so intense that the veterans did not even stop for their habitual "smoke break." Although Bonhoeffer wrote his essay in another era and for a different readership, one that was confronted with a different set of problems, the veterans were fascinated by the topics he addressed. They identified with the implications of his subtitles, for example, "No ground under our feet," "Who stands fast?" "Of folly," "Contempt for humanity?" "Of suffering," "Are we still of any use?" and "The view from below."[46]

Capitalizing on the veterans' instant and profound connection with Bonhoeffer, Siemon-Netto interprets their conviction that God went AWOL in Vietnam via Bonhoeffer's *theologia crucis* and his concept of the "world come of age." According to Siemon-Netto, Vietnam vets are men whose pain has taken them across the threshold of a new world. As hardened citizens of this world, veterans instinctively comprehend Bonhoeffer's claim that "man is challenged to participate in the sufferings of God in a godless world."[47] These insights help the vets recognize God in their own experiences: "You see, as you are suffering with God in a godless world, god is suffering with you in a world you have experienced as godless. So what does that say to you? That God is a Vietnam vet!"[48]

With encouragement from Bethge, Siemon-Netto comes to regard his veterans as the vanguard of a "godless grown-up world," a group whose despair is a major step in the maturing process of this "young nation."[49] Yet despite this book's occasional profundities (Siemon-Netto observes that Bonhoeffer's image of having no ground under one's feet is an apt description of post-traumatic stress disorder, and that "god as a working hypothesis in morals, politics, philosophy, and religion" is the very God the veterans "flipped off" in Vietnam),[50] the parallels it draws between America's involvement in Vietnam and Nazi Germany on one hand, and between Vietnam veterans and the German resistance on the other, are often forced.[51] Still, *The Acquittal of God* is a profound example of the way Bonhoeffer's writings can bring healing power to persons and situations far removed from his own experience.

Model of Mature Faith

The impulse to establish Bonhoeffer as a paradigm of spiritual maturity is evident in a number of studies in the field of "faith development." The seminal work in this area is James W. Fowler's *Stages of Faith*, which presents a taxonomy of human faith development in six stages.[52] Fowler describes the last of these with reference to Bonhoeffer's spiritual achievement. In the middle of Fowler's account of "universalizing faith," he writes: "When asked whom I consider to be representatives of this Stage 6 outlook I refer to Gandhi, to Martin Luther King, Jr., in the last years of his life and to Mother Teresa of Calcutta. I am also inclined," Fowler adds, "to point to Dag Hammarskjöld, Dietrich Bonhoeffer, Abraham Heschel and Thomas Merton."[53] There is nothing shocking here. Asked to catalog the spiritual giants of the past century, many of us would cite these very names. Nor is it surprising—given Bonhoeffer's bold stand against Nazism, his steadfastness unto death, and his own interest in Gandhi[54]— that Fowler honors the German theologian by including him among these modern faith heroes.

In a subsequent study in this genre, Robin W. Lovin and Jonathan P. Gosser attempt to demonstrate that Bonhoeffer belongs in this select company by applying faith development theory to what is known of his life.[55] Lovin and Gosser trace Bonhoeffer's progress through successive faith stages, beginning with the "deep sense of security that emerged from the trustworthy environment of the Bonhoeffer family home," his experience of his older brother's death in 1918, his profound enjoyment of music, his quest for experience beyond his own land, and his "faith crisis," which they interpret in developmental terms as "a transition from a critical attitude of exploration to a stance of commitment."[56]

The authors identify evidence of Bonhoeffer's progression through faith stages three, four, and five. Then, based on his prison poetry and reports of those who knew him in captivity, they suggest that Bonhoeffer's faith underwent a further transformation "beyond the acquiescence of the obedient servant to a heartfelt, even joyful, acceptance of the role he had been called to play."[57] In particular, Bonhoeffer's poem "The Death of Moses" appears to represent his arrival at stage six—"the universalizing vision in which all things are related to God and God's kingdom becomes a present, tangible reality."[58]

This analysis of the dynamics of Bonhoeffer's spiritual development is impressive; yet a nuanced picture of stage six faith leads us to wonder whether Bonhoeffer is a suitable representative of "universalizing faith." Fowler notes that stage six faith represents a triumph over the paradoxes of stage five ("conjunctive faith"), in which the self is caught between universalizing apprehensions "and the need to preserve its own being and well-being." If stage five is characterized by loyalty to the present order, Fowler explains, the stage six self is spent in the transformation of that order. Those reaching this stage have achieved enlarged visions of universal community that "disclose the partialness of our tribes and pseudo-species." Naturally, their leadership initiatives often involve strategies of nonviolent suffering through which they evince "redemptive subversiveness" in situations of concrete oppression.[59]

Fowler's further elaborations of stage six faith clarify his naming of Bonhoeffer as one of its exemplars. Stage sixers exhibit "costly" love and openness, according to Fowler, and frequently become martyrs. These "universalizers" often die at the hands of those they hope to change, and are "often more loved and revered after their death than during their lives."[60] Such descriptions of faith's telos draw upon Fowler's teacher H. Richard Niebuhr's concept of "radical monotheism," which Fowler defines as "a faith relationship characterized by total trust in and loyalty to the principle of being."[61] This radical monotheism regards the forms of religious life as "relative representations or modes of response to that determinative center of power and value that is the sovereign reality . . ." Thus, bearers of stage six faith represent a qualification of the penultimate by a vision of the "commonwealth of being [as] universal."[62]

"Inclusive" and "universal" are the watchwords of stage six faith, while "being" is its ultimate concern. But applying these terms to Bonhoeffer elicits the mistaken impression that he ultimately exchanged the affirmations of Protestant Christianity for a universal religious vision emancipated from historical particularity. There is no doubt that Bonhoeffer possessed instincts which for his time and place were remarkably inclusive and tolerant. Yet for him Christ was "that determinative center of power and value that is the sovereign reality . . . ," not a "relative representation or mode of response" to that reality. Thus Bonhoeffer's Christ-centered apprehension of reality does not easily conform to Fowler's Niebuhrian monotheism. Nevertheless, the compelling nature of Bonhoeffer's universal portrait is strikingly clear in those who regard him as an exemplar of mature faith.

Moral Leader

Bonhoeffer is often cast as a paragon of moral courage by those who seek to universalize his legacy by emphasizing its broad human dimensions. The *Saturday Evening Post* commends Bonhoeffer as "a voice of clarity and compassion that speaks to the moral confusion of our time," while Martin Doblmeier, director of the feature-length documentary *Bonhoeffer*, affirms that "Bonhoeffer is one of the great examples of moral courage in the face of conflict" and Geffrey Kelly and Burton Nelson argue that he stands out as a moral leader because of "his willingness to suffer the harshness of imprisonment for his faith and to endure the loss of his freedom."[63]

Perhaps the most energetic advocate of Bonhoeffer's image as exemplar of moral leadership is psychiatrist-author Robert Coles. In two books—*Lives of Moral Leadership: Men and Women Who Have Made a Difference* and *Dietrich Bonhoeffer* (his contribution to Orbis Press's Modern Spiritual Masters Series)—Coles fashions a portrait of Bonhoeffer as a modern moral hero.[64] *Lives of Moral Leadership* depicts Bonhoeffer as an "idealist," "a compelling moral and spiritual leader" who expressed an "unyielding opposition to evil." He was a "moral witness" who exemplified a unique sort of "leadership." His life was an "extended moral vigil" that evinced "a leader's chosen moral transcendence." Bonhoeffer was a "principled fighter" who possessed unforgettable "stoicism" and exhibited a "will" that simply would not "take no for an answer" (and in this regard was similar to both Edith Stein and Simone Weil).

How well does Coles help us understand Bonhoeffer? By placing him in a diverse company of moral heroes that includes Robert Kennedy, Dorothy Day, Gandhi, and Albert Jones (a Boston bus driver), Coles can eschew sectarian language and portray Bonhoeffer's life and death in its universal dimensions. Since Bonhoeffer is so often perceived as a solitary hero without confidant or peer, there is a measure of clarity that emerges from this analysis. Placing him in the same moral universe as other modern "witnesses" enhances our appreciation of the locations Bonhoeffer-like courage emerges in our world—even among city bus drivers.

However, as in Fowler's case, there is a price for exchanging Bonhoeffer's legacy into the currency of "moral leadership." Bonhoeffer certainly possessed the qualities identified by Coles. But in communicating these qualities in the quasi-secular language of morals, values, and convictions, Coles presents a lowest-common-denominator Bonhoeffer who is less than the man himself. Just as the Holocaust is distorted when it is made a chief example of "man's inhumanity to man," its survivors exemplars of humanity's resilience, so Bonhoeffer is disfigured if we transform him into a model of the human spirit's triumph. Like Fowler, Coles composes a picture of Bonhoeffer that foregrounds the values of a pluralistic society—including tolerance, service, comfort with ambiguity, and commitment to universal truth—but in the process obscures the particularity of his religious commitments.

Agent of Reconciliation

In a world that is hyperconscious of racial and ethnic antagonisms, Bonhoeffer's contemporary "message" is naturally extended to the challenge of reconciling peoples. Indeed, a prominent aspect of Bonhoeffer's universal portrait is his willingness to transgress barriers of kith and kin to speak out on behalf of the oppressed other.

Contemporary interpreters have elaborated Bonhoeffer's relevance for racial reconciliation from a variety of perspectives. The evangelical Bonhoeffer is remembered as one who throughout his life opposed "the sin of racism." And, not surprisingly, this characteristic is quite pronounced in liberal portraits. Clifford Green asserts that because Bonhoeffer "confronted and repudiated" racism in America and Germany, "churches and societies that transcend the divisiveness of racism and nationalism reflect Bonhoeffer's spirit."[65] John D. Godsey maintains that "at its core and at every stage" Bonhoeffer's theology was "utterly opposed to racist attitudes and practices."[66] On all sides, opposition to anti-Semitic prejudice is cited as the reason Bonhoeffer risked his life in opposing Nazism.[67]

Many point to the influence of his Harlem experience in awakening Bonhoeffer to the reality of human oppression. Eberhard Bethge writes that "when we remember the delicate relationship between black and white in the United States, we must marvel at the depth to which Bonhoeffer penetrated the intimate sphere of the Harlem outcasts."[68] And Bonhoeffer's teacher and friend Paul Lehmann recalls the impressive way the young German explored the problem of racism "to its minute details through books and countless visits to Harlem through participation in Negro youth work, but even more through a remarkable kind of identity with the Negro community so that he was received there as though he had never been an outsider at all."[69] Lehmann judges that if Professor Eugene Lyman was "at the centre of Bonhoeffer's theological explorations, the Negro community in Harlem was at the centre of his social exploration" in America.[70]

Taken by his forays into Harlem and his defense of German Jews, contemporary memory has made Bonhoeffer the epitome of Christian concern for racial rapprochement. This is particularly true among those who are engaged with the intractable problems of race in South Africa and North America. Bonhoeffer's theology is applied to the American situation by a number of authors, most notably Victoria Barnett and Josiah Ulysses Young III. Barnett makes the underappreciated point that Bonhoeffer's thinking on the church's response to racial ideology was influenced by international ecumenism. From the beginning, Barnett notes, the ecumenical movement sought "the conciliation of class and race antagonisms."[71] Bonhoeffer reflected this goal in his critique of racial notions that were infiltrating German theology even prior to the Nazi seizure of power. Chief among these was the elevation of race or nationality to the status of an "order of creation." To this concept, which he feared could be used to rationalize war, class struggle, and exploitation, Bonhoeffer contrasted "orders of preservation" which affirm the divine gifts that structure and preserve life but keep open "the revolutionary possibility" of breaking an order that becomes "closed, rigid, and no longer permits the proclamation of revelation."[72]

Having identified the burgeoning racism in European culture and theology before 1933, Bonhoeffer recognized that the Jewish Question "raised central questions about the church's ability to critique cultural, national or racial ideologies." His resistance to Nazism, then, should be viewed as the extension of an intellectual process that began prior to 1933—"the search for a form of Christian witness and identity that could withstand the onslaught of a totalitarian ideology." The parallel with our own time and place, Barnett writes, is to be found in "the interweaving of culture, ideology and belief that prevents us, still, from being not just the church for others, but the church for one another."[73]

In *No Difference in the Fare: Dietrich Bonhoeffer and the Problem of Racism*, Josiah Ulysses Young III utilizes Bonhoeffer's theology to explicate the enduring challenge of racial reconciliation. While acknowledging Bonhoeffer's sexist, elitist, and even antidemocratic qualities, Young insists that denouncing racism was a crucial dimension of Bonhoeffer's life and thought, and that he offers useful theological insights for those who are committed to racial justice. Four aspects of Bonhoeffer's life reveal the antiracist dimensions of his legacy, according to Young: his commitment to reality, which entailed the distinction between faith and religion; his sojourn in Harlem; his desire to study with Gandhi (and thus "to edify himself through more contact with people of color"); and his struggle against Hitler.

For Young, Bonhoeffer's intense engagement with African American culture during his year at Union Theological Seminary is the key to comprehending his antiracist spirit. Young claims that Bonhoeffer's Harlem experience was formative not only for his understanding of America's "Negro problem," but for his distinctive way of doing theology. He even connects Bonhoeffer's celebrated "conversion" with a transformation that began in Harlem. The academic dissertation on the church Bonhoeffer completed before coming to New York, Young suggests, came alive at Abyssinian Baptist Church, where he discovered a community not unlike the *Herrschaftsverband* (the pure association of authority) described in *Communio Sanctorum*.[74] Young also maintains that Bonhoeffer's commitment to obeying Christ concretely was rooted in the "visible emotion" of black worship in Harlem, and that his interest in ethics was akin to the "ebullient experience" he both witnessed and participated in there. As a way of underscoring the black church's influence on Bonhoeffer's theology, Young interweaves passages from his writings with words from some of the Negro spirituals Bonhoeffer would have heard and sung in America.

More recently, in an article on "Bonhoeffer's New York," Scott Holland argues that some of the German theologian's most distinctive phrases—including "cheap grace" and "world come of age"—actually had their origin in the pulpit work of Abyssinian's pastor Adam Clayton Powell Sr.[75] These attempts to demonstrate the resources in Bonhoeffer's life and thought for the ongoing struggle against racism illuminate the way he serves as a guide for those concerned with the reconciliation of peoples. For many who perceive a direct link between Bonhoeffer's American experience and his advocacy for German Jews, Bonhoeffer's affinity for the oppressed comprises the very essence of his contemporary relevance.

Rescuer and Righteous Gentile

Images of an antiracist Bonhoeffer are nourished in the conviction that his opposition to National Socialism stemmed from a decision to defend the Jewish people at all costs. Understandably, the portrait of a Christian theologian willing to relinquish his own security on behalf of Jews has considerable appeal in the post-Holocaust world. Yet, Bonhoeffer's identity as a "righteous Gentile" who sacrificed his life to oppose Nazi anti-Semitism is one of the more conflicted dimensions of his legacy.

Pictures of Bonhoeffer as a consistent philosemite animate popular narratives of his life. *Bonhoeffer: Agent of Grace*, the award-winning film that aired nationally on PBS in 2001, was promoted as the story of "a Christian theologian who gave his life to save Jewish people . . ."[76] A church bulletin insert published by the Christian History

Institute asserts that Bonhoeffer "was condemned for his involvement in 'Operation 7.'"[77] And virtually the only thing about Bonhoeffer of which Biblical Discernment Ministries approves is his arrest, which "arose from his direct involvement in smuggling fourteen Jews to Switzerland."[78]

This portrait of Bonhoeffer the pro-Jewish crusader is elaborated in great detail in Denise Giardina's critically acclaimed biographical novel *Saints and Villains*. If the Bonhoeffer fashioned by Michael Phillips in *The Eleventh Hour* is the quintessential evangelical, Giardina's Bonhoeffer is the consummate liberal. He smokes cigarettes, engages in premarital sex, is a committed pacifist, and is influenced by ecumenical contacts in other countries and denominations. The two novels are united, however, in the assertion that Bonhoeffer's contemporary relevance lies in his perception of the intimate connection between Christians and Jews. Both books celebrate a camaraderie with and empathy for threatened Jews, and both make clear that Bonhoeffer's concern for Jewish suffering is what launched him on the path toward political resistance.

Saints and Villains is the story of Bonhoeffer's public opposition to the Nazis, and the story's plot is fueled by his private aversion to anti-Semitism. The novel's opening chapter implies that this aversion was virtually innate in Bonhoeffer. While hiking through the Thüringer Wald, Dietrich and his twin sister Sabine are caught in a snowstorm. A woman who shelters the teenagers remarks offhandedly that their hometown of Berlin contains "too many Jews." "Why do you say that? Do you know any Jews?" Dietrich testily responds.[79] This incident dramatizes Bonhoeffer's natural inclination to champion Germany's Jews, and foreshadows his inevitable collision with Nazism. As the story unfolds, both themes are central.

Dietrich's affinity for things Jewish is underscored when he falls in love with a Jewess named Elisabeth Hildebrandt. As the narrator points out, Bonhoeffer's first act of treason occurs when he makes love to Elisabeth in violation of the Nazi Nuremberg laws. In subsequent passages, Bonhoeffer's sympathy for Jews as Jews is repeatedly confirmed. His parishioners describe him as "obsessed with the Jewish Question"; he wanders through Berlin's Jewish district in search of Elisabeth, whom he later helps escape from Germany; he pleads with his coconspirators to do something for the Jews, though his brother-in-law must remind him that "the saving of Jews is not your assignment"; he daydreams of pulling a trainload of Jews to freedom; he walks the streets of the German capital while "thousands of people wearing yellow stars flowed past him—some carrying suitcases and boxes, others wandering confused and empty-handed—beneath the watchful eyes of armed SS guards"; Schindler-like, he bribes an SS official in an effort to save Elisabeth's husband from deportation.[80] Then, in the book's final scene, while he is being transported to his own execution site, Bonhoeffer passes

> a caravan of Jews being driven on foot from Auschwitz and Treblinka to the Reich. Dietrich watches through a crack between the slats of the truck's wooden sides as the scarecrow men, women, and children make their painful way, driven by armed guards like draft horses ready to die in the traces. The passing truck forces them from the road, and they do not look at it but stand with heads bowed taking what rest they can as they wait to be forced on.
> "The absent ones," Dietrich says.
> And thinks he is better off on the road with them.[81]

Artificial though it may be, in highlighting Dietrich's longing to identify and suffer with Jewish victims of the Third Reich the scene is faithful to the Bonhoeffer Giardina has portrayed in the previous 450 pages.

Mary Glazener's *The Cup of Wrath* is another work of historical fiction that accentuates Bonhoeffer's response to anti-Jewish persecution.[82] It does so through references to documented history (such as Bonhoeffer's opposition to his church's adoption of the Aryan clause, his reaction to *Kristallnacht*, and his role in "Operation-7"), accounts of his influence on other characters in the novel, and fabricated episodes in which Bonhoeffer comes to the aid of vulnerable Jewish men. In one such scene, Bonhoeffer and his cousin are walking the streets of Berlin when two members of the SA forcibly remove a Jew from an "Aryan only" bench. As the brownshirts prepare to give the offending "non-Aryan" a thrashing, Bonhoeffer moves into action:

> With three quick steps Dietrich passed the storm troopers, addressing the hapless victim as he went, "Ah, Johannes, have I kept you waiting? I'm terribly sorry. I was held up at the university." He

winked at the startled Jew, put his hand on his shoulder, and steered him to the path, where Hugo waited in obvious amazement. In a voice loud enough to be heard by the storm troopers, Dietrich said, "I'd like you to meet my cousin, Herr Councilor von der Lutz, of the Justice Department." He tried to reassure the frightened man with a look, then turned to Hugo. "My friend, Herr Johannes Ertzberger." Without a backward glance, Dietrich nudged them forward. Hugo, three inches taller than Dietrich, towered above the man walking between them.

"We'd better hurry or we'll be late for the matinee," said Dietrich, and continued in the same vein until they were out of earshot of the SA men . . . [The Jew] said, with tears in his eyes, "Thank you. Thank you very much. Those men—there's no telling—."[83]

Such episodes unmistakably reflect the image of a post-Holocaust Bonhoeffer who recognizes Jews' unique vulnerability under Nazi rule and Christians' singular duty to protect them. They assure us that, at least with regard to the issue of anti-Semitism, Bonhoeffer's heart and mind were in the right place from the beginning.[84] But while these novelistic creations faithfully reflect the traits Bonhoeffer exhibited when he exited a New York restaurant that refused to serve his African American friend Frank Fisher or decided he could not accept a German parish as long as that privilege was denied his non-Aryan companion Franz Hildebrandt, they leave readers with the mistaken impression that Bonhoeffer publicly and consistently intervened on behalf of Jews he did not know.

If portraits of Bonhoeffer as an instinctive opponent of Nazi anti-Semitism are deceiving, they do reflect a common apprehension of the man. For instance, when Catholic theologian Harry James Cargas wrote in 1982 that the Vatican ought to acknowledge Bonhoeffer as a saint, he spoke of "a Protestant who sacrificed his life in great measure for what he did on behalf of Jews." The precedent for such a "generous ecumenical act," Cargas wrote, was "the Jewish practice of recognizing righteous gentiles, non-Jews who, at great personal risk, aided Jews during the Nazi era." That Bonhoeffer deserved such an honor, Cargas opined, was beyond question.[85] Within a few years, a concerted effort was under way to honor Bonhoeffer on Jerusalem's "Avenue of the

Righteous." The endeavor to have Bonhoeffer accorded "Righteous Gentile" status—which to this point has yielded only a series of official petitions, published articles, popular pleas, and conference sessions—provides a unique window on Bonhoeffer's role in the post-Holocaust Christian imagination.[86]

The campaign to have Bonhoeffer recognized as a "Righteous Gentile" received new momentum in 1998 when Stephen A. Wise published an appeal in the *Christian Century* titled "Why Isn't Bonhoeffer Honored at Yad Vashem?"[87] Wise noted that the thirteen thousand persons honored as "Righteous among the Nations" include men such as Armen Wegner who did not actually rescue Jews. Bonhoeffer did so, according to Wise, and he provides the details of "Operation-7," a wartime *Abwehr* plot to spirit German Jews across the Swiss border disguised as government agents. Responding to the objection that most of these rescuees were converts to Christianity, Wise reminds us that "according to Nazi law, a person with a single Jewish grandparent or great-grandparent was considered Jewish, even if he or she had been baptized."[88]

Not only was Bonhoeffer directly involved in rescuing Jews, Wise maintains, but he opposed Hitler in other ways. In addition to speaking out repeatedly against mistreatment of Jews by the Nazis, Bonhoeffer violated the High Treason Law by sending descriptions of deportation procedures to Wise's grandfather, who had ties to President Roosevelt.[89] Wise recounts these and other features of Bonhoeffer's opposition to Nazi Jewish policy in an attempt to demonstrate that he risked "life, freedom, and safety" to protect Jews (a direct appeal to Yad Vashem's requirements).

Despite this seemingly unassailable argument, Wise's twenty-six-page petition (which included an affidavit from an "Operation-7" rescuee and a newly found copy of the indictment charging Bonhoeffer with trying to help an imprisoned Jewish professor) was rejected. In an October 1998 letter, Mordechai Paldiel, director of Yad Vashem's Department for the Righteous among the Nations, informed Wise that in Bonhoeffer's case three important pieces of data were lacking: evidence of personal involvement in assisting Jews at considerable risk to himself, open defiance and condemnation of Nazi anti-Jewish policies, and "direct linkage between the man's arrest and his stance on the Jewish issue."[90]

Yad Vashem's position was further delineated in a *Jerusalem Post* article in which Paldiel acknowledged that although Bonhoeffer was a martyr in the struggle against Nazism, he was not among those "non-Jews who specifically addressed themselves to the Jewish issue, and risked their lives in the attempt to aid Jews." In Paldiel's view, Bonhoeffer had opposed Hitler on church-state issues and his imprisonment and execution stemmed from "involvement in the anti-Hitler plot of July 1944, and not, to the best of our knowledge and the known record, [from] any personal aid rendered to Jews." As for "Operation-7," Paldiel opined that since the action had "the full backing of the highest authority in the *Abwehr*," honoring those involved would make a "laughing matter" of the Righteous program. The same article quoted Peter Hoffman, a scholar of the German resistance, who confirmed that Bonhoeffer's close ties to government insiders in the resistance were a chief obstacle to his recognition by Yad Vashem.[91]

The question received rigorous scholarly attention at the 2000 annual meeting of the American Academy of Religion, where the AAR's Bonhoeffer Group sponsored a session dealing with "Bonhoeffer, the Jews, and Judaism." The session was timely, since in July of that year Yad Vashem had again refused to honor Bonhoeffer with the designation "Righteous among the Nations." In a letter explaining the most recent decision, Paldiel elucidated a new dimension of Bonhoeffer's case. "On the Jewish issue," Paldiel wrote, "the record of Bonhoeffer is to publicly condone certain measures by the Nazi state against the Jews (save only baptized Jews), and to uphold the traditional Christian delegitimization of Judaism, coupled with a religious justification of the persecution of Jews." Paldiel went on to argue that while Bonhoeffer's condemnations of Nazi anti-Jewish measures were uttered "in private and among trusted colleagues; his denunciations of Judaism and justification of the initial anti-Jewish measures were voiced in writing."[92]

The AAR session featured a paper by Richard L. Rubenstein titled "Was Dietrich Bonhoeffer a 'Righteous Gentile'?" as well as responses from leading Bonhoeffer scholars. While Rubenstein disputed some of Yad Vashem's conclusions, he stressed that such institutions have the right to bestow honors as they see fit. Yet he did insist that it is quite possible to regard Bonhoeffer as a "righteous Gentile," with or without Yad Vashem's imprimatur. For in considering Bonhoeffer's words and deeds under Nazism, one must keep in mind two things. First, Bonhoeffer "transcended the time and culture that produced him to do what only a handful of his fellow Germans were prepared to do, risk and finally sacrifice his life in the struggle to bring to an end the terrible evil that had overtaken his people." Second, the resources for his opposition to Hitler and National Socialism were located precisely in Bonhoeffer's faith, even if "that faith was a seamless garment that included a harshly negative evaluation of Jews and Judaism."[93]

The issue shows no signs of being resolved. In fact, pique among Bonhoeffer's supporters was intensified in October 2003 when Hans von Dohnanyi, Bonhoeffer's brother-in-law and comrade in the conspiracy, was named "Righteous among the Nations" in an official ceremony in Berlin. This matter of Bonhoeffer's legacy vis-à-vis Jewish-Christian relations will be taken up in a subsequent volume.

Assessing the Universal Bonhoeffer

Bonhoeffer's universal portrait translates his life and thought to a broad audience by employing a non-sectarian language of sacrifice, morality, spirituality, and mature faith. These idioms no doubt clarify Bonhoeffer's universal significance; but do they also obscure his particularity?

Given modern developments in the concept of martyrdom, it seems appropriate to remember Bonhoeffer as one "martyred by the Nazis." As long as we do not lose sight, that is, of what distinguishes Bonhoeffer's experience under National Socialism from that of victims whose range of moral choice was considerably narrower than his. Lawrence Langer has coined the term "choiceless choice" to describe the moral universe in which many Jewish victims of the Nazis were forced to exist. Langer writes that they "were plunged into a crisis . . . where crucial decisions did not reflect options between life and death, but between one form of abnormal response and another, both imposed by a situation that was in no way of the victim's own choosing."[94] We are often reminded that Bonhoeffer's decision to return to Germany in 1939 was made before "the terrible alternative of either willing the defeat of [his] nation in order that Christian civilization may survive, or willing the victory of [his] nation and thereby destroying our civilization."[95] This was a terrible alternative indeed. But, as Bonhoeffer himself realized, it was one he could have

made "in security." Thus it should not be equated with the truly choiceless choices faced by millions of other Nazi victims.

More troubling consequences result from attempts to universalize
Bonhoeffer's legacy on the part of Robert Coles and James Fowler. Bonhoeffer, Coles tells us, "forsook denominational argument, oaths and
pledges and avowals. In the end he reached out to all of us who crave,
in hunger and in thirst, God's grace."[96] Thus Coles establishes Bonhoeffer's relevance for the contemporary seeker who is put off by dogma
and tradition but who seeks a guide through life's difficult passages.[97]
Similarly, when Bonhoeffer is observed through the lens of Fowler's
faith development theory, he models the "universalizing apprehensions" necessary to liberate us from captivity by the present order.

But this picture privileges Bonhoeffer's actions while virtually ignoring his theological convictions. Because he personified the universal
hero who pours out his life in sacrificial love, Bonhoeffer is cast as a
spiritual pioneer who was able to pierce the clouds of human perception to catch a glimpse of "being itself." Lost in this drama, however, is
the Bonhoeffer who stubbornly clung to traditional forms of religiosity
and never sought a spiritual plateau from which the reality of Jesus
Christ might be relativized. When the German theologian is portrayed
in these ways, what accrues to the Bonhoeffer of myth is forfeited by the
Bonhoeffer of history. We gain a religious hero in the image of Gandhi,
King, and Mother Teresa, a "stage-sixer" who broke the confines of tradition to realize a universal faith based in compassion. But we lose a
theologian and pastor who struggled to balance contemporary relevance and Christian identity during a period of social crisis.

What of Bonhoeffer's popular image as a guide for contemporary
efforts at racial reconciliation? This image is cultivated by interpreters
who are keen to explore the influence of Bonhoeffer's New York
sojourn on his subsequent career. They remind us that while studying
at Union Theological Seminary during 1930–31 Bonhoeffer engaged
the race issue on a deeper level than most white Americans at the
time; that he befriended black student Frank Fisher; that he became
active in ministry at Abyssinian Baptist Church and "spent nearly
every Sunday and many evenings" in Harlem; that he immersed himself in the culture of the Harlem Renaissance and collected phono-
graph records of black gospel music; that he wrote an essay on James
Weldon Johnson's *The Autobiography of an Ex-Colored Man* for

Reinhold Niebuhr; that he interacted with blacks only a generation removed from slavery; and that he experienced firsthand the sting of racial discrimination.[98]

Yet there are problems with assuming that Bonhoeffer's engagement with black culture in Harlem motivated his confrontation with Hitler on behalf of Jews. For instance, although in 1930 New York boasted the largest Jewish population of any city in the world and the campus of Jewish Theological Seminary was visible from the front door of UTS, there is "no evidence that Bonhoeffer manifested any curiosity concerning Jews or Judaism" during his stay in America.[99] Further, assessment of Bonhoeffer's German resistance in light of his experience in New York can lead to a blurring of important historical and ideological distinctions and encourage the equation of contempt for African Americans with Nazi anti-Semitism and "Germany's extermination camps— the *Vernichtungslager* . . . [with] America's lynching posts."[100]

And what of Bonhoeffer's reputation as a rescuer of Jews? Forty years ago, some likened Bonhoeffer to Pope John XXIII based on the influence the men were likely to have on the future of Christianity.[101] But today Bonhoeffer appears to have more in common with Pope Pius XII, who is presently being considered for canonization but whose wartime career vis-à-vis Jews is the subject of a debate that spans the academic-journalistic divide.[102] In assessing the theological and institutional dimensions of the European Christian response to Nazism, Richard L. Rubenstein finds it fruitful to consider Bonhoeffer and Pius together.[103] But one likeness Rubenstein does not consider is the similar roles these men play in post-Holocaust soul-searching within their respective religious communities. For Catholics and Protestants are equally in need of the symbolic comfort provided by heroic churchmen who stood up to fascism in order to mitigate Jewish suffering.

A further similarity between Bonhoeffer and Pius is the reaction precipitated by critical assessments of their responses to Jewish suffering. Just as Pius XII's relationship to the Holocaust is inevitably viewed in light of his imminent canonization and the desire to maintain the purity of the institutional church (a purity painstakingly preserved in "We Remember: A Reflection on the Shoah"),[104] perceptions of Bonhoeffer are affected by the need to identify authentic Christian faith, which is what Protestants scramble to protect when the institutional church fails them. And just as recent criticism of

Vatican activities affecting Nazis and their Jewish victims has created a Catholic backlash, the failure of Bonhoeffer to receive Righteous Gentile status has produced resentment among Protestants.

Indeed, Yad Vashem's refusal to honor Bonhoeffer as one of the "Righteous among the Nations" indicates that his legacy vis-à-vis the Jewish people is more conflicted than his universal portrait suggests. At the very least, it appears that Bonhoeffer's reputation as exemplar of post-Holocaust Jewish-Christian rapprochement rests on complex historical and theological issues that require further analysis.

PART TWO

INTERPRETING THE

BONHOEFFER

PHENOMENON

[Bonhoeffer's] testimony, in life and death, has tended to restore the heroic dimension to Christian existence.

—DON C. HARBUCK

Our own lamentable history of war and persecution has produced genuine martyrs for the sake of Christ (such as Dietrich Bonhoeffer) who were not Roman Catholics. Many of these persons were not only personally holy but led paradigmatic lives; they taught useful new ways of incarnating the Christian message into real life. In the common estimation, these people are saints; in these cases, it is the vox populi that has spoken.

—LAWRENCE S. CUNNINGHAM

Just as you would have to redefine martyrdom to make Bonhoeffer a martyr, so you would have to redefine sanctity to make him a saint, but that latter would be a worthwhile effort if it were undertaken, not to give Bonhoeffer extra credit but to rehabilitate, perhaps, the notion that some kind of holiness has some place in our profane world . . .

—THEODORE A. GILL

SAINT

FUNCTION AND FORM OF CHRISTIAN HAGIOGRAPHY

The time has come to consider more precisely how the concept of "sainthood" broached in the book's introduction illuminates Bonhoeffer's role in the religious imagination.

Many admirers of Bonhoeffer have suggested that he be thought of as a saint. Seeking to explain the unprecedented interest in Bonhoeffer among Roman Catholics, William Kuhns argues that his appeal is related to Catholics' "instinctive search for a model of sanctity." The tradition of saints, he writes, has impressed Catholics with the need to follow a pattern of holiness. While older patterns of sanctity encourage retreat from the world, "the semiconscious need to discover a pattern of holiness directed to the world has been met by precious few thinkers. Bonhoeffer is one of them."[1] Harry James Cargas proposes that "the Vatican consider actually canonizing this great Protestant martyr."[2] And Leo Zanchettin and Patricia Mitchell honor Bonhoeffer as one of only two non-Catholic "Christian Heroes."[3]

But it is not only Roman Catholics who cite Bonhoeffer when enumerating twentieth-century heroes of faith. In fact, Bonhoeffer is featured in virtually every publication devoted to the identification of modern "saints." One of the first studies in this genre was Howard V. Harper's *Profiles of Protestant Saints*, published in 1968. Harper's nineteen "great Protestants who have become 'canonized' in people's minds" include Bonhoeffer, Martin Luther, John Calvin, John Wesley, David Livingston, D.L. Moody, Jane Addams, and Albert Schweitzer.[4] Over three decades later, catalogues of unofficial sainthood continue to treat Bonhoeffer as a prototype. Robert Ellsberg's *All Saints: Daily Reflections on Saints, Prophets, and Witnesses for Our Time*, devotes April 9 to "Dietrich Bonhoeffer, theologian and confessor."[5] And James C. Howell's *Servants, Misfits, and Martyrs: Saints and Their Stories* treats Bonhoeffer in chapters on "prisoners" and "martyrs."[6] These tributes to "Bonhoeffer the saint" are reflective of sentiments in the broader population. When Beliefnet asked readers in 2002 whom they would canonize if given the opportunity, Bonhoeffer was the first nominee.[7]

These expressions of admiration should not be taken as claims that Bonhoeffer meets some set of objective criteria for sainthood. Yet in order to determine whether the designation "saint" is more than honorific in Bonhoeffer's case, we will review the phenomenon as it developed within the Christian tradition.

History: The Evolution of Sainthood

For centuries saints have been a fundamental part of Roman Catholic piety. According to *The Catholic Encyclopedia,* "Catholics, while giving to God alone adoration strictly so-called, honor the saints because of the Divine supernatural gifts which have earned them eternal life, and through which they reign with God in the heavenly fatherland as His chosen friends and faithful servants."[8] The public veneration of saints, which is known to have existed since the second century, developed in local communities, was centered around the saint's tomb, and emerged from the conviction that a martyr who had shed blood for Christ was in heaven and able to exercise intercessory prayer on behalf of believers.[9] During the fourth century, devotion to the martyrs spread rapidly as entries in the calendar of one church were embraced by others and cults developed around selected confessors and virgins. Over time asceticism came to be regarded as something of a substitute for martyrdom, and those who faithfully pursued the ascetic life were considered worthy of the same honor. In addition, zealous bishops were perceived as sharing the teaching role of Christ. Thus, while the earliest saints were martyrs such as Polycarp, Ignatius, and the Martyrs of Lyons, soon Antony and Athanasius in the East, Augustine and Martin in the West were also venerated after their deaths.[10]

As venerated martyrs came to be viewed as loci of spiritual authority, early legends and hagiographies were rife with evidence of their thamauturgic powers. Particularly after the peace of Constantine in 313, the saint came to be viewed less as a model than "a locus of power and a source of beneficence."[11] As requirements for sainthood were codified in canon law, miracle increasingly became the determinative factor in canonization and saints were regarded primarily as "power agents."[12] The "lives" written during the twelfth and early thirteenth centuries provided vivid personal portraits of the saint. Although miracles were demanded both by popular devotion and the official procedure for canonization, writers presented the known facts of the saint's life as material for human portraiture as well as spiritual edification.[13]

Despite the changing role of saints in the lives of believers, their importance in official Catholic piety has not waned. In 1982, Pope John Paul II introduced a simplified process for recognizing saints. After a rigorous examination of a candidate's life, work, and writings undertaken by the Postulator of the Cause, the pope may accept that the Servant of God has practiced the Christian virtues in a heroic degree and declare them Venerable, the first of three steps on the path to sainthood. Following a physical miracle, such as an unexplained healing, the candidate is beatified by the pope and declared blessed. A further physical miracle is required before the person is canonized and declared a Saint of the Church.

While the concept of sainthood is often identified with Roman Catholicism, in fact many religious traditions honor saints or their equivalents. Hinduism extends the title of *sri* or *guru* to some mystics. In Buddhism the concept of *bodhisattva* is limited to enlightened beings, sages, and masters. The Qur'an refers to "close friends" of God known as *walis*. Within the Jewish community, an unofficial consensus can render certain Jews "saintly" (Abraham Joshua Heschel appears to be the modern "saint" with the broadest acceptance.) Orthodox Christians, while lacking any official procedure for recognizing sanctity, have classified six categories of saints, including the Just—"those who led exemplary lives as clergy or laity, becoming examples for imitation in society."[14] Traditionally, Protestants have adhered to the Reformation custom of including all believers under this heading. But Episcopalians, Lutherans, and Methodists maintain lists of honored "saints" who, while neither venerated nor prayed to, are regarded as spiritual exemplars whose pious lives may instruct believers.[15] Even evangelical Protestants, traditionally resistant to anything remotely "Catholic," have been known to evince an interest in the concept of sainthood.[16]

How does this overview of the phenomenon relate to Bonhoeffer and his reception? First, it discloses that sainthood is a widespread, if not universal, characteristic of religion. Second, it reminds us that the original arbiter of Christian sainthood was the collective voice of the faithful. As Lawrence Cunningham writes, "until the tenth century, saints were proclaimed by the simple device of listening to the *vox populi*."[17] Third, it reveals that prior to emergence of the formal canonization process sainthood was nearly synonymous with martyrdom in both the Roman Catholic and Orthodox traditions (and martyrs were automatically considered saints).[18] Thus this overview of sainthood suggests that Bonhoeffer's "martyrdom" places him in the company of early Christian heroes whose suffering for the faith provided the basis for their popular veneration. Encouraged by these connections, let us consider more carefully the modern meaning of saints.

Function: The Meaning of Sainthood

An unexcelled guide to the social functions of sainthood is Lawrence S. Cunningham's *The Meaning of Saints*.[19] A Roman Catholic theologian and scholar of contemporary culture, Cunningham is uniquely qualified to inform our inquiry into the saint's role in Catholic tradition and Western culture more generally. Cunningham's goal is twofold: identifying the presence of "heroic sanctity" in our age, and making the concept of concern to modern persons. He is hopeful on both counts, since at the "precise time when interest in the intercessory or cultic power of the saints is in some decline, there has been a corresponding interest in religious figures as paradigms."[20] Unfortunately, the church's "bureaucratization of sanctity" has tended to produce saints that are "outside the interest of the average intelligent modern Christian," and has created a bifurcation in Catholic life between "a neglected official list of saints and those contemporary heroes of the faith who, in fact, attract the attention and the idealism of the modern Catholic."[21]

Aware that commending heroic sanctity to modern persons will require a radical rethinking of the relationship between sainthood and the miraculous, Cunningham offers a generic definition of sainthood that disregards veneration, canonization, and miracle: "A saint is a person so grasped by a religious vision that it becomes central to his or her life in a way that radically changes the person and leads others to glimpse the value of that vision."[22] Where are such persons to be found? If saints are signs of God, Cunningham writes (paraphrasing Thomas Merton), we should expect to discover such signs among "poets, novelists, diarists, prisoners of conscience, resisters, prophets, fools, and other wrestlers with God."[23] Naturally, such nontraditional saints are likely to live in dialectical tension with the structured church. Existing at the Christian community's cutting edge, they are harbingers and prophets of "what the Church needs to be and needs to do in a given historical moment."[24] "What should concern us," according to Cunningham, "is the side of the saint that emphasizes the prophetic, the exemplary, the moral dimension, and the challenge."[25]

In several ways, Cunningham's revision of the concept of sainthood illuminates Bonhoeffer's own saintly identity. First, Cunningham's emphasis on restoring the vox populi as a criterion for recognizing heroic sanctity encourages us to privilege his popular, as opposed to institutional, reception. Catholic de-emphasis on the ecclesiastical canonization process would be a generous ecumenical gesture, Cunningham maintains, since it would allow "the vox populi of the entire Christian community [to] give their equal approbation to a pastor Bonhoeffer and a Maximilian Kolbe as well as a Gandhi or a Schweitzer."[26] It would also be a force for democratization within the church, since saint's "lives" have always related "Christianity from below rather than from above." Second, Cunningham elucidates Bonhoeffer's role in the religious imagination by underscoring saints' emblematic value for a people or culture. Often they are "symbols or talismans for certain ideas, sentiments or aspirations," he observes. "Their place of honor is assured because of some function they fulfill in the popular imagination."[27] In a passage that might have been penned with Bonhoeffer's reception in mind, Cunningham writes that "the Saint is one who in this or that extreme cultural circumstance says, by life and word, that there is a way in which the life of the gospel can be lived." In the presence of such persons, Christians must feel "more uncomfortable, more unexamined, and less smug."[28]

Finally, despite Cunningham's clear intention of viewing sainthood in broad perspective, he returns again and again to Bonhoeffer in order to illustrate his points. More often than Catholic figures such as John

Henry Newman, Simone Weil, and Dorothy Day, or universally admired religious heroes like Tolstoy and Gandhi, Bonhoeffer serves as Cunningham's archetype of heroic sanctity in the modern world:

> When Western Christianity as an institution seemed cravenly incapable of dealing with Hitlerism in Germany, it was the individual—the Dietrich Bonhoeffers, Maximilian Kolbes, and their confreres—who made it possible to salvage the vision of Christianity in a totalitarian setting.
>
> What strikes one about a Dietrich Bonhoeffer is not that he died at the hands of the Gestapo but that he reflected, prayed, wrote, counseled, and lived under the extreme circumstances of a Gestapo regime . . . The example of Dietrich Bonhoeffer sets forth the saintly personality in the most extreme of positions.[29]

Cunningham's repeated utilization of Bonhoeffer is based in part on how neatly he embodies what Cunningham calls the "hiddenness" of modern sanctity, which

> derives from the fact that large parts of twentieth-century culture are either indifferent or positively hostile to religious values. The active life of Pastor Dietrich Bonhoeffer, for example, was an exemplary one. He was a political activist, a concerned pastor, and a fertile Christian theologian and thinker. It was, however in the crucible of a Gestapo prison cell that his person changed from heroism to sanctity. Bonhoeffer has been important for subsequent generations of Christians because he was able to maintain and nourish his deep faith in an essentially dehumanizing and alien environment. The posthumous publication of his *Letters and Papers from Prison* permitted us to see a person who was not merely heroic but saintly. It was only because those papers were saved that we could glimpse a spiritual life that would have meaning for us being developed. The hidden witness of his religious fidelity became apparent almost fortuitously.[30]

For Cunningham, the life and witness of the saint signifies one of three things: (1) the perennial value of the religious by showing it in a vigorously lived fashion; (2) a model for new ways of living out the religious vision of a given tradition; or (3) a prophetic judgment on those who share the religious tradition but fail to reach up to its claims and/or ideals.[31] Based on the preceding chapters, it would not be difficult to argue that Bonhoeffer exercises each of these functions in the contemporary religious imagination.

Structure: Saints and Their "Lives"

In the Christian tradition, the meaning of saints always has been inseparable from their written "lives." Thus, in order to explore Bonhoeffer's role as a modern saint it is necessary to become familiar enough with Christian hagiography to identify the conventions that delineate this genre and the structures that comprise its literary template. The patterns in medieval hagiography are consistent enough to lead one scholar to claim, "when you've read one saint's Life, you've read them all." Obviously, this is hyperbole; yet if it is meaningful at all to refer to Bonhoeffer as a saint, we would expect hagiographical patterns to be discernible in the literature generated by his memory.

The most helpful study of the literary conventions in classical hagiography is Alison Goddard Elliott's *Roads to Paradise: Reading the Lives of the Early Saints.*[32] Saints' lives reveal so many similarities, Goddard contends, not because they "borrow" from one another, but because in a profound sense they tell the same story. Focusing on the "generative narrative matrix" underlying accounts of saints' lives, she offers a synchronic reading of hagiography that understands various legends as "chapters of a single megatext."[33] Elliott distinguishes between two types of saints' stories—*passiones* (accounts of martyrs' lives) and *vitae* (tales of confessor saints, including desert hermits). The *passio* is "a unified narrative depicting a single, heroic action," animated by the confrontation of saint and tyrant. "In the climactic confrontation scene the tyrant attempts to persuade the saint to recant; the saint defiantly refuses, confesses his (or her) faith, and assails pagan religion." Thus the martyr-hero of the *passio* is distinguished by "his diametrical opposition to pagan culture," which is by definition an embrace of Christianity.[34]

The structure of the *vita* is gradational rather than binary; that is, it relates a series of events designed to reveal the distinctive qualities of the confessor saint: "The motivating thrust of the narrative is not the comparatively static opposition between good and evil, Christian and pagan," Goddard notes, "but a fluid scale of values that moves from good to better to best." Such plots often involve a journey or quest, as the saint withdraws from the world in search of greater sanctity.[35] In the *vita*, "the symbolic nexus of the drama" lies in images of interiority—including the saint's secret flight from his family or his surrogate death and burial in a cave or tomb—not the public images of confrontation and execution that animate the *passio*.[36]

On the surface, Bonhoeffer's story appears to resemble both *passio* and *vita*. It brings to mind the former inasmuch as it depicts the hero's path to martyrdom as an extended confrontation with a pagan tyrant. It resonates with the medieval *vita* to the extent that it narrates a journey toward sanctity which calls for withdrawal from the world, traffics in images of interiority, and includes a surrogate burial (his imprisonment).[37] But to argue convincingly that Bonhoeffer's story has assumed hagiographic form, we must establish not only the genre's typical plots but its literary conventions as well. These are easily gleaned from a popular hagiographic collection such as *Butler's Lives of the Saints*.[38] According to my review of the brief "lives" in this text, the basic conventions of Christian hagiography include:

Fortunate birth. Even in the briefest "lives," this detail is supplied where appropriate. The family's means not only distinguish the future saint, but highlight the perquisites of wealth that will be rejected in favor of a holy vocation when the secular glory to which the saint has been born is shunned for the heavenly glory for which he is reborn.[39] Often the saint's prospects for worldly acclaim exacerbate the consternation of parents when he or she indicates an attraction for the religious life.

Notable childhood. The saint's childhood typically contains evidence of religious devotion or interest in the spiritual disciplines. Some future saints evince a strange attraction to asceticism and/or monasticism, while those who are not yet converted toward spiritual things reveal their precociousness in secular endeavors. This literary convention reaches back to the extracanonical gospels, which feature stories of Jesus and his mother demonstrating miraculous powers.[40] In his *Life of Cuthbert*, Bede ascribes to Cuthbert both natural and spiritual precocity, writing that "in his earliest youth [Cuthbert] put his neck to the yoke of monastic discipline." Yet he also loved games: "He was naturally agile and quick-witted and usually won the game . . . He used to boast that he had beaten all those of his own age and many who were older at wrestling, jumping, running, and every other exercise."[41]

Concern for the socially marginal. The saint's innate rejection of the material privilege into which he or she has been born is often reflected in a concern for "the poor." Typical is St. Luke the Younger (tenth century), "a pious and obedient boy, [who] . . . from a child . . . often went without a meal in order to feed the hungry, and sometimes . . . would strip himself of his clothes that he might give them to beggars. When he went forth to sew, he was wont to scatter half the seed over the land of the poor . . ."[42]

Commitment to the church. Not uncommon is the saint who is called to serve the church in some official capacity (bishop, archbishop, pope), is reluctant to do so, but overcomes this instinctive humility out of devotion to Christ's bride. For instance, when chosen bishop of Poitiers, St. Hilary "did all in his power to escape the promotion, but his humility only made the people more earnest in their choice . . ." Similarly, St. Francis de Sales, resistant to the idea of succeeding his bishop, submitted "to what he ultimately felt was a manifestation of the Divine Will."[43] Bede writes of Cuthbert's tenure as bishop that "he strictly maintained his old frugality and took delight in preserving the rigours of the monastery amidst the pomp of the world."[44]

Chastity. Hardly anything is ever written about what moderns would call saints' "sex lives." However, while marriage is not regarded as a boon to sanctity, it is not always a hindrance.[45] Conveniently enough, many saints are widows or widowers, have chosen celibacy in order to enter the ascetic life or the priesthood, or are engaged in "spiritual" marriage.[46] According to Elliott, the heroes of medieval *vitae* often take flight to escape an unwelcome marriage, and later endure temptation in the reappearance of their abandoned bride. In hagiographical literature virginity is considered a form of spiritual martyrdom.[47]

Defining conflict. Saints' "lives" are often dominated by perpetual struggle with some problem, temptation, or heresy. The trials emerging from this struggle underscore the alternative between genuine faith and infidelity and illuminate the saint's heroic sanctity. Not infrequently, the saint's defining conflict is a dispute with other Christians. "Even among the canonized saints," Robert Ellsberg writes, "there are countless stories of those who suffered persecution or humiliation—not from ostensible 'enemies of the faith' but at the hands of their fellow Christians."[48] St. Hilary, St. Methodius, and St. Boniface are just some of those who suffered persecution at the hands of the faithful.[49] Whatever the nature of this defining conflict, the dramatic tension it creates enhances the story's appeal.

Suffering. Persecution, exile, imprisonment, and death are common fates among the saintly. Zeal for theological orthodoxy naturally leads to confrontation with enemies of the gospel. But persecution can come at the hands of family members (faithfulness to the heavenly father leads to sustained conflict with the earthly father), nation, or— during a season of heresy—the church itself. Elliott identifies flight into the desert as a recurring motif in medieval *vitae*, where it expresses the themes of departure and journey. "A number of medieval works," she writes, "contain heroes who are exiles."[50]

Liminality. Related to persecution and exile is the saint's liminal relationship to social and ecclesiastical communities. The desert saint in particular is a loner, his story "pervaded with symbols of marginality." Analyzing the biographies of modern religious leaders, Andre Droogers concludes that they too show "an affinity for wandering or travel, for isolation and seclusion, for poverty, hardship, and ordeal. All, moreover, [have] contact with marginal people and [count] marginals among their followers, and all [manifest] strained relationships with the establishment."[51]

Courage in the face of death. Saints fear neither punishment nor death. They quickly come to terms with personal mortality and calmly face their own ends. In fact, many saints derive peace from an intimation that death is at hand. St. Francis de Sales "had a premonition that his end was not far off." St. Colette and St. John Joseph-of-the-Cross both foretold their own deaths.[52]

Final testament. The saint's last words, uttered for the benefit of his or her disciples, are recorded for those who will later encounter the saint's story. Typically, they summarize the saint's struggle and affirm his or her triumph. As Bede writes at the conclusion of his *Life of Cuthbert*: "When I asked him rather urgently what counsel he was going to leave us as his testament or last farewell, he launched into a brief but significant discourse on peace and humility, and exhorted us to be on our guard against those who, far from delighting in these virtues, actively foster pride and discord."[53]

The Bonhoeffer Vita

Are these conventions of hagiographic literature discernible in the Bonhoeffer metanarrative? There is no doubt that Bonhoeffer's *fortunate birth* is the traditional starting point for relating his biography; indeed, this aspect of his background is rarely omitted. A recent text informs us that Bonhoeffer's father Karl was "a professor of psychiatry in Breslau, on the Oder River, now a part of Poland. Dietrich spent the first six years of his life in a huge mansion in a forest of birch trees situated next door to the mental hospital in Schneitniger park. The staff included a cook, a housemaid, a parlor maid, a governess, a French governess, a chauffeur, a receptionist and a gardener." Like most prosperous families, the author continues, the Bonhoeffers owned a summer home.[54] Bonhoeffer's comfortable upbringing, in fact, highlights two other aspects of his biography that mirror hagiographic tradition — his remarkable ability to relate to persons of low estate and his relatively easy adjustment to the deprivations of prison.

Nor is it difficult to find evidence of his *notable childhood* in the biographical literature that has grown up around Bonhoeffer's memory. Invariably, Bonhoeffer is described as a precocious child of considerable academic and musical prowess, not to mention spiritual sensitivity. We are told that as children Dietrich and his twin sister would lie awake imagining eternal life. "We endeavored every evening to get a little nearer to eternity by concentrating on the word 'eternity' and excluding any other thought," Sabine recalls.[55] Bonhoeffer's intellectual acumen is witnessed to by a fellow student who remembers seeing this "blond young student contradicting the revered polyhistorian, his excellency von Harnack, contradicting him politely but on objective grounds."[56] In part because of his intellectual precocity, Bonhoeffer's choice of a church vocation shocks the other members of his family.

Similarly, Bonhoeffer's *concern for the socially marginal* is underscored in most accounts of his life. Evidence of this concern is traced from Barcelona (where Bonhoeffer encountered real poverty for the first time) to New York (where he was drawn to the religious and cultural life of Harlem), to Wedding (the working-class district of Berlin where he taught a confirmation class), and ultimately to Tegel and Flossenbürg (where he was led by his decision to oppose the Nazi regime on behalf of suffering Jews). Geffrey B. Kelly writes that "Christ's coming was not, for Bonhoeffer, a once a year reaching out at Christmas to the cuddly babe of Bethlehem, but an everyday opportunity to welcome Christ in the person of the outcast in torn clothing or the homeless beggar in need of shelter."[57]

Bonhoeffer's special affinity for Germany's marginalized and vulnerable Jews is communicated in episodes that appear in virtually every account of his life: his outrage at the pogrom of November 1938 (in response to which he underlined a passage from Psalm 74, wrote the date in the margin of his Bible, and vigorously denied that this outbreak of violence represented God's judgment), his involvement in "Operation-7" (the plot to smuggle German Jews to Switzerland disguised as *Abwehr* agents), and his part in assembling a "Chronicle of Shame" documenting Nazi crimes. Bonhoeffer's concern for Jews is also linked to the grand story of his grandmother's defiance of the Nazi boycott of Jewish shops in April 1933.

Commitment to the church is also emphasized in most versions of Bonhoeffer's biography. This commitment begins with his early decision to become a pastor and theologian and intensifies in response to his family's attempts to discourage him. Bethge tells us that when Bonhoeffer was about fourteen, his brothers and sisters "tried to persuade him that he was taking the path of least resistance, and that the church to which he proposed to devote himself was a poor, feeble, boring, petty bourgeois institution, but he confidently replied: 'In that case I shall reform it!'"[58] After 1933 Bonhoeffer's ecclesiastical career—his role in the church struggle, his tireless efforts to get the Confessing Church to take a strong stand on the "Jewish Question," his ecumenical activities, his acceptance of the assignment to lead a Confessing Church seminary, his supervision of "collective pastorates," and his return from his American safe haven—mirrored his unwavering commitment to serve the church and reform it if possible. Episodes indicative of Bonhoeffer's commitment to the church include his presence at Palm Sunday Mass in St. Peter's Square during a trip to Rome with his brother Klaus in 1924, and the "great liberation" of 1931 when he realized that "the life of a servant of Jesus Christ must belong to the Church."

Chastity may seem an extraneous feature of Bonhoeffer's story; yet its importance should not be underestimated. "He was not, on the whole, interested in women," one biographer tells us, because he was so dedicated to his work. "His most fundamental, personal sacrifice," according to another chronicler, was the decision "to renounce marriage and end a relationship with a woman who meant a lot to him and whom in 'normal' times he certainly would have married."[59] Yet chastity born of distraction is not the stuff of sainthood. In accordance with the hagiographical pattern, Bonhoeffer's engagement to Maria von Wedemeyer ensures that his perpetual chastity will be forged in the midst of passion, not lack of interest or opportunity. The strength of this passion is revealed in the letters Bonhoeffer wrote from prison to fiancée Maria von Wedemeyer: "The thing that draws and binds me to you in my unspoken thoughts and dreams cannot be revealed, dearest Maria, until I'm able to fold you in my arms. That time will come, and it will be all the more blissful and genuine the less we seek to anticipate it and the more faithfully and genuinely we wait for each other."[60]

Since this amorous relationship was never consummated,[61] its ardor can be described in terms that invest Bonhoeffer's portrait with both drama and sanctity: "He could not believe at first that she was the same girl. She was no longer shy, and she met his gaze with eyes that were deep and lustrous, yet soft and unassuming." "Now, at a beautiful 18, she could not avoid notice. Poised, fresh, cultured, filled with vitality, she was the image of everything Dietrich would have longed for in a wife." "Her nearness, the fragrance of her hair, the touch of his hand upon her waist, was more than enough pleasure for him . . ."[62] These word pictures are worthy of a Harlequin Romance and have a similar function: They bespeak a Bonhoeffer who is passionate, but remains chaste, a man who longs for his absent love like any prisoner, but whose fervor is not expressed carnally. In this sense, Denise Giardina's creation of Elisabeth Hildebrandt, the Jewess with whom Bonhoeffer has sexual relations in *Saints and Villains,* is a gross violation of the saintly portrait fashioned by other writers.

Bonhoeffer's *defining conflict,* obviously, is his extended confrontation with Nazism and its Christian sympathizers. The conflict begins with Bonhoeffer's radio address on "leadership" the day following Hitler's accession to power and from that moment frames his decisions and determines his fate. Indeed, every dimension of Bonhoeffer's

Table 1 Bonhoeffer's "Vita" and the Hagiographic Template

Themes and Episodes	Hagiographic Feature
Pastors and academics in mother's family Father's stature as prominent psychiatrist Large home, servants, etc.	Fortunate Birth
Achievement in sports, music Intellectual prodigy	Notable Childhood

Decision to study theology, 1920
    "In that case I shall reform [the
    church]!"
Holy Week in Rome, 1924
"Conversion," 1931
Church Struggle, 1933–
Return to Germany, 1939
	Commitment to the Church

The poor in Barcelona, 1928
"Negroes" in Harlem, 1930–31
    Indignant departure from
    a restaurant that refuses to serve
    Frank Fisher
Working-class youth in Berlin, 1931
Jews in Germany, 1933–
    Julie Tafel Bonhoeffer's defiance of
    Nazi boycott of April 1933
    Outrage at the pogrom of November 1938
    Involvement in "Operation-7"
    Contributions to "Chronicle of
    Shame"
	Concern for Socially Marginal

Immediate opposition to Nazism
    Radio address critical of the
    Führerprinzip, February 1933
Opposition to "German Christians" and
Confessing Church leadership
    Confrontation with Gestapo, 1933
Work for the Resistance, 1938–45
	Defining Conflict

Table 1 *(continued)*

Themes and Episodes	Hagiographic Feature

Censure
  Prohibited from teaching (1936–)
  Prohibited from residing in Berlin
  (1938–)
  Prohibited from preaching (1940–)
  Prohibited from speaking or publishing
  in Germany (1941–)
Arrest and imprisonment (1943–45)
	Suffering/persecution

London, 1933–35 ("into the wilderness
  for a while")
Finkenwalde & Collective Pastorates,
  1935–39
New York, 1939
"Disguised" existence as double agent
    Public Hitler salute at café,
    June 1940
    "Incognito" of death as enemy
    of the state, 1945
	Liminality/exile

Devotion to work Engagement to Maria von Wedemeyer	Chastity

Prison demeanor
    Serenity during Allied bombing raid
    Refusal to escape
Death "entirely submissive to the will
  of God"
	Courage in the Face of Death

Prison writings Last words: "For me this is the end, but also the beginning of life"	Final Testament

suffering—his frustration with the church, his relentless advocacy of peace, his agonizing decision to join the political resistance, his endurance of the loneliness, deprivation, and indignity of prison, and his execution as a traitor—arises from his clash with National Socialism.

The hagiographic theme of *liminality* is expressed in the exile that is a product of Bonhoeffer's opposition to National Socialism. Georg Huntemann observes that Bonhoeffer never held the office of pastor in a congregation of the Protestant Church of Germany, and that even before he joined the resistance he "lived on the edge of illegality."[63] Eberhard Bethge reminds us that at the age of thirty Bonhoeffer was barred from his academic post; at thirty-four, the pulpit was closed to him; at thirty-five, he was forbidden from publishing; and, with his imprisonment at age thirty-seven, he was denied even conversation with is friends.[64] These dimensions of his "inner exile" reflect Bonhoeffer's liminal existence under Nazism, as does Bethge's description of the "incognito" he donned in conspiracy and death.[65] So complete was the anonymity of this "enemy of the state" that his family only learned of his death months after the fact.[66] Significantly, the motifs of liminality common to the saint's *vita* include disguise, a theme that emerges in Bonhoeffer's role as a double agent in the conspiracy and his dissembling under interrogation.[67] An episode that highlights this double consciousness is Bonhoeffer's response to the news of France's surrender to Germany in 1940. Raising the Hitler salute, Dietrich tells a stunned Bethge, "we shall have to run risks for very different things now, not for that salute."

Courage in the face of death is another hagiographic convention that is strikingly apparent in accounts of Bonhoeffer's life. In fact, every description of Bonhoeffer's imprisonment underscores this theme. Episodes that illuminate Bonhoeffer's courage include his serenity in the midst of an Allied air raid on Tegel prison, and his refusal to escape with Corporal Knobloch lest he endanger members of his family. According to Payne Best, a fellow prisoner during Bonhoeffer's last days, the theologian "was all humility and sweetness; he always seemed to me to diffuse an atmosphere of happiness, of joy in every smallest event in life." On the morning before his death, Best writes,

> Pastor Bonhoeffer held a little service and spoke to us in a manner which reached the hearts of all, finding just the right words to express the spirit of our imprisonment and the thoughts and

resolutions which it brought. He had hardly finished his last prayer when the door opened and two evil-looking men in civilian clothes came in and said, "Prisoner Bonhoeffer, get ready to come with us."[68]

His last hours at Flossenbürg are recounted by the prison doctor, who "saw Pastor Bonhoeffer still in his prison clothes, kneeling in fervent prayer to the Lord his God." "The devotion and evident conviction of being heard that I saw in the prayer of this intensely captivating man," this eyewitness wrote, "moved me to the depths."[69] Like St. Stephen looking to heaven as his accusers pummel him with stones or St. Perpetua losing herself in spiritual ecstasy while being attacked by wild animals, Bonhoeffer the martyr is placid in the face of death.

Finally, Bonhoeffer's *final testament* is represented by his prison writings, sealed until after his death, preserved and transmitted by his hagiographer. Bonhoeffer's last recorded words—"For me this is the end, but also the beginning of life"—constitute a more concise summation of his message.[70]

The major themes in Bonhoeffer's biography, the episodes that are used to express them, and the features of the hagiographic template to which they correspond, are listed in table 1 (episodes are indented under their associated themes in the first column).

Gospel: Bonhoeffer and Jesus

Lawrence Cunningham observes that saints function like the "paradigmatic personages of the Gospels . . . [by] enflesh[ing] Christian ideals in concrete historical situations and widely divergent historical epochs."[71] And in their introduction to the "lives" of Near Eastern holy women written between the fourth and seventh centuries, Sebastian P. Brock and Susan Ashbrook Harvey write that "since the primary call for Christians was the imitation of Christ, the life and death of the believer were understood as meaningful always in relation to the Gospel model . . ."[72]

Thus, if the story of Bonhoeffer's life possesses formal similarities with classical hagiography, it should not surprise us to learn that it also reflects the life of Christ portrayed in the gospels. One hagiographic motif linking Bonhoeffer's biography with the gospel tradition is incarnation. Robert Ellsberg defines saints as "those who, in some partial way, embody—literally incarnate—the challenge of faith in their time and place."[73] Similarly, Brock and Harvey write that "through the holy one God acts in, participates in, and is present in the world in which we live." In these ways hagiography echoes the promise of incarnation, a promise that is especially salient when cultural conditions make heroic sanctity dangerous or impossible. As the medieval saint was able to "accomplish deeds of power and meaning where people perceive themselves to be helpless,"[74] Bonhoeffer maintained faith in God's presence through the rise of fascism, world war, and the Holocaust. In the process he witnessed to the incarnational reality that God suffers in and with the world.

Another christological element in Bonhoeffer's biography is its conformity with the narrative logic of Christ's life. Like the Jesus of the canonical gospels, Bonhoeffer is a divine man on a mission, unwilling to avoid danger, committed to liberating his people even though it requires his death. Surely this is one reason the term "martyrdom" is so freely applied to Bonhoeffer, despite the definitional problems. As early Christian communities venerated the *martyres* who suffered at the hands of pagan authorities, Bonhoeffer is Christ's witness before the modern pagans.

At times, biographers have made Bonhoeffer's similarities with Jesus Christ quite explicit:

> Bonhoeffer was a Christ-like man. There are dramatic parallels between the two lives. Both had temptations to turn aside from the inevitable disastrous end, and both had opportunities to do so. Both were unmovable. Jesus "set his face like a rock" to go to Jerusalem, where He knew the cross was waiting for Him; Bonhoeffer could not be kept out of Germany even though the gallows or the firing squad was almost a certainty. Both were executed for crimes against the state. And both died young, while life was "still going up and up and up."[75]

Robert Huldschiner confesses that "somehow you feel that the man who wrote about the Man for others lived and died for you, too."[76] Michael van Dyke observes that for Bonhoeffer faith was no escape hatch from the power of evil men, and asks, "hadn't Jesus Himself provided a demonstration of this truth?"[77] The same author depicts Bonhoeffer's decision to return to Germany in 1939 as a Gethsemane experience: "In the steamy heat of a summer night in 1939, Dietrich had walked up and down Times Square, agonizing over the news from Europe. Alone, he sought to reject the cup of suffering he knew would be his."[78] Even Henry Smith Leiper, the friend who arranged Bonhoeffer's trip to America, compared Bonhoeffer to the man "who had, long centuries ago, taken the road to Golgotha as he 'set his face steadfastly toward Jerusalem.'"[79]

Indeed, portraying Bonhoeffer as a Christ figure has been a singular temptation for authors. Elizabeth Berryhill's play *The Cup of Trembling* reiterates this theme in several ways—in Bonhoeffer's Gethsemane experience in his parents' garden, as he "breaks bread" in his cell, during a prison worship service in which words from the Suffering Servant passages in Isaiah are recited, in the prominence of a cross that hangs above the stage, and in references to Hitler as Antichrist and his henchmen as fiends.[80] Similarly, Mary Glazener's historical novel *The Cup of Wrath* uses Isaiah 53 to frame the final hours of Bonhoeffer's life:

> *And with his stripes we are healed.* The words of Isaiah came again to Dietrich's mind as the car sped north on the narrow road. The two men, grim and silent, sat in front. Dietrich handcuffed in the back seat, hardly noticed them. In the face of death, Dietrich thought, a man tries to arrange his affairs. For him there were left the affairs of heart and spirit, and these could be arranged through prayer alone.
>
> • • • • • • • •
>
> At a crossroad stood a small wayside crucifix made of wood, with a little pointed roof to protect the figure of the broken Christ. *All we like sheep have gone astray; we have turned every one to his own way; and the Lord hath laid on him the iniquity of us all.*[81]

Transported to Flossenbürg by two thieves, Bonhoeffer is turned over to the camp guards with the words, "The lost sheep. We found him . . ." During the ensuing trial, the prosecutor strikes Dietrich in the face; at the foot of a scaffold supporting three nooses Dietrich traces the sign of the cross in the dirt. "Then he rose and surrendered his life into the hands of the Father," Glazener writes. Resurrection is hinted at in the book's final sentence: "The sun was rising."[82]

Links with the Christian master narrative can also be communicated more subtly. The nexus between Bonhoeffer's story and the life of Christ is implied, for instance, in references to the theologian's spell on those with whom he came into contact. In a popular version of his life, Bonhoeffer—"large boned, muscular, and blond"—encounters a working-class youth who is awed by "Dietrich's strong looking shoulders and hands, and the steel blue determination in his eyes."[83] Indeed, Bonhoeffer is quite often portrayed with the dual qualities of strength and tenderness Christians associate with Jesus.

On one hand, Bonhoeffer is a manly figure who chooses to suffer rather than retreat from his convictions. In the words of Theodore J. Kleinhans, Bonhoeffer "did not look like a professor of theology. He was a big man, well over six feet tall, an athlete, round in the face, almost boyish. He had his mother's blue eyes and blond hair."[84] Leo Zanchettin and Patricia Mitchell add that whether Bonhoeffer was performing classical music, competing in track-and-field events, or engaging in heated discussions, he "approached every act with an aggression that impressed many who knew him."[85] Howard Harper concurs that whatever Bonhoeffer did, "from playing tennis to serving Christ, he gave it everything he had."[86] These descriptions of Bonhoeffer—this "handsome, blond, athletic, young man," this "man among men" who "stood out in a crowd," whose piety was "manly, bracing, and rugged in every way"[87]—echo the sort of muscular Christianity that traffics in images of the strapping carpenter who fearlessly confronted his enemies, took no care for his personal safety, stubbornly walked the path of resistance, and stoically endured the cross.

On the other hand, biographers emphasize that Bonhoeffer was a gentle creature, a devoted brother and son, and a faithful friend. He was loved by children,[88] acted charitably toward his captors, was a pastor to fellow prisoners, and exuded a remarkable calm during bombing raids. Dietrich's charm won over many, his twin sister writes. "Everybody felt his warm-heartedness; his big strong hand seized the hand of the other person so kindly. He always turned his gaze fully towards him to whom he was speaking; . . ."[89] Those who met him, a biographer tells us, were impressed by "the feeling he was really listening to you and no one else."[90]

Michael Novak has wondered whether Bonhoeffer's admirers try a little too hard to portray him as gentle, kind, friendly, "almost as if he had given the impression that he might not be."[91] But there is no need to suspect compensation for presumed flaws in Bonhoeffer's character. Rather, these stylized descriptions seem to be driven by an unconscious impulse to depict Bonhoeffer the saint in religious-heroic terms.

The Hagiographer

Heroes of the faith who become included in popular Christian devotion are blessed with disciples who record the details of their lives and thereby set the parameters for official memory. Regardless of its historicity, this disciple's chronicle establishes the orthodox perspective on the saint's life. Typically, this disciple has a role in creating the saint's cult as well, since he or she often is in possession of the dead hero's personal effects. The chronicling disciple becomes known simply as the Hagiographer.

Saint Dietrich's Hagiographer was Eberhard Bethge, the relative, confidant, and disciple who spent a lifetime making the details of Bonhoeffer's life and thought accessible to a wide audience. Because Saint Dietrich was also a theologian—and a very fruitful one—his hagiographer was called to serve as a one-man committee of authenticity whose duty it was to establish the limits for faithful appropriation of Bonhoeffer's memory. This role was performed through Bethge's own writing on particular aspects of Bonhoeffer's legacy, his presence at conferences, his role in sustaining institutions of memory, and his practice of placing his *imprimatur* on studies that he regarded as faithful to the master. During his lifetime, Bethge's seal of approval (in the form of forewords, introductions, or endorsements) became an indispensable sign of orthodoxy in Bonhoeffer studies.[92]

Identifying Bethge's role as Saint Dietrich's Hagiographer is not to impugn his remarkable biographical work or to question his interpretation of Bonhoeffer's theological legacy. It is simply to acknowledge his role in establishing the portrait of Bonhoeffer by which all others are measured. In the next chapter, we will explore still other expressions of Bonhoeffer's sainthood.

There are times in which lectures and publications no longer suffice to communicate the necessary truth. At such times the deeds and sufferings of the saints must create a new alphabet in order to reveal again the secret of the truth.

—MICHAEL BAUMGARTEN

The witness to Christ borne even to the shedding of blood has become a common inheritance of Catholics, Orthodox, Anglicans and Protestants.

—POPE JOHN PAUL II

Saints are people whose faith is so much a part of their being that it leaves visible traces, just as the work we do leaves lines on our faces and alters our posture. By this standard, Bonhoeffer was indeed an ecumenical saint, one who continues to offer us a vision of other possibilities.

—VICTORIA J. BARNETT

O God our Father, who art the source of strength to all thy Saints, and who didst bring thy servant Dietrich Bonhoeffer through imprisonment and death to the joys of life eternal: Grant that we, being encouraged by their examples, may hold fast the faith that we profess . . .

—ANGLICAN PRAYER

CULT

EXPRESSIONS OF THE BONHOEFFER PHENOMENON

H aving established that the Bonhoeffer metanarrative is often transmitted according to the conventions of hagiography and gospel, we are prepared to explore other aspects of Saint Dietrich's "cult."

Pilgrimage

As I began researching this book, I traveled to Germany in the hope of visiting as many Bonhoeffer sites as possible in a week. Superfluously it turns out, I carefully planned my own Bonhoeffer "pilgrimage." My wife and I flew to Munich and drove north to Berlin, where we visited many of the locations associated with the Bonhoeffer family and their involvement in the German resistance. Along the way, we took in Flossenbürg and Buchenwald. When we returned home and I started the book in earnest, I learned that Bonhoeffer pilgrims have resources at their disposal I had not dared to imagine.

These include the DB Ministry and Travel Service, Inc., which offers an annual eighteen-day guided excursion to Germany and Poland called the "Basic Bonhoeffer." In Berlin, pilgrims visit the Bonhoeffer-House at Marienburger Alee 43, the state archives where Bonhoeffer's writings are deposited, several churches associated with his ministry, and the prisons where he was incarcerated. Pilgrims also travel to Ettal, where Bonhoeffer spent the winter of 1940–41, and Flossenbürg KZ, where he was murdered. The tour is assisted by Germans who knew Bonhoeffer, including a niece, first cousin, and daughter of his fiancée. According to president Marlan Johnson, a retired ELCA pastor from Minnesota, DB Ministry and Travel Service is "a losing proposition for us business-wise, but this is our calling." Johnson discovered Bonhoeffer—the man who "changed him forever"—in 1993 while making his own pilgrimage to Flossenbürg. Johnson and wife Sharon now travel the country giving lectures and slide presentations on Bonhoeffer and Paul Schneider, "martyred witnesses in the resistance to Hitler and Nazism."[1]

During the summer of 2004, Bonhoeffer devotees could choose between two group pilgrimages. In June, the Johnsons offered "The Dietrich Bonhoeffer-Paul Schneider 18 Day Tour to Germany and Poland" immediately following the International Bonhoeffer Congress in Rome. In May, Professors Peter Frick and A. James Reimer of Waterloo, Ontario, led "Bonhoeffer: Life and Legacy," a two-week excursion through Germany, Poland, and the Czech Republic that "trace[d] the route of Bonhoeffer's last journey." In addition, the ELCA Wittenberg Center announced a "Dietrich Bonhoeffer and Martin Luther" seminar in Wittenberg, Germany, for 2005.

Would-be Bonhoeffer pilgrims can also find guidance in published travelogues. *The Steps of Bonhoeffer: A Pictorial Album* was first published in 1969.[2] Before that time, books, papers, lectures, and sermons had been written to provide insight into the times and people that shaped Bonhoeffer's life. However, as coauthor J. Martin Bailey observes, no similar effort had been made "to deal with the places which he himself described so effectively in his writings." Bailey's volume fills that void with a collection of photographs taken a quarter century after Bonhoeffer's death.[3]

To Pomerania in Search of Dietrich Bonhoeffer is an account of a journey to northwest Poland by nine Minnesotans, as well as a guide for those who would follow in their footsteps. The book contains maps, photographs, excerpts from letters, and other documents that elucidate the various tour sites, and accounts by previous pilgrims. Author Jane Pejsa notes of Pomerania that "very few Bonhoeffer pilgrims have explored this beautiful, sparsely settled region that Bonhoeffer came to love."[4] In 1996 she and the other "Bonhoeffer pilgrims" visited six locations associated with the theologian's "underground" work between 1935 and 1943 and marked each with a memorial plaque. Because the sites had not been maintained during the communist period, these pilgrims were also detectives:

Exiting the autos, the travelers begin the search. Behind the bushes they discover clues—the partial outline of a foundation, the remains of an entrance stoop, and finally, a well, with an old millstone as its cover. This was Sigurdshof! The forest has closed in on all sides; yet one tree stands out from all the rest, a stately oak far older than Bonhoeffer's time. The travelers nail to this tree the appropriate memorial plaque.[5]

At one of the sites—a former Lutheran church taken over by Roman Catholics—the pilgrims discover that the International Bonhoeffer Society had left their own commemorative plaque just a year earlier.

British scholar Keith Clements recently offered an account of his own Bonhoeffer odyssey in "Bonhoeffer's Last Days: A Pilgrimage."[6] Traveling to Flossenbürg in 2002 by the same route along which Bonhoeffer was transported in 1945, Clements kept a journal of his thoughts and emotions. As he passed significant landmarks, Clements strained to imagine Bonhoeffer's thoughts: "What must it have been like," he wonders, "to see all this and know that one would soon be saying farewell to it all, and perhaps horribly? . . . What were his thoughts about family and friends—Eberhard and Renate, and of course Maria?"[7] Stopping in Schönberg, where Bonhoeffer was held for several days prior to his execution, Clements reflects on Dietrich's final sermon. In the local church he pens "a prayer of thanks in German—'for Dietrich Bonhoeffer who preached his last sermon here in Schönberg, April, 1945.'"[8] The journey ends at the Flossenbürg memorial to Bonhoeffer and other members of the anti-Hitler conspiracy. For Clements,

> simply to stand at that spot and before that memorial tablet is enough to convey that one is on holy ground. And we can be sure that whatever he went through in those last moments, Dietrich Bonhoeffer did pray as he drank his last drop of sharing the sufferings of God in the world, the final stage on the way to freedom, the end which was for him the beginning of life. So all one can do there is pray, in silence, oneself. But what to pray? For anyone who goes to Flossenbürg and stands there, I would counsel simply to pray the prayer we all know best: 'Our Father . . . ,' pondering every phrase. I guarantee it will never mean quite the same—ever again.[9]

Narration

While moving, these journeys to locations associated with Bonhoeffer's life and death fail to do justice to the uniqueness of his role in the religious imagination. For students of theology have been known to travel to Basel to encounter Barth's spirit (I am one), or visit New Harmony, Indiana, in hopes of communing with the ashes of Tillich. However, among those who count theologians as their heroes there is nothing quite like the compulsion to narrate Bonhoeffer's life.

As we have seen, Bonhoeffer resembles previous Christian saints inasmuch as his story is a compelling tale of Christian faith overcoming adversity. Thus, Bonhoeffer's popularity bespeaks the perennial need for religious heroes who embody courage, perseverance, and the triumph of conviction over suffering and death. However, the volume and variety of biographical literature inspired by Bonhoeffer distinguishes him from every other modern theologian. Under the category of "narration" we shall consider popular biographies, works of historical fiction, and documentary films that communicate Bonhoeffer's story.

One of the first fictionalized biographies of Bonhoeffer to appear remains among the best. Donald Goddard's *The Last Days of Dietrich Bonhoeffer* is powerful reading, even for those who are familiar with the history it relates (Bonhoeffer's imprisonment, trial, and execution).[10] Goddard narrates what is known of Bonhoeffer's incarceration at Tegel and Prinz Albrecht Strasse prisons, dramatizes the repeated interrogations he endured in these places, and includes lengthy excerpts from his "letters and papers." The book bespeaks an abiding popular interest in Bonhoeffer's prison experience, and thus reflects the hagiographic tradition in at least two ways. First, Goddard's narrative—with its interrogations and maneuverings on the part of Bonhoeffer's Nazi enemies—is reminiscent of the medieval *passio* and its climactic confrontation between saint and tyrant. Second, Goddard highlights Bonhoeffer's courage in the face of impending death that so impressed his fellow prisoners and that, as we have seen, is profoundly typical of Christian hagiography. According to Goddard, Bonhoeffer neither feared nor resented these proceedings [of his summary court-martial], for they could alter nothing, and when the time came for him to speak in his own defense he declined to do so for the same reason. Back in his cell, he prayed on his knees through the night.

He now willed nothing for himself. He had surrendered everything at last—his past, his pride, his own self. He awaited what was to come with the purest concern, wholly involved and yet wholly at peace.[11]

Even in the moment of death, Goddard's Bonhoeffer exudes peace: "Then he was alone, blindly trusting. As he heard the trap creak, he yielded humbly to the rope, and in the sudden wrench, was no longer separate from his God."[12]

Earlier chapters of this book included references to a number of narrative treatments of Bonhoeffer's life, including Mary Glazener's *The Cup of Wrath*, Denise Giardina's *Saints and Villains*, Theodore J. Kleinhans's *Till the Night Be Past*, Elizabeth Raum's *Dietrich Bonhoeffer: Called by God*, Renate Wind's *A Spoke in the Wheel*, Michael Phillips's *The Eleventh Hour*, Michael van Dyke's *Dietrich Bonhoeffer: Opponent of the Nazi Regime*, and Susan Martins Miller's *Dietrich Bonhoeffer*. Some of these—particularly the works of Glazener, van Dyke, and Miller—stay remarkably close to the details of Bonhoeffer's life supplied by Eberhard Bethge. As Glazener writes, "there was no need to try to create exciting events. They were already there."[13]

Yet one of the more popular narrative strategies in this literature is heightening the story's drama by foreshadowing Bonhoeffer's death. Kleinhans, for instance, begins at the story's end:

The weeks before the hanging had been filled with calm hope. Dietrich Bonhoeffer was only 39 years old and genuinely in love for the first time in his life. The awakening of spring always had brought him a kind of pagan delight, perhaps too primitive for a professor of theology. From the woods around the ruins of his castle at Flossenbürg, he could smell the nectar of blossoming linden and hawthorn. At dusk he could hear the nightingales, a pleasant change from the constant rumble of bombs that had

been his melody in Berlin. At dawn came the lilting call of mat-
ing cuckoos.[14]

This passage typifies the combination of biographical fact and literary
embellishment that is the emblem of popular narrative treatments of
Bonhoeffer's life.

The story of Bonhoeffer has been narrated in four documentary
films, including one still in production.[15] The first of these to appear
was *Dietrich Bonhoeffer: Memories and Perspectives* (1983).[16] Slow-
moving and shot entirely in black and white with one camera and no
musical background, this haunting film opens with Susanna Bonhoeffer Dress sitting before a family picture album and revealing the
fate of each of the eight Bonhoeffer children whose images it contains. The next fifteen minutes deal with Dietrich's death, alternating
between the reactions of close friends and still shots of Flossenbürg.
The film then reaches backward to explore Bonhoeffer's prison
period, the rise of Nazism, and his sojourn in New York. Finally, it
moves forward to the Church Struggle and Finkenwalde, Bonhoeffer's
response to *Kristallnacht*, and his move into the conspiracy. *Dietrich
Bonhoeffer: Memories and Perspectives* highlights a thread of resistance in Bonhoeffer's life that links pacifism and conspiracy. But it is
most notable as an archive of interviews with those who knew him,
including Eberhard and Renate Bethge, Julius Reiger, Paul and Mar-
ion Lehmann, Inge and Joachim Kanitz, Werner Koch, Emmi Bonhoeffer, and Winfried Maechler.

If *Dietrich Bonhoeffer: Memories and Perspectives* foregrounds the
liberal Bonhoeffer who resisted military service and saw Christ as the
brother of all persecuted human beings, *Hanged on a Twisted Cross*
(1996) is more attentive to Bonhoeffer's spiritual sensibilities.[17]
Underscoring the theologian's piety, the film pays special attention to
Bonhoeffer's spiritual awakening around 1931. In a section titled
"The Conversion," this "great liberation" is depicted as the major
transition in Bonhoeffer's life. *Hanged on a Twisted Cross* also stresses
the daily Bible reading, prayer, and singing that were part of Bonhoeffer's prison routine, as well as his pastoral role with other prisoners. "Bonhoeffer found the answer to all his questions in his
continuous living in Christ," the narrator tells us. The film's longest
reference to Bonhoeffer's writings is an excerpt from *The Cost of*

Discipleship which warns of the church's replacement of faith with doctrine about faith.

Martin Doblmeier's widely acclaimed *Bonhoeffer* (2003) provides contemporary audiences with a remarkable sense of the place and time in which Bonhoeffer lived.[18] The film uses Holocaust images, as well as interviews with scholars and Bonhoeffer's contemporaries, to establish that Hitler's persecution of the Jews was the primary impetus for Bonhoeffer's decision to join the resistance. After the film was turned down for official entry into the Sundance Film Festival, the filmmaker arranged to have it screened in local churches. As a result of word-of-mouth publicity, through May 2003 the film had shown at more than two dozen church venues on the East Coast, the Midwest, and the West Coast (including Catholic, Episcopal, Methodist, Presbyterian, Lutheran, Baptist, and Bible churches). In July 2003 *Bonhoeffer* was playing by theatrical engagement in about ten U.S. cities.[19]

Lawrence Cunningham reminds us that the tradition of the saints has always been "rooted in story," and that the practice of writing saints' "lives" continues today in a variety of forms.[20] In its many shapes and reiterations, Bonhoeffer's biography confirms both observations. New versions of his story continue to appear, even though precious little about Bonhoeffer's life or death has remained unknown to us since the appearance of Bethge's definitive biography nearly four decades ago. The compulsion to re-narrate Bonhoeffer's life and death no doubt reflects the forces that are always at work in the production of saints' "lives." Stories that are such suitable conduits for spiritual power demand continual retelling.

Dramatization

Bonhoeffer's life has been dramatized more than that of any other theologian—perhaps more than any religious figure of the twentieth century. "Dramatize" may be the wrong term, however, since the plays, movies, and fictionalized biographies based on Bonhoeffer's life do not so much introduce drama as accentuate it. Many of the theatrical elements in his story emerge from Bonhoeffer's mortal conflict with Nazi totalitarianism. But dramatic tension also results from the paradoxes that attended his own life: "How could a boy who had almost never warmed the seat of a pew grow up to preach in Berlin's most illustrious pulpits?" asks Theodore Kleinhans. "How could a young theologian who hated war and fled to America rush home and apply for a chaplaincy just before the Nazi panzers trampled Poland? How could a preacher volunteer to work as a spy for the German *Wehrmacht*? How could a professor of theology plot to blow up Hitler."[21] Indeed, enigmas proliferate the story of this Prussian pacifist, this pastor-in-training who becomes fascinated by the Spanish bullfight.[22]

In dramatic portrayals of his life, Bonhoeffer's story is structured by a series of representative incidents. In addition to those cited in the previous chapter, the following have become standard episodes in the Bonhoeffer drama:

- his drilling with fraternity brothers at a secret military camp, the deprivations of which send him home in a huff
- his failure to receive an American driver's license due to his stubborn refusal to offer the examiner a bribe
- his three-week visit to Karl Barth's seminar in 1931 in which he impresses the older theologian
- his bold stand regarding war and peace at the World Alliance conference at Fäno in 1934
- teaching the Finkenwalde brethren a lesson in servanthood by locking himself in the kitchen and washing the dinner dishes
- his letter to Reinhold Niebuhr in which he expresses the "terrible alternative" facing German Christians ("I will not have the right to participate in the reconstruction of Christian life in Germany after the war if I do not share the trials of this time with my people")
- the gathering in Hans von Dohnanyi's house in Berlin, where he and other family members practice a cantata for Karl Bonhoeffer's seventh-fifth birthday and await word on the latest attempt on Hitler's life
- his realization that his freedom is at an end when a phone call to his parents' house is answered by an unknown voice

In addition, a few remarkable "sayings" stories are used to construct the Bonhoeffer drama. Among these are "if you boarded the wrong train, could you get where you wanted by running through the corridor in the opposite direction?" (in response to a Finkenwalde student who wondered whether one could remain a member of the *Reichskirche* and simply ignore its errors); "I hope God will give me the power not to take up arms" (directed at a student who asked him what he would do if called up); "only he who cries out for the Jews may sing Gregorian chant" (following the promulgation of the Nuremberg Laws in 1935); "if the synagogues burn today, the churches will be on fire tomorrow" (his warning to fellow Christians after *Kristallnacht*); and "if one watches a madman driving through a crowd of people, one can either bandage the wounded or wrest the wheel from the driver" (in response to a question about his decision to join the resistance).

The first stage production inspired by Bonhoeffer's life was Elizabeth Berryhill's *The Cup of Trembling* (1958), which tells "in dramatic form, the story of the life of a man who, the author imagines, was very like or might almost have been Dietrich Bonhoeffer." The character's name is Erich Friedhoffer, and the play commences with a preview of his death:

The houselights and stage lights go down to blackness. In the dark we hear music: harsh, discordant, threatening—recalling the sounds of marching feet and blunt commands. On a side platform, lights come up to reveal a gallows in silhouette, to which an EXECUTIONER enters. Across the stage area, also seen in silhouette, a MAN with his hands tied behind him enters, followed by a GUARD. They march slowly to the gallows, where the guard leaves the man with the executioner and steps back, standing rigid. The executioner steps to the man, takes the rope in both his hands and places it around the man's neck. Lights go out instantly.[23]

The events leading to Friedhoffer's execution unfold as a play within a play, featuring seven actors. The characters include Friedhoffer's mother, father, and sister, Ernst Metzger (Eberhard Bethge), Christopher Elliott (Payne Best), Heinz Schmidt (a Tegel prison guard), and Heinrich Müller (a student acquaintance of Friedhoffer who later becomes a Gestapo agent). The "Stations on the Road to Freedom" chorale that frames the action functions as "a kind of mirror in which to see that journey" that was Friedhoffer's life.

Act 1 is punctuated with signs of the impending conflict between Friedhoffer and the Nazi state. Friedhoffer discovers a copy of *Mein Kampf* on his professor's desk; background sounds include "Deutschland, Deutschland über alles," the Horst Wessel song, "a truculent and snarling drum roll," a montage of Sieg Heils, and a series of radio news bulletins tracing Hitler's accession to power. Contrasted with these symbols of the Nazi revolution are strains of "Now Thank We All Our God," "Jesu, Joy of Man's Desiring," and "A Mighty Fortress Is Our God." At one point, bits of racist rhetoric spewed by a NAZI ORATOR echo against Friedhoffer's reading of Jesus' Beatitudes. The two worlds collide when Müller arrives at the Friedhoffer home to warn Erich: "You are a man of God. Stay with that. Hang onto it like grim death. Friedhoffer, for God's sake, stay with the next world and leave this one to those who really think it matters."[24]

Friedhoffer retreats to the garden of his parents' home to be alone with his thoughts, but is ambushed there by the sounds of *Kristallnacht*: "Out of the humming air, come sounds and voices. A crash of glass, as of a rock thrown through a window." Jewish voices cry, "Help us . . . please . . . help us . . ." but Friedhoffer replies, "No! I will not listen." "Brother, we seek you—we call you! Can you hear us? Can you hear us?" the voices plead. And Friedhoffer: "I cannot! Ask of me what you will . . . but I cannot kill!" Kneeling in the garden, the young Christian cries out: "O my Father, if it be possible, let this cup pass from me: nevertheless, not as I will, but as thou wilt. Father, if thou be willing, remove this cup from me: nevertheless, not my will, but thine be done. O my Father, if this cup may not pass away from me, except I drink it, thy will be done." Erich then returns to the house and announces to his sister that he will join the conspiracy.[25]

Many hagiographical conventions are evident in Berryhill's representation of Bonhoeffer/Friedhoffer. His mother describes him as "the happiest child I ever saw—full of wonder, . . . life spilling out of him as if there were too much of it to be contained in one small boy."[26] His intellectual precocity is demonstrated in one of Karl Barth's seminars where he humiliates Müller the future Gestapo agent for his shallow understanding of Martin Luther. His courage in the midst of death mesmerizes fellow prisoners. "Perhaps tomorrow you will tell me . . . what it feels like . . . not to be afraid," stammers one anxiety-stricken inmate who is calmed by "Pastor Friedhoffer."

Wilfred Harrison's *Coming of Age: A Play* (1973) is a meditation on the relevance of Bonhoeffer's prison writings for the church's future in a secular world. A meeting called to determine "what is to be done with the Church" (now that keeping the place open is "uneconomic") is introduced by an AUCTIONEER who instructs the audience: "In making your bids, ladies and gentlemen, you may make speeches, call witnesses, demonstrate, stand on your heads if you think it will stress your offer . . . So make your bids, ladies and gentlemen, for this desirable property and the land on which it sits."[27] A member of the audience named Marsh, quite familiar with *Letters and Papers from Prison* and its notion of "religionless Christianity," invokes Bonhoeffer "as evidence that the Church—this property—will serve the people best by becoming secularized at the Church's own will."[28]

The rest of the play is driven by Marsh's dialogue with characters who are less certain about the church's function in a world "come of age." They know something of Bonhoeffer, too, and have their own interpretations of his legacy. While the meeting is inconclusive, the play does provide an answer of sorts to the question "what is to become of this Church?" "We shall all answer," the AUCTIONEER explains at the play's end, "not only by what happens within the Church itself, whatever use these premises are put to, we shall honour [Bonhoeffer], or not, in whatever we do, within the Church and without, in the world in which we live."[29] *Coming of Age: A Play* is a remarkably insightful application of Bonhoeffer's mature thought to the church's role in a postwar world.[30]

In 1982 Douglas Anderson published *The Beams Are Creaking*, another drama based on Bonhoeffer's life. The play is "the fascinating story of Dietrich Bonhoeffer told in a creative theatrical way"—that is, with the aid of six radios that dominate the stage and intermittently broadcast a narrative account of German political life between 1930 and 1945. A central theme is Nazi persecution of the Jews and its role in pushing Bonhoeffer toward resistance. This theme is broached in a discussion between Dietrich and Klaus Bonhoeffer comparing the plight of American Negroes and German Jews. "I must tell you," Dietrich says to Klaus, "what impressed me so much about the black man in America."

I don't know if it is due to his poverty, or oppression, or whatever, but his religion is much more a way of life than it is for us. It over-flows into his music and even his conversation. There is a real sense of . . . of being part of a Christian community that the Ger-man Church seems to lack. *(Pause)* I think if German Christian-ity were more of a way of life, instead of merely a Sunday's obligation, something like the Nazi movement would never have taken root. Now our Church seems powerless to oppose it.[31]

Throughout the play, in fact, African Americans carry a message for the German people. Watching Jesse Owens perform at the 1936 Olympics, Bonhoeffer is in awe: "He's just a beautiful thing to look at, isn't he? . . . Perfectly proportioned . . . a beautiful Negro."[32]

With Bonhoeffer's exposure to American racism as background, the play projects romantic notions of the Confessing Church's dedication to relieving Jewish suffering. In a dramatic meeting with Nazi leaders Müller and Goering, Bonhoeffer calls the Aryan clause a "boldfaced, anti-Semitic decree" and is undeterred by the threat of imprisonment. In a meeting with Bishop Bell he refers to the Confessing Church as "our resistance movement" and laments that "the German Church decides to ignore anyone who happens to be of Jewish descent. Do you think that Christ would ignore anyone who happened to be of Jewish descent? It's shocking."[33] Bonhoeffer's decision to join the conspiracy is precipitated by his realization that his sister, whose husband is non-Aryan, "is no longer welcome in her own country."[34]

Act 2 of *The Beams Are Creaking* is set in Bonhoeffer's cell in Tegel prison. The main dialogue is between Dietrich and fiancée Maria, but the play also highlights Bonhoeffer's relationship with Knobloch, the prison guard who offers to help him escape. As Bonhoeffer is led away to his death, the two are singing "A Mighty Fortress Is Our God." Knobloch speaks for the play's implied reader when he says to his friend: "I've never met anyone like you before, Padre. I think I would die for you. *(Pause)* I'm embarrassed. But it's true."[35]

To date the only feature film dealing with the German theologian's life is *Bonhoeffer: Agent of Grace* (1999), which won "Best Film" at the Monte Carlo Television Festival and subsequently aired on public tel-evision stations in the United States.[36] Any film drama based on his-torical events must invent dialogue, develop certain characters while ignoring others, and generally take liberties with its subject matter. But giving cinematic expression to the life of a German theologian presents a special challenge for the filmmaker. Among the sacrifices in *Bonhoeffer: Agent of Grace* are Dietrich's identity as a professional theologian and any references to the German Church Struggle. Viewers are given a sense of Dietrich's pastoral sensitivities (in one powerful scene he calms a frightened prisoner by praying through the wall that separates them). But there are only vague indications of his theology in brief scenes where he expresses affection for Gandhi or ruminates on the role religion in a "world come of age."

Like other feature films that emphasize their subject matter's universal appeal, *Bonhoeffer: Agent of Grace* makes Dietrich's fiancée Maria von Wedemeyer his virtual costar. The love affair is the defining relationship in Dietrich's life (Eberhard Bethge appears only once) and scenes are devoted to the couple's flirtations at the von Kleist estate, to Dietrich's attempts to comfort Maria when she learns that her father and brother have been killed in action, to Maria's visits with Dietrich at Tegel prison, to their first kiss in the presence of prosecutors and guards, and to Maria's fruitless attempts to locate Dietrich toward the end of the war.

Bonhoeffer: Agent of Grace presents Bonhoeffer's defining conflict with Hitler in a series of dramatic scenes: Dietrich and a colleague surreptitiously cut down Nazi church banners; Dietrich warns a group of clergy that it is impossible for Christians to take the loyalty oath to Hitler; when Dietrich returns to Finkenwalde following a Gestapo raid, the cross in the seminary chapel has been transformed into a swastika. Added tension is created by the presumed conflict between Bonhoeffer's identity as a pastor and his work for the resistance. A German officer on a suicide mission asks for Dietrich's blessing; his Nazi prosecutor reminds him of Paul's words in Romans 13; and a Jewish rescuee warns amid planning for "Operation-7": "Please, Dietrich, don't win the war only to lose your soul."

Not surprisingly, publicity for *Bonhoeffer: Agent of Grace* underscores the universal dimensions of Dietrich's story: This is "a true story of love, courage and sacrifice" about a man who "struggled inside himself and chose to resist the Nazis" and "paid the ultimate price" for his beliefs. Bonhoeffer challenges us to consider "what is a moral person to do in a time of immorality." Indeed, for director Eric Till "the essence of the real story itself" is Bonhoeffer's heroism.[37] This essence is captured in Dietrich's final words to Maria: "Believe in the future no matter what. Remember it was courage that brought us here."

Nearly thirty years before the appearance of *Bonhoeffer: Agent of Grace*, Theodore A. Gill published *Memo for a Movie*, a "factual work of the imagination" exploring "the narrative facts and interpretive possibilities for a projected film" on Bonhoeffer.[38] In an effort to entice "an artist among filmmakers," Gill provided a thumbnail sketch of Bonhoeffer's life:

> A child of plenty, personable, brilliant, many-talented, develops sweetly in his family privilege. He travels, he plays, he excels at the university, he enters the Lutheran ministry. He proclaims a solidly biblical gospel and enforces a traditional piety. He honors the government, preaches no politics, exalts the church, considers pacifism. He gets a great kick out of being around. Then his nation accepts a mad suitor, the atmosphere is suddenly electric with threat, Bonhoeffer goes into the Resistance. At home he opposes, abroad he exposes the lie of his government and too many of its people. On the move or hiding out, he writes, preaches, teaches, exhorts, schemes. He refuses safety, operates as a kind of double agent in his own country and a courier to the enemy, enters a conspiracy against the life of the head of state, is misunderstood by the church, betrayed by colleagues, imprisoned, hanged, burned to lost ashes in the Nazi ovens. Years after the war, a friend collects and publishes letters and poems written by Bonhoeffer from prison. Realistic young students find in these fragments more suggestive for twentieth-century faith and life than in any of their teachers, and the fascination and fame of Dietrich Bonhoeffer begins its enormous spread and usefulness.[39]

Bonhoeffer's life, Gill contends, is worth filming on its own account, for in essence it is the story of "a complex hero [who] is swept into historic events and the scenario quite honestly explodes into razzle-dazzle, hanky-panky, and derring-do with a real martyrdom for toppers." Gill predicts that "such an account of personal development in the midst of earth-shaking, earth-shattering events, all true, will spark dramatic treatment in all media in all time ahead."[40]

Gill's "screenplay" takes the form of seven stories and interpretive notes. He emphasizes the cinematic possibilities of familiar episodes, including the Roman Easter of 1924 ("If done cinema verité, this footage of Easter Week could be stunning: high mass at St. Peter's on Palm Sunday, in a throng of monks, priests, seminarians, of all colors, in all garbs, from all continents; . . ."); a visit to the Spanish bullring in 1928, the almost trip to India and Gandhi; Dietrich and Frank Fisher being refused seating in a New York restaurant; the road trip to Mexico with Tean Lasserre; the visit with Karl Barth in 1931; the introduction to a confirmation class of working-class youths ("garbage rains down on him as he climbs the stairs to his first meeting with them, but he doesn't miss a beat. They test him, and he waits them out"); the interrupted radio lecture of February 1, 1933; the discussion with Martin Niemöller of the imminent implementation of the "Aryan paragraph" and his anger when the older man counsels caution; Dietrich's ninety-one-year-old grandmother violating the Nazi boycott of Jewish shops (Grandmother Bonhoeffer should be introduced when Dietrich is at Tübingen, Gill tells us, "if only to prepare for a great episode in which she stands out years later"); the commission at Bethel; the introduction to George Bell in London; the fateful leaking of the Confessing Church's memorandum to Hitler; the trip with his students to the Berlin Olympics; *Kristallnacht*; discussing the conspiracy with his sister Christine; wandering around Times Square in July of 1939; the bogus Nazi salute that symbolizes his acceptance of a conspirator's identity; his sojourn at Ettal monastery near Munich where he finds *The Cost of Discipleship* being read at lunchtime; the gathering of the Bonhoeffer clan to rehearse a cantata as they await news of the latest attempt on Hitler's life; his arrest; prison guards capitulating to the Bonhoeffer charm; roaming the prison as an ambulance man; visits in prison from Maria and his mother's cousin, General Paul von Hase; his calm amid the rain of Allied bombs ("moving down the aisle of locked in prisoners clamoring to be taken to the bomb shelters, he invokes no religious phrases, but with steady good sense reinforces common life in the midst of death"); his discovery that coconspirator Hans von Dohnanyi is being held in the same prison; Maria scouring Germany for Dietrich, lugging a suitcase full of warm clothes for him; and the dreaded arrival of Gestapo agents who announce, "Prisoner Bonhoeffer, get ready and come with us."[41]

Like other narratives of Bonhoeffer's life, Gill's begins at the end—with Bonhoeffer climbing the executioner's scaffold. But if suspense about Bonhoeffer's fate is thus diminished, "there is surging drama in the desperate fight to stay alive."[42] Indeed, the real cinematic possibilities of Bonhoeffer's life are revealed as we near the end of the "memo." Gill imagines a "savage cut"

> from the quiet, twilight woodsiness of the part around the big family houses, to the tiny, chilling, empty cell into which Dietrich Bonhoeffer is pushed in Tegel prison. The sound track fills in the screen's barren outline. The clanging of opened and closed doors, the banging on closed doors that will not open. The wretched sobbing of the man in the next cell. Far away, through many doors, the terrifying screams of a prisoner under torture, the incoherence of sudden relief, the renewed screaming screwed up higher, the babble of mad acquiescence.[43]

Another series of "slashing" cuts moves from Hitler slamming Canaris's notebook onto his desk, to a prison hospital in Berlin where Christine von Dohnanyi sits with her husband during his final moments, to a Nazi officer receiving secret orders and leading a column of cars headed for Flossenbürg. The final scene is a veritable montage of terror: "Perhaps as Dietrich Bonhoeffer crosses the prison yard to the gallows his scene can be slowed and dimmed as on other parts of the screen Klaus and Rudiger march to the Berlin wall where they are shot and Hans is carried to his execution." These scenes too might fade, Gill notes, as Maria is found "making her way from shattered city to shattered city, camp to camp, climbing through rubble, looking, asking, calling."[44]

While never losing sight of the history in which this story is inscribed, Gill's enthusiasm for a feature film based on Bonhoeffer's life is rooted in his conviction that Dietrich has a message for the world. Because Bonhoeffer is "a man for our seasons," this movie will not be another anti-Nazi film. If it is faithful to Bonhoeffer and what he was about, then it will be "a film about us, too."[45]

Significantly, Gill's attempt to interest filmmakers in Bonhoeffer's story touches on a theme emphasized throughout this study—the "impressive unity" between thought and action. Gill acknowledges

that "ideas are not necessarily photogenic and theological development is not immediately cinematic." But with Bonhoeffer, he claims,
that doesn't matter. For "the point of all his teaching is there, in the
concreteness—the graspable detail, the tellable event, the picturabil-
ity—of his existence and ours."[46] Gill reminds us that concreteness is
not only a theme of Bonhoeffer's theology, but the key in which his life
was written. In this sense he is made for the movies.

Commemoration

Organized commemoration of Bonhoeffer's life and legacy takes
many forms. Bonhoeffer's prison poem "By Gracious Powers" has
been set to music and today can be found in the hymnbooks of many
denominations.[47] In 1992 an original work titled *Bonhoeffer Triptychon* premiered in New York with the Dresden Chamber Choir.[48]
More recently, British composer and organist Philip Moore has set to
music three of Bonhoeffer's prison prayers ("Morning Prayers,"
"Prayers in Time of Distress," and "Evening Prayers") and made them
available on CD.[49] Commemorating the fiftieth anniversary of Bonhoeffer's death, churches of the Northwestern Pennsylvania Synod of
the ELCA sponsored an original play titled *The Demands of Conscience: The Inner Struggles of Dietrich Bonhoeffer*, and Augsburg College in Minneapolis has created a pictorial exhibit titled *Dietrich
Bonhoeffer-A Life in Photographs.*[50]

In addition, Bonhoeffer's life is routinely commemorated in special worship services. An example may be found in Douglas A.
Huneke's book *The Stones Will Cry Out*. "For the Life and Service of
Dietrich Bonhoeffer: A Service of Remembrance and Gratitude"
includes an invocation, call to worship, litany of confession and
thanksgiving, assurance of pardon, affirmation of faith, confession,
and benediction based on Bonhoeffer's writings, notes for a sermon
on cheap and costly grace (among other themes), and the hymn "By
Gracious Powers." W. H. Auden's poem "Friday's Child" (dedicated
to Bonhoeffer) is suggested as suitable text for a sermon ending or a
printed bulletin.[51]

The Bonhoeffer-House in Berlin ("A Memorial and Place of
Encounter") maintains a permanent exhibition dealing with

Bonhoeffer's life and work. Pilgrims can visit his study, restored to the condition in which he left it when arrested by the Gestapo.[52] And London's Westminster Abbey now features a sculpture of Bonhoeffer, unveiled in July 1998 as one of "ten limestone statues commemorating twentieth-century Christian martyrs" at a service attended by Queen Elizabeth II and Archbishop George Carey. "The gleaming, nearly life-size figures," sculpted from French Richemot limestone and placed over the Abbey's West door, include likenesses of Martin Luther King Jr., Oscar Romero, and Maximilian Kolbe. Before the statues' unveiling, congregants listened to a Commemorative Concert by Jon Hardy titled "De Profundis," which incorporated quotations from Bonhoeffer and King. A sermon preached in the Abbey two weeks later called Bonhoeffer a true martyr whose "whole life became an authentic witness to Christ and to God's justice."[53]

Since 1972 Bonhoeffer commemoration has been institutionalized in a series of International Bonhoeffer Congresses held every four years—in Kaiserwerth, Germany (1972), Geneva (1976), Oxford (1980), East Berlin (1984), Amsterdam (1988), New York (1992), Cape Town (1996), Berlin (2000), and Rome (2004). Participants hail from Europe and North America, as well as from Asia, Africa, Australia, and Latin America. "I am not aware of any other theologian, ancient or modern," writes the organizer of the Cape Town congress, "who has attracted quite the same worldwide attention on such a regular basis."[54]

Often drama and commemoration merge when Bonhoeffer is celebrated, as they did in 1999 at a conference on the campus of Penn State University. "Bonhoeffer's Dilemma: The Ethics of Violence" was part of a semester-long teaching initiative sponsored by Penn State's Institute for Arts and Humanistic Studies involving a dozen courses in various departments. The conference also was the occasion for the unveiling of an opera titled *Bonhoeffer* based on the relationship of Dietrich and Maria von Wedemeyer.

Conclusion

The forms of pilgrimage, narration, dramatization, and commemoration described in this chapter vary greatly in terms of aesthetic quality and historical faithfulness. Each, however, testifies to Bonhoeffer's unique location in the contemporary religious imagination. So why criticize them? The answer lies in the next chapter.

[North Americans] tend to be consumers in theology as in all other things, and go about the world with [their] shopping carts looking for interesting, marketable religious ideas that are the results of other peoples' pain.

　　—DOUGLAS JOHN HALL

Bonhoeffer, like Christ, belongs to all of us. . . . He belongs to everyone who can pick up his book at the library, the bookstore, or from a friend.

　　—POSTING AT BONHOEFFERSCELL@YAHOOGROUPS.COM

We must . . . avoid turning Bonhoeffer into a cult figure instead of a witness to Jesus Christ.

　　—JOHN W. DE GRUCHY

DOMESTICATION

THE PERILS OF PROTESTANT SAINTHOOD

The preceding chapters have sought to elucidate the Bonhoeffer phenomenon by exploring his identity as a modern saint and the ways this identity is reflected in various aspects of his reception. In assessing the portraits of the German theologian that sustain communities of interpretation, we have indicated areas of exaggeration and misappropriation but have refrained from dismissing these portraits because they fail to conform to some canonical image. In fact, we have seen evidence that by inviting honest debate within their respective communities of memory, the portraits are self-correcting. At this point, however, we must consider the ways Bonhoeffer's sainthood contributes to distortions of his legacy by encouraging domestication and sanctification.

A Time to Kill?

As was alluded to in our discussion of "the conservative Bonhoeffer," evangelicals' admiration for the German theologian has led some to enlist him in support of an antiabortion agenda. A text often cited in this connection is Bonhoeffer's statement in *Ethics* that

> destruction of the embryo in the mother's womb is a violation of the right to live which God has bestowed upon this nascent life. To raise the question whether we are here concerned already with a human being or not is merely to confuse the issue. The simple fact is that God certainly intended to create a human

being and that this nascent human being has been deliberately deprived of his life. And that is nothing but murder.[1]

In fashioning a pro-life Bonhoeffer, however, symbolic links have proven more effective than proof-texts. The fundamental symbolic connection is forged by likening state-sanctioned abortion of America's "defenseless children" with the Nazi Final Solution, and the church's accommodation to Nazism with Christian passivity before the "American holocaust."

As we have seen, Erwin Lutzer claims that the current assault on traditional values by liberal elites is "reminiscent of Hitler's Germany," and that the growing power of the secular state confronts us with "the American version of Hitler's 'positive Christianity.'" When America is perpetrating a "silent 'holocaust' in which five thousand tiny victims lose their lives every day," Lutzer proclaims, Bonhoeffer calls Christians to action.[2] No pro-life figure, however, has been more passionate than James Dobson in attempting to establish the analogy between Nazi Germany and America in the aftermath of *Roe v. Wade*:

> What if today were 1943 and you were in Nazi Germany and knew that Hitler and his henchmen were killing Jews and Poles and Gypsies and homosexuals and the mentally handicapped, among other "undesirables"? You knew these helpless people were being gassed, and that little children were standing all day, on one occasion in a freezing rain, for their turn to die in the gas chambers. Would you have said if you were there, "We're not going to get political in my church! That's somebody else's problem. I'm not called to address controversial issues!" Would you try to make a case for silence in the church?

"I thank God," Dobson concludes, "that Dietrich Bonhoeffer did not shrink in timidity when he saw unmitigated wickedness being perpetrated by the Nazis. He spoke out boldly, even though he had to know it would cost him his life." Having set up Bonhoeffer as a guide for the church's opposition to abortion, Dobson adapts his confession of guilt to the American church's complicity in the deaths of "thirty-nine million babies [that] have been killed by abortionists since 1973." "By her own silence," Dobson writes quoting Bonhoeffer, the church "has rendered herself guilty because of her unwillingness to suffer for what she knows is right."[3]

If these mainstream conservative spokespersons hint at parallels between Nazi crimes and legal abortion, others leave no doubt that we are living in the midst of a second holocaust. In the symbolic universe of radical antiabortionists, clinics are "abortion chambers" and "death camps," and information on abortion providers is collected in "Nuremberg files."[4] Groups such as Missionaries to the Unborn compile "graphic pictorial[s]" that purport to draw parallels between "what the Jews suffered at the hands of Nazi Germany, and what unborn babies currently suffer at the hands of American abortionists."[5] Obviously, when one inhabits this symbolic world the task of justifying anti-abortion violence becomes much easier.

In the past decade religious rationales for attacking abortion providers and the institutions that sustain them have been personified by two men: Paul Hill and Michael Bray. Hill is the better known of the two. In September 2003 he became the first American executed for antiabortion violence after being convicted of murdering a physician and his security escort outside a Pensacola, Florida abortion clinic in 1993. After the murders, Hill reflected on criticism of his actions from the Christian community:

> Before World War II the church in Germany also shrank from resisting the evils of an unjust, oppressive government. Dietrich Bonhoeffer is an example of a church leader who, as an individual, sought to protect innocent life by plotting the death of Hitler. He is now considered a hero and his *Ethics* is used as a college text. A holocaust was going on and no civil leaders arose (they are hard to find under totalitarian rule). Few people today, looking back, would say that the active civil disobedience of that time should have been restrained. We can be certain that the counsel of restraint today will be regretted by those who look back on it in the future.[6]

Hill's supporters fervently embrace the Bonhoeffer analogy, which was only strengthened when the government executed him. Following his death, one pro-Hill Web site reminded readers that "in September of 1935 the Confessing wing of the Protestant Church in Prussia met in

the city of Steglitz," where Marga Meusel, Bonhoeffer, and a few others "urged that the persecution of the Jews under the increasingly
restrictive Nuremberg Laws be placed on the Synod's agenda." Doing
nothing in the face of "unspeakable injustice" was not an option for
these brave Christian men and women, the site contended, just as
"doing nothing was not an option for Paul Hill. Is it an option for us?"[7]
Another site, titled "Men of Courage: Paul Hill and Dietrich Bonhoeffer," featured photographs of these "martyrs for Christ" and placed a
picture of corpses stacked at Dachua alongside a photo of aborted
fetuses in a waste receptacle. Bonhoeffer and Hill, according to author
Joe Pavone,

> were clergymen who were at odds with the passivity and cow-
> ardice of their fellow Christians to resist a holocaust . . . An evil
> government that allowed the extermination of a segment of its
> population, and the silence of an emasculated church, intimi-
> dated neither man . . . To the very end of their lives, Bonhoeffer
> and Hill refused to recant their beliefs that their actions were jus-
> tified. There was no retreating for these men of God. They were
> not ashamed that their fight against murder had put them in
> prison. With their lives at stake, they bravely upheld the princi-
> ple of active resistance to evil and evil governments. The Nazi
> holocaust and the American murder of 45 million unborn chil-
> dren did not conquer the spirit of these men. They followed
> Christ in life and death and challenge us to do the same today.[8]

If Paul Hill is the hero-martyr of violent antiabortionists, Michael
Bray is the movement man, "the spiritual godfather of anti-abortion violence."[9] Not surprisingly, Bray relies on the very same symbolic links to
Nazi Germany proclaimed by activists and implied by mainstream abortion opponents. The same year Hill murdered John Britton and James
Barrett, Bray authored A Time to Kill: A Study concerning the Use of Force
and Abortion, "the definitive book on the ethical justification for antiabortion violence."[10] In this work and in subsequent interviews, Bray has
likened American politicians to Hitler and called America "comparable
to Nazi Germany."[11] Theologically, Bray is influenced by Dominion theology and its reconstructionist agenda, but also looks for support among
mainstream theologians—particularly Reinhold Niebuhr and Dietrich

Bonhoeffer—who were forced to respond to the Nazi threat in their own day. Bonhoeffer, of course, is Bray's chief "moral exemplar," the model of Christian sacrifice par excellence.

The compulsion to draw parallels between radical opposition to abortion and the anti-Hitler resistance is reflected as well in the White Rose Banquet, organized by the American Coalition of Life Activists and held each year since 1996 near Bray's hometown of Bowie, Maryland. The banquet, named for the resistance cell that operated at the University of Munich in 1942–43, is scheduled on the eve of the anniversary of the *Roe v. Wade* decision. The program honors "prisoners of Christ" who have been sentenced for antiabortion activities and dispenses the Order of the White Rose to activists recently released from prison.

Despite being wrapped in honorable images, the resort to violence has made reasonable pro-lifers quite nervous and discouraged them from citing Bonhoeffer as a paragon of Christian activism. In response, the radicals criticize this loss of nerve and underscore their devotion to the German theologian. A few months after Hill's murders, John Brockhoeft, who at the time was serving time in federal prison for firebombing an abortion clinic, wondered why certain pro-lifers no longer mentioned Bonhoeffer's name.[12] Brockhoeft took the opportunity to remind his readers that Bonhoeffer was not only "an ordained Lutheran minister (like our own Mike Bray)" but an example of "absolute, Christian commitment to the cause of innocent human life."[13] Brockhoeft explained that the radical antiabortion movement naturally regards Bonhoeffer as a hero in its war against "America's ongoing holocaust" because of "the perfect parallel between the Nazi's slaughter of innocent people, not so long ago, and America's exact same wickedness today." In particular, "the wickedness practiced on these little [aborted] babies is exactly identical to what the Nazis in Europe did during WWII!" When Bonhoeffer began to see the horror "from below—from the viewpoint of those who suffer oppression," he decided to fight for the lives of the innocent.[14]

It should be emphasized that responsible pro-life leaders have explicitly condemned the sort of violence advocated by Hill, Bray, Brockhoeft, et al.[15] Nevertheless, there is no doubt that invocations of Bonhoeffer which condemn Christian passivity in the face of the "American holocaust" provide symbolic encouragement for radical antiabortion activists. When Erwin Lutzer notes that, like Bonhoeffer, "many of our Christian heroes were law breakers," and adds that abortionists commit murder "just as Hitler's emissaries . . . [despite] not breaking any laws,"[16] he is not offering an explicit sanction for violence. But he is playing into the hands of Bonhoeffer devotees on the radical right who agree that America's Nazi-like culture must be resisted and conclude that Bonhoeffer's relevance lies in his reluctant decision to wield the sword to fend off chaos and protect the defenseless.

A similar form of ideological assistance is offered when Charles Colson cites Bonhoeffer as a model for Christian civil disobedience, arguing that there are times when believers must stand against an "unjust regime"; when James Dobson applies Bonhoeffer's confession of guilt to the "murder of innocents" in America; when Georg Huntemann argues that the anti-Christian forces that animated Nazism have reappeared on the contemporary theological and political left; and when Erwin Lutzer decries the American version of "positive Christianity" and asserts that "liberalism" is the threat linking us to fascist Germany.

Some Bonhoeffer scholars have responded directly to this abuse of the German theologian's legacy by calling attention to the distinction between murder and tyrannicide.[17] But in focusing on what Bonhoeffer *meant*, they ignore the more crucial issue of what Bonhoeffer *means*, a task that would require a thorough critique of all attempts to make Bonhoeffer "ours" by establishing parallels between Nazism and contemporary movements or programs we find distasteful. As we have seen, this way of confirming Bonhoeffer's significance is featured in portraits of the Protestant saint across the theological spectrum.

Indeed, liberals have been as guilty as anyone of ascertaining Bonhoeffer's relevance for contemporary political life by portraying their own governments in Nazi images. This tendency became evident during the Vietnam era, when progressive thinkers such as Daniel Berrigan and Robert McAfee Brown insisted on viewing American "warmongering" through the prism of National Socialist genocide. Although Brown tried to aviod making "facil comparisons between Nazi Germany and the United States," as the Vietnam war intensified he could not resist viewing America as an "evil government" in the Nazi mold. Berrigan went further, citing Bonhoeffer as a model for his own moral resistance to the war, which he claimed was "a parable in its genocidal character" to Hitler's Holocaust.

The liberal proclivity for affirming parallels between American conservatism and Nazi fascism continued during the 1980s and 1990s, when Larry Rasmussen, Geffrey Kelly, Donald Shriver, G. Clarke Chapman, Wayne Whitson Floyd Jr., and others invoked Bonhoeffer in order to undermine religious legitimations of the Republican vision for America. Internationally, the relationship between fascism and reactionary politics was located in support for third-world totalitarian regimes that Kelly represented as "Nazism metastasized," or in the Cold War nuclearism described by Chapman as an idolatrous "totalism" endangering peace.

Thus, the despicable appropriation of Bonhoeffer by antiabortion activists only highlights the problem of domestication that is endemic to the Bonhoeffer phenomenon more generally. This domestication of Bonhoeffer's legacy can be effectively countered only when we are prepared to examine the compulsion to make his life and times analogous to our own. And this compulsion is evident in every portrait of the Protestant saint that seeks to translate his heroic sanctity into contemporary inspiration.

Bonhoeffer and the Jews

If Bonhoeffer's sainthood encourages *domestication* of his legacy by placing it in the service of contemporary questions, needs, and concerns whose connection with his own is sometimes tenuous and often more symbolic than real, it also gives rise to *sanctification* of the theologian's memory by making criticism of his life and thought seem disrespectful or even sacrilegious. As was mentioned in the preface, I had a personal encounter with a sanctified Bonhoeffer when I sought to examine his relationship to the "Jewish question" before members of the International Bonhoeffer Society in 1995.

The problem of sanctification in Bonhoeffer scholarship is a matter that will require further exposition. But it is no doubt exacerbated by the fundamental dynamics of the Bonhoeffer phenomenon. Throughout this book, we have seen that Bonhoeffer's unique contemporary influence is rooted in the integrity between thought and deed, belief and action that he has come to personify. On one hand, this unity has helped to establish Bonhoeffer's place in the contemporary religious imagination. William Kuhns notes that Catholic enumerations of twentieth-century saints generally include Bonhoeffer, "not simply because his life ended in martyrdom but because [he was] a man whose original thoughts were mirrored in life . . ."[18] This nexus between sainthood and integrity has ancient roots. In medieval saints' "lives," according to Allison Goddard Elliott, "what men say corresponds to what they do. The saint confesses his faith, then translates words into action." This is especially true of martyrs' stories, Elliott stresses, since "the speaker must be willing to back up the confession of faith with deeds."[19]

On the other hand, Bonhoeffer's reception as a modern representative of heroic sanctity gives rise to a presumption of integrity between deed and word that may not always exist. That this presumption affects the way Bonhoeffer's theology is interpreted is borne out in the image of Bonhoeffer as a guide for post-Holocaust Christian theological reflection. Impressed by Bonhoeffer's sacrificial actions on behalf of Jews, the remarkable integrity between his thought and behavior creates the presumption that Bonhoeffer must have thought in ways that were radically pro-Jewish as well. Thus, catalyzed by Bonhoeffer's remarkable integrity, the conviction that Jewish suffering was "the decisive stimulus to [Bonhoeffer's] repudiation of the regime from the beginning"[20] gives rise to the image of a man whose actions were an outgrowth of his theology. This image will be carefully scrutinized in a subsequent study.

NOTES

Preface

1. Robert Ellsberg, "The Mystery of Holiness: Taking Saints Seriously for the Needs of Our Time," *Sojourners* 26 (September–October 1997), at http://www .sojo.net, August 2002.

2. See Frits de Lange, "Saint Bonhoeffer? Dietrich Bonhoeffer and the Paradox of Sainthood," at http://www.home.hetnet/nl/~frits.lang/artsaintbonhoeffer.htm.

3. For a published response to the paper, see Andreas Pangritz, "Sharing the Destiny of His People," in *Bonhoeffer for a New Day: Theology in a Time of Transition*, ed. John W. de Gruchy (Grand Rapids, Mich.: Eerdmans, 1997), 258–77; 259–60.

4. John S. Conway, "Coming to Terms with the Past: Interpreting the German Church Struggles 1933–1990," *German History* 16:3 (1998): 377–96.

Chapter 1: Introduction

1. Dietrich Bonhoeffer, *Letters and Papers from Prison*, ed. Eberhard Bethge (New York: Macmillan, 1972), 369.

2. See Manfred Kwiran, *Index to Literature on Barth, Bonhoeffer and Bultmann* (Basel: Friedrich Reinhardt Verlag, 1977).

3. John W. de Gruchy, "Bonhoeffer's Legacy: A New Generation," *Christian Century* 114 (April 2, 1997): 343–45 (at firstsearch.oclc.org, November 2002).

4. James Patrick Kelley, "Bonhoeffer Studies in English: How Theologians Become Popular," *Lexington Theological Quarterly* 3:1 (1968): 12–19; 16.

5. See Wendy Murray Zoba, "Decoding Generations," *Christianity Today* 118 (April 2, 2001). For an analysis of Generation X spirituality that utilizes some of Bonhoeffer's theological categories, see Tom Beaudoin, *Virtual Faith: The Irreverent Spiritual Quest of Generation X* (San Francisco: Jossey-Bass, 1998).

6. Similarly, in August 2002, http://www.barnesandnoble.com listed 144 new books on Bonhoeffer, in addition to 105 out-of-print titles. There were 166 matches

for "Tillich," but most of these were scholarly studies that dealt almost exclusively with Tillich's theology. "Bultmann" yielded only 47 matches.

7. Zoba, "Decoding Generations."

8. John A. T. Robinson, *Honest to God* (Philadelphia: Westminster, 1963).

9. Ibid., 25.

10. Without apology, Robinson wrote: "I have made no attempt to give a balanced picture of Bonhoeffer's theology as a whole, which cannot be done by concentrating as I have been compelled to do, on this final flowering of it" (ibid., 36n1).

11. John D. Godsey, *Preface to Bonhoeffer: The Man and Two of His Shorter Writings* (Philadelphia: Fortress Press, 1965), 7.

12. "Introduction," in *The Place of Bonhoeffer: Problems and Possibilities in His Thought*, ed. Martin E. Marty (New York: Association Press, 1962), 12–13.

13. Wayne Whitson Floyd Jr., "Bonhoeffer's Many Faces," *Christian Century* 112 (April 26, 1995): 444–45.

14. John D. Godsey, *The Theology of Dietrich Bonhoeffer* (Philadelphia: Westminster Press, 1960), 13.

15. Robert E. Huldschiner, "A Review Article—The Quest for the Historical Bonhoeffer," *Lutheran Forum* 3 (September 1969): 12–13. J. Martin Bailey claims that Bonhoeffer's *Cost of Discipleship* and *Life Together* were for the resistance movement among German Christians what *Mein Kampf* was to the Nazis. See J. Martin Bailey and Douglas Gilbert, *The Steps of Bonhoeffer: A Pictorial Album* (Philadelphia: Pilgrim Press, 1969), 14. David H. Hopper argues that Bonhoeffer actually lived between rather than through the crucial events of the twentieth century (World War I and the aftermath of World War II). See David H. Hopper, *A Dissent on Bonhoeffer* (Philadelphia: Westminster Press, 1975), 136.

16. In Bonhoeffer, Robert Coles observes, "we see little of the zig and zag so aptly evoked by a masterful observer of human psychology. In Bonhoeffer's life the march of his feet, step upon step, is directed, relentless, all too foretellable, an insistent and persistent and resounding antiphon of dissent to the legions of hate that paraded across Germany, then other countries. . . ." See *Dietrich Bonhoeffer*, Modern Spiritual Masters Series (Maryknoll, N.Y.: Orbis, 1998), 27.

17. For a study of interwar religious movements that tended toward fascism, see Zeev Sternhell, *Neither Right Nor Left: Fascist Ideology in France*, tr. David Maisel (Berkeley: University of California Press, 1986).

18. "Dietrich Bonhoeffer in Pomerania," and Albrecht Schönherr, "The Single-heartedness of the Provoked," in *I Knew Dietrich Bonhoeffer*, ed. Ronald Gregor

Smith and Wolf-Dieter Zimmerman, tr. Käthe Gregor Smith (New York: Harper & Row, 1966), 113; 126.

19. W. A. Visser 't Hooft, "Dietrich Bonhoeffer, 1945–1965," *Ecumenical Review* 17 (July 1965): 224–31; 225.

20. "Theologian of Life," *Time* 75 (May 9, 1960): 53–54.

21. John T. Elson, "A Man for Others," *Life* 58 (May 7, 1965): 108–16; 108.

22. Eberhard Bethge, *Dietrich Bonhoeffer: A Biography*, rev. and ed. Victoria J. Barnett (Philadelphia: Fortress Press, 2000), xiii; and "Dietrich Bonhoeffer 1906–1945," *Christianity and Crisis* 25 (April 19, 1965): 75. See also Karl Barth, "From a Letter to Superintendent Herrenbrück," in *World Come of Age*, ed. Ronald Gregor Smith (Philadelphia: Fortress Press, 1967), 91: "Why should one not allow oneself to be addressed like this by a man of whom it was asked and to whom it was also given that he not only thought it and said it, but also lived it?"; William Kuhns, *In Pursuit of Dietrich Bonhoeffer* (New York: Image Books, 1967), xii: "Perhaps no single truth is so striking about Bonhoeffer as his personal synthesis of life and theology"; and 281–82: "It is indeed possible that Bonhoeffer, with his life and finally with his martyrdom, has provided the epitaph to a long and ultimately sterile tradition of theology in which the theologian's personal life matters little"; and "A Catholic Looks at Bonhoeffer," *Christian Century* 84 (June 28, 1967): 830–33; 832: "The real inspiration of Bonhoeffer lies not only in his thought but also in the tensions and heroism of his life . . . Perhaps this integrity, this embodiment of theology in the world, has beyond all else served to attract Catholics to his writings. Perhaps this integrity will do much to make Bonhoeffer a source of renewal in the Catholic Church"; Godsey, *Preface to Bonhoeffer*, 21: "It is our contention that much of the respect paid to Bonhoeffer's words is due to the overall witness of his life"; Bailey and Gilbert, *The Steps of Bonhoeffer*, 14: "His whole life was of a piece. W. A. Visser 't Hooft has called him the 'least schizophrenic of men'"; Benjamin A. Reist, *The Promise of Bonhoeffer* (Philadelphia and New York: J. B. Lippincott, 1969), 37: "Simply the recounting of Bonhoeffer's life in somewhat detailed perspective is enough to suggest that events provide the clues to his theology"; *The Christian Century* 90 (January 10, 1973): 50: Bonhoeffer "was one of those rare individuals in whom word and action were one . . ."; Clifford J. Green, "Bonhoeffer in the Context of Ericksen's Luther Study," in Roger A. Johnson, *Psychohistory and Religion: The Case of Young Man Luther* (Philadelphia: Fortress Press, 1977), 162–96: Bonhoeffer has "exerted a personal magnetism on modern Christians seeking to weld faith and identity"; James H. Burtness, *Shaping the Future*, 173: "He was one of those people who said what he did and did what he said, so that his life is a commentary on his writings, and his writings on his life";

Albrecht Schöenherr, "Dietrich Bonhoeffer: The Message of a Life," *Christian Century* 102 (November 27, 1985): 1090–94; 1090–91: "What moves us to ponder Bonhoeffer's life today? Why is there an obviously growing interest in him? I think it is because his was such a unified life . . . Life for him consisted not of different compartments, but of a single reality"; Georg Huntemann, *The Other Bonhoeffer: An Evangelical Reassessment of Dietrich Bonhoeffer*, tr. Todd Huizinga (Grand Rapids, Mich.: Baker, 1993), 150: "He hated the dualism of learning and living, doctrine and spiritual life"; Wayne Whitson Floyd Jr., "Bonhoeffer's Literary Legacy," in John W. de Gruchy, *The Cambridge Companion to Dietrich Bonhoeffer*, ed. John W. de Gruchy (Cambridge: Cambridge University Press, 1999), 71–92; 71: "One might conclude then that it is his remarkable life, not the substance of his thought and writing, that provides Bonhoeffer's legacy with its coherence, its integrity"; and Paul Cleverly, "An Overview of Dietrich Bonhoeffer's Theology: Interpretations and Possibilities of 'Religionless Christianity' and Other Principal Themes," http://www.thesumners.com/bonhoeffer/essay03.html, April 2003: "The attraction of Dietrich Bonhoeffer for many Christians and non-Christians alike over the years has been because of the way his lifestyle reflected his beliefs. Indeed, his actions exemplified his beliefs whilst his beliefs illuminated his actions. The integrity of his witness which ended with his death gives weight to his theology, and in a remarkable way, he brought together faith and political responsibility; faith and works; freedom and obedience; justification and sanctification; the sacred and the secular; and the Church and the world."

See also Frederick K. Wentz, "Lay Renaissance: Europe and America," *Christian Century* 76 (May 13, 1959): 576–79; 576; William E. Hull, "Review of Dietrich Bonhoeffer, *The Way to Freedom: Lectures and Notes, 1935–1939*," and Wolf-Dieter Zimmerman and Ronald Gregor Smith, eds., "I knew Dietrich Bonhoeffer," Christian Century 85 (July 12, 1967):920-21; and Clifford Green, "Bethge's Bonhoeffer," *Christian Century* 87 (July 1, 1970): 822–25.

23. Marilynne Robinson, *The Death of Adam: Essays on Modern Thought* (Boston: Houghton Mifflin, 1998), 110.

24. Wentz, "Lay Renaissance: Europe and America," 577.

25. Eckard Minthe, "Bonhoeffer's Influence on the Younger Generation of Ministers in Germany," *Andover Newton Quarterly* 2 (September 1961): 13–45; 45.

26. Michael Novak described Bonhoeffer and Camus as "the major heroes of many young Christians." See "Bonhoeffer's Way," *Book Week* 4 (February 19, 1967): 5–6; 5. Camus was in France during World War II where he worked for the resistance and undertook the editorship of the Parisian daily *Combat*, which first appeared clandestinely in 1943. See also Peter L. Berger, "Camus, Bonhöffer and

the World Come of Age," *Christian Century* 76 Part 1 (April 8, 1959): 417–18 and Part 2(April 15, 1959), 450–52; Robinson, *Honest to God*, 129; and Larry L. Rasmussen, *Dietrich Bonhoeffer: Reality and Resistance*, Studies in Christian Ethics (Nashville: Abingdon, 1972), 129.

27. Stephen C. Rose, "Bethge's Monument," *Christianity and Crisis* 30 (July 20, 1970): 154–55; 154.

28. Godsey, *The Theology of Dietrich Bonhoeffer*, 282. Also in 1960 Martin Marty admitted that he himself had once dismissed Bonhoeffer "as an expert devotionalist and exegete who held fascination because he was martyred" and noted "the temptation to foster a Bonhöffer cult." But he concluded that seminarians were identifying with the substance of Bonhoeffer's theology as well as with the single-mindedness of "one who kept the eternal purpose of Christian sacrifice before himself and others." See Martin E. Marty, "Bonhoeffer: Seminarians' Theologian," *Christian Century* 77 (April 20, 1960): 467–69; 467. When he edited *The Place of Bonhoeffer* in 1962, Marty asked each contributor to locate the German theologian within the history of theology, lest he "be regarded either as demigod or obsolete idol" (Marty, *The Place of Bonhoeffer*, 10, 18).

29. "Bonhoeffer: Representative Christian," *Christian Century* 82 (April 7, 1965): 420–21; 420; and Henry P. Van Dusen, letter to the editor, *Christian Century* 90 (January 10, 1973): 50. See also W. W. Bartley III, "The Bonhoeffer Revival," *New York Review of Books* 3 (August 26, 1965): 14–17; 14. In 1962 Martin Marty confidently wrote "that Bonhoeffer deserves critical analysis as 'a very sophisticated theologian' goes without saying," and observed that younger Christian thinkers in Europe and America could be divided into two camps: those who acknowledged their debt to Bonhoeffer and those who did not (Marty, *The Place of Bonhoeffer*, 18).

30. "Bonhoeffer: Representative Christian," 420.

31. The citation is from a 1967 article published in *Saturday Review*. Cited in Hopper, *A Dissent on Bonhoeffer*, 20. The same year John Macquarrie commented on Bonhoeffer's "special fascination for students . . . Here was a man who really lived out his faith." See Macquarrie, *New Directions in Theology Today, Volume III: God and Secularity* (Philadelphia: Westminster, 1967), 37–38. Cf. Thomas W. Ogletree, "The Church's Mission to the World in the Theology of Dietrich Bonhoeffer," *Encounter* 25 (autumn 1964): 457–69: 457: "Few of the younger theologians of our time have excited as much attention in seminaries and student groups . . ."

32. Hopper, *A Dissent on Bonhoeffer*, 21–22.

33. See especially ibid., ch. 2. In 1952 Karl Barth described the author of *Letters and Papers from Prison* as "an impulsive visionary thinker who was suddenly

seized by an idea to which he gave lively form, and then after a time he called a halt
. . . with some provisional last point or other." In 1961 Eberhard Bethge wrote that
while ecumenical representatives had honored Bonhoeffer as a martyr, "they let
the shadow of ignorance prevail as to whether or not [he] was a theologian of some
status" (cited in Hopper, *A Dissent on Bonhoeffer*, 15, 27). In 1970, John Macquarrie noted in *New York Times Book Review* "a tendency to overrate Bonhoeffer
as a theologian. His work is too fragmentary for him to stand in the first rank in that
respect" (cited in Clifford Green, *Bonhoeffer: A Theology of Sociality* rev. ed.
[Grand Rapids, Mich.: Eerdmans, 1999], 6). In 1971, Theodore A. Gill wrote that
Bonhoeffer could be interpreted as a "brisk but secondary figure in Christian letters." See Theodore A. Gill, *Memo for a Movie: A Short Life of Dietrich Bonhoeffer*
(New York: Macmillan, 1971), 15.

34. In 1955, Gerhard Ebeling wrote that "in dealing with the person and
work of Dietrich Bonhoeffer it is very difficult to resist the tendency to dwell
upon the close tie between the theological and the human aspects, as it speaks to
us above all in the collection of *Letters and Papers from Prison* . . . We [are
tempted to] speak of Bonhoeffer's theological and spiritual ancestry and his place
in the most recent history of theology, of the development he himself underwent,
and of his personal life which presents . . . the unforgettable commentary on his
theological thinking." A decade later, in *Christ for Us in the Theology of Dietrich
Bonhoeffer* (New York: Harper, 1967), John A. Phillips stressed "Bonhoeffer's
freedom from the events of his life and of the time in which lived" (23). More
recently, Wayne Whitson Floyd Jr., General Editor of the English Edition of *Dietrich Bonhoeffer Werke*, has argued that this project makes it possible to "view the
entire written legacy, resisting all temptations to reduce Bonhoeffer's enduring
significance to his remarkable biography alone." See "Bonhoeffer's Literary
Legacy," in de Gruchy, *The Cambridge Companion to Dietrich Bonhoeffer*,
71–92; 71.

35. Kelley, "How Theologians Become Popular," 19.

36. See Reist, *The Promise of Bonhoeffer*, 15, 116.

37. André Dumas, *Dietrich Bonhoeffer: Theologian of Reality* (New York:
Macmillan, 1971); James Woelfel, *Bonhoeffer's Theology: Classical and Revolu-
tionary* (Nashville: Abingdon, 1970); Clifford Green, *Bonhoeffer: The Sociality of
Christ and Humanity* (Missoula: Scholars, 1972); Rasmussen, *Dietrich Bonhoeffer:
Reality and Resistance*; Heinrich Ott, *Reality and Faith: The Theological Legacy of
Dietrich Bonhoeffer* (Philadelphia: Fortress Press, 1972); Ronald Gregor Smith,
ed., *World Come of Age* (Philadelphia: Fortress, 1967); and Phillips, *Christ for Us
in the Theology of Dietrich Bonhoeffer*.

Bonhoeffer's reception has also been interpreted diachronically, that is, in terms of the various texts that over time have come to symbolize his legacy. Eberhard Bethge writes that "in the 1950s, all over the world, theologians and churchmen concerned that faith in Christ should still be capable of presentation, discovered the author of *Cost of Discipleship* and accordingly drew for themselves a picture of the martyr for such a faith. In the 1960s, it was the author of the letters from Tegel Prison who was discussed, who finally acknowledged the irreversibility of the Enlightenment. . . . Today we are in a period when Bonhoeffer's *Ethics* has shifted to the centre of interest. This is as true in Japan and the United States as in Germany itself." See Bethge's foreword to Keith W. Clements, *A Patriotism for Today: Love of Country in Dialogue with the Witness of Dietrich Bonhoeffer* (London: Collins Liturgical Publications, 1984). While it is true that Bonhoeffer looks different depending on what text one is reading, it is also true that many admirers of Bonhoeffer identify with a particular text because it represents the image of Bonhoeffer to which they are attracted.

38. Some have even concluded that Bonhoeffer's biography is an indispensable key for interpreting his theology. In 1972, Ernst Feil asserted that the unity of Bonhoeffer's life provides the foundation for understanding the continuity in his thought. In particular, Feil argued, the movement from "thought" to "deed" in Bonhoeffer's theology is paralleled by his move from an academic vocation to increasing involvement in the ecclesiastical and pastoral spheres. See Hopper, *A Dissent on Bonhoeffer*, 41, 73, 117. The same year, Larry L. Rasmussen wrote that Bonhoeffer's life bore with unquestionable integrity "the very conformation to Christ which he set at the center of his ethics." See Rasmussen, *Dietrich Bonhoeffer: Reality and Resistance*, 149. In another work originally published in 1972, Clifford Green argued for the centrality of the "autobiographical dimension" in Bonhoeffer's theology, without a knowledge of which "understanding of Bonhoeffer's theological development would be darkened by inner obscurity or externally imposed speculation, or both" (Green, *A Theology of Sociality*, 3). According to Green, Bethge's biography revealed "that a deep, personal concern is at work along with the theological, philosophical, exegetical, ecclesiastical, and political factors which informed [Bonhoeffer's] thinking" (ibid.). In 1985 James H. Burtness wrote that the connection between Bonhoeffer's life and work is "absolutely essential," due to the shortness of his life and the fragmentary character of much of his writing, the coincidence of his career with the Nazi dictatorship, and the integrity between thought and deed. See James H. Burtness, *Shaping the Future: The Ethics of Dietrich Bonhoeffer* (Philadelphia: Fortress, 1985), 173. In 1994 Douglas John Hall observed that Bonhoeffer "crossed over the invisible but absolutely decisive boundary between professional theology or theology as profession and 'theological

existence'." See "Ecclesia Crucis: The Disciple Community and the Future of the Church in North America," in Wayne Whitson Floyd Jr. and Charles Marsh, eds., *Theology and the Practice of Responsibility: Essays on Dietrich Bonhoeffer* (Valley Forge, Pa.: Trinity Press International, 1994), 59–73; 62. In 1998, Josiah Ulysses Young III contended that "what gives more credibility to [Bonhoeffer's] witness than his scholarship *(actus reflexus)* was his hands-on experience *(actus directus)* with African-Americans." See *No Difference in the Fare: Dietrich Bonhoeffer and the Problem of Racism* (Grand Rapids: Eerdmans, 1998), 87.

39. According to Paul Lehmann, Bonhoeffer exhibited in his life and writings "the paradox of discipleship," one mark of which "was the combination in Bonhoeffer of conservative and revolutionary passions and concerns. Aristocratic by heritage and taste, he could abandon luxury and even comfort for a larger claim upon him as a human being and as a Christian. His conservatism prevented a doctrinaire espousal of socialist theories and programmes of social change. On the other hand, his revolutionary sensitivity to the injustices of a colonial and capitalist society prevented an equally doctrinaire resistance to social change." See "The Paradox of Discipleship," in Smith and Zimmerman, *I Knew Dietrich Bonhoeffer*, 42.

40. Woelfel, *Bonhoeffer's Theology*, 299.

41. Thomas I. Day does so by attempting to correct the "notoriously poor English translations [that] have added to the difficulties in Bonhoeffer scholarship." See *Bonhoeffer on Christian Community and Common Sense*, Toronto Studies in Theology 11 (New York: Mellen, 1975). Of the book's ten endnotes, eight deal with mistakes in translation Day claims distort Bonhoeffer's meaning.

42. J. Carl Ridd, "A Message from Bonhoeffer," *Christian Century* 83 (June 29, 1966): 827–29; 827.

Chapter 2: Seer

1. Craig L. Nessan, "The American Reception: Introduction to Bonhoeffer's *Christ the Center*," in Dietrich Bonhoeffer, *Who Is Christ for Us?*, Facets, ed. Craig L. Nessan and Renate Wind, tr. Craig L. Nessan (Minneapolis: Fortress Press, 2002), 20. John W. de Gruchy writes that prior to 1963 Bonhoeffer "was known in the English-speaking world as a martyr of the Confessing Church struggle *(Kirchenkampf)* in Germany, and the author of *The Cost of Discipleship*." See "The Reception of Bonhoeffer's Theology," in *The Cambridge Companion to Dietrich Bonhoeffer*, ed. John W. de Gruchy (Cambridge: Cambridge University Press, 1999), 93–109; 93.

2. Ronald Gregor Smith," Introduction," in *World Come of Age*, ed. Ronald Gregor Smith (Philadelphia: Fortress Press, 1967), 10.

3. Paul L. Lehmann, "Faith and Worldliness in Bonhoeffer's Thought," in *Bonhoeffer in a World Come of Age*, ed. Peter Vorkink II (Philadelphia: Fortress Press, 1968), 26. See also Regin Prenter, "Dietrich Bonhoeffer and Karl Barth's Positivism of Revelation," 93–130; William Hamilton, "'The Letters Are a Particular Thorn: Some Themes in Bonhoeffer's Prison Writings," 131–60; and Rudolf Bultmann, "The Idea of God and Modern Man," 256–74, in Smith, *World Come of Age*.

4. Since 1960 Bonhoeffer research in Germany has been a vibrant enterprise about which it is difficult to generalize. What can be affirmed is that for some time Bonhoeffer research has been carried on mainly in doctoral dissertations, that the impact of Bonhoeffer's theology has been more pronounced in the former German Democratic Republic than in the Federal Republic, and that interest in Bonhoeffer shows no sign of abating. Also, like the English-language studies that are the focus of this book, interpretations of Bonhoeffer in Germany reveal differing emphases and arrive at "diametrically opposed positions." The reason for this, Ernst Feil explains, "lies not so much in Bonhoeffer's own work as in the fact that the prison letters have had an especially strong fascination for many who have studied them and seem to be especially prone to being interpreted according to the interpreter's own pre-understanding. This interpretation of the letters then becomes the basis for interpreting all of Bonhoeffer's theology." See Ernst Feil, *Bonhoeffer Studies in Germany: A Survey of Recent Literature*, ed. James H. Burtness, tr. Jonathan Sorum (Philadelphia: Bonhoeffer Center, 1997), 7.

5. Reinhold Niebuhr, "The Death of a Martyr," *Christianity and Crisis* 5:11 (June 25, 1945): 6. Erwin Sutz, a Sloane fellow at Union who had studied with Karl Barth and Emil Brunner, is credited with deepening Bonhoeffer's appreciation of "crisis theology." See Geffrey B. Kelly and F. Burton Nelson, *The Cost of Moral Leadership: The Spirituality of Dietrich Bonhoeffer* (Grand Rapids, Mich.: Eerdmans, 2003), 11.

6. John T. Elson, "A Man for Others," *Life* (May 7, 1965): 108–16; 111. Bonhoeffer continues to be remembered as a neoorthodox thinker. See Douglas John Hall, *Remembered Voices: Reclaiming the Legacy of "Neo-orthodoxy"* (Louisville, Ky.: Westminster John Knox, 1998). Hall claims that neoorthodox theology can be characterized by its starting point in revelation, its emphasis on the Bible, its historical consciousness, the influence of the Reformation, and its ecumenical character. Certainly Bonhoeffer would qualify as a neoorthodox thinker under this definition.

7. In the 1960s there were attempts to translate Bonhoeffer's musings on "the world come of age" and "religionless Christianity" for the benefit of pastors in the

American suburbs. Theodore O. Wedel of Union Theological Seminary noted that certain Bonhoeffer catchphrases had become part of the "'gossip theology' currently regnant in our seminary common rooms." He acknowledged that Bonhoeffer's "daring paradoxes lend themselves to the now fashionable critical assaults on the contemporary church, captive, so we are told, in suburban ghettos, and awaiting the advent of liberating knights in Bonhoeffer armor." But Wedel sought to demonstrate the significance of these Bonhoefferian paradoxes for the training of ministers. See "Man Come of Age," *Union Seminary Quarterly Review* 18:4 (May 1963): 326–40; 326–27.

8. Eberhard Bethge, *Bonhoeffer: Exile and Martyr* (New York: Seabury, 1975), 19.

9. Ronald Gregor Smith, *The New Man: Christianity and Man's Coming of Age* (New York: Harper & Row, 1956), 110.

10. Ibid., 112.

11. John D. Godsey, *The Theology of Dietrich Bonhoeffer* (Philadelphia: Westminster, 1960), 260.

12. Godsey suggested that during his earliest period (up to 1931) Bonhoeffer focused on *Jesus Christ as the revelational reality of the church*; during his middle period (1932–39) upon *Jesus Christ as the Lord over the church*; and in his final period (1940–45) upon *Jesus Christ as Lord over the world*.

13. Godsey, *The Theology of Dietrich Bonhoeffer*, 280. Indeed, some of the earliest academic courses on Bonhoeffer were offered at Princeton Seminary and Union Seminary (New York), bastions of neoorthodoxy that trained a great number of mainline Protestant ministers during the 1950s and 1960s.

14. "Dietrich Bonhoeffer: Religionless Christianity: Maturity, Transcendence, and Freedom," in Roger A. Johnson and Ernest Wallwork, *Critical Issues in Modern Religion* (Englewood Cliffs, N.J.: Prentice-Hall, 1973). On Berrigan, see chapter 3. In truth, Bonhoeffer remained virtually invisible to many students of Protestant theology in the mid-1960s. A case in point is the book *Creative Minds in Contemporary Theology*, ed. Philip E. Hughes (Grand Rapids, Mich.: Eerdmans, 1966). Bonhoeffer is strangely absent from this text—even from its index—though it contains chapters on thirteen American and European theologians, including five from Germany or Switzerland who were his rough contemporaries.

15. Benjamin Reist, cited in John W. de Gruchy, *Bonhoeffer and South Africa: Theology in Dialogue* (Grand Rapids, Mich.: Eerdmans, 1984), 12.

16. W. W. Bartley III, "The Bonhoeffer Revival," *New York Review of Books* (August 26, 1965): 14–17; 14. Bartley notes that it was not until the late 1950s that serious criticism of these thinkers began to appear in America—precisely the time

that Bonhoeffer's letters and papers, which "contained some implicit (and a few explicit) criticisms, from within the ranks of the church, of the efforts of thinkers like Tillich and Bultmann," began to be widely read in English.

17. William Hamilton, "A Secular Theology for a World Come of Age," *Theology Today* 18 (January 1962): 435–59; 458.

18. Peter L. Berger, "Camus, Bonhöffer and the World Come of Age," *The Christian Century* 76, part 1 (April 8, 1959): 417–18; part 2 (April 15, 1959): 450–52.

19. Ibid., part 2, 451.

20. David H. Hopper, *A Dissent on Bonhoeffer* (Philadelphia: Westminster, 1975), 31.

21. John A. T. Robinson, *Honest to God* (Philadelphia: Westminster, 1963), 23.

22. Ibid., 76.

23. Ibid., 25. According to Robinson, Bonhoeffer was one with Julian Huxley "in discarding the supranaturalist framework" (ibid., 127).

24. Bartley, "The Bonhoeffer Revival," 14. Michael Novak made a similar observation in 1967: "Bonhoeffer's *Letters* reached the United States at a time when the giants of two generations — Tillich and the Niebuhrs — were growing old . . ." See Michael Novak, "Dietrich Bonhoeffer," *The Critic* (June–July 1967): 38–45; 45.

25. Bethge, *Bonhoeffer: Exile and Martyr*, (New York: Seabury, 1975), 24.

26. James W. Woelfel made this point in 1970. Woelfel included Robinson's *Honest to God* in the "liberal" school of interpretation because it views Bonhoeffer in terms of his commonalities with Tillich and Bultmann. However, whatever Robinson's own theological bearings, the popular reception of *Honest to God* certainly linked it with others in the radical mode. See *Bonhoeffer's Theology: Classical and Revolutionary* (Nashville: Abingdon, 1970).

27. Paul van Buren, *The Secular Meaning of the Gospel: Based on an Analysis of Its Language* (New York: Macmillan, 1963), 1.

28. Ibid., 123, 132; see also 163.

29. Ibid., 171. Hamilton argues that while van Buren cited Bonhoeffer's plea for a nonreligious interpretation of the gospel, he is in fact best understood as a linguistic analyst influenced by Bultmann's demythologizing project. See Thomas J. J. Altizer and William Hamilton, *Radical Theology and the Death of God* (Indianapolis: Bobbs-Merrill, 1966), 32.

30. Gabriel Vahanian, *The Death of God: The Culture of Our Post-Christian Era* (New York: Braziller, 1961); and *No Other Name* (New York: Braziller, 1966). Vahanian was cautious about attempts to base contemporary theology in

Bonhoeffer's notion of "religionless Christianity": "The drama of Bonhoeffer's thought, anchored as it is in the conviction of the insurmountable incompatibility between faith and religion, is to succeed only in substituting a new dichotomy, that of atheism and theism, for the traditional cleavage between the sacred and the profane or the religious and the secular, and in laying the foundations for an innerwordly millenarianism instead of the otherworldly and transcendental millenarianism that Christian traditionalism based on the dyad of this world and the next" (*No Other Name*, 21). See also, "What Is Meant by 'The End of the Age of Religion'?" in *The Death of God Debate*, ed. Jackson Lee Ice and John J. Carey (Philadelphia: Westminster, 1967), 264ff.

31. Harvey Cox, *The Secular City: Secularization and Urbanization in Theological Perspective*, rev. ed. (New York: Macmillan, 1966).

32. Ibid., 2.

33. Ibid., 211.

34. The book was actually an anthology of writings from the previous decade that heralded the death-of-God movement.

35. Peter C. Hodgson, "The Death of God and the Crisis in Christology," *Journal of Religion* 46 (October 1966): 446–62; 446, 447.

36. F. Thomas Trotter, "Variations on the 'Death of God' Theme in Recent Theology," and William Hamilton, "Questions and Answers on the Radical Theology," in Ice and Carey, *The Death of God Debate*, 101, 216–17.

37. Ibid., 40. In "Dietrich Bonhoeffer," an article originally published in *Nation* in 1965, Hamilton described Bonhoeffer's "decisive influence" on an entire generation of younger Protestant theologians (ibid., 113–18).

38. Hodgson, "The Death of God and the Crisis in Christology," 452.

39. Altizer and Hamilton, *Radical Theology and the Death of God*, 39. In another place, Hamilton announced that "you cannot follow Bonhoeffer because, for the most part, it is impossible to figure out exactly what he meant. His work cannot, in spite of Eberhard Bethge's valiant efforts, be shaped into a developmental unity . . ." See "Bonhoeffer: Christology and Ethic United," *Christianity and Crisis* 21 (October 19, 1964): 195–98; 195.

40. Altizer and Hamilton, *Radical Theology and the Death of God*, 7.

41. Ice and Carey, *The Death of God Debate*, 16.

42. William Blair Gould, *The Worldly Christian: Bonhoeffer on Discipleship* (Philadelphia: Fortress Press, 1967), 80. See also Benjamin A. Reist, *The Promise of Bonhoeffer* (Philadelphia: J. B. Lippincott, 1969), 116; and Paul L. Lehmann, "Faith and Worldliness in Bonhoeffer's Thought," in Vorkink, *Bonhoeffer in a World Come of Age*, 27–28.

43. "What Price Insight: A Reply to 'Camus, Bonhoeffer and the World Come of Age,'" *Christian Century* 76 (May 20, 1959): 618–19.

44. Reginald H. Fuller, "Introduction," in *Two Studies in the Theology of Bonhoeffer*, ed. Jürgen Moltmann and Jürgen Weissbach, tr. Reginald H. Fuller and Ilse Fuller (New York: Scribner's, 1967), 15.

45. Ibid., 15. Bethge noted in an interview that "'Nonreligious interpretation' means Christological interpretation. It might not mean that for others, but it did for Bonhoeffer." See H. Elliott Wright, "Aftermath of Flossenburg: Bonhoeffer, 1945–1970: An Interview with Eberhard Bethge," *Christian Century* 87 (May 27, 1970): 656–59; 657. In 1968 Bethge noted that the seeds of "Christianity without religion" were sown in a letter Bonhoeffer wrote in 1932. See "The Challenge of Bonhoeffer's Life and Theology," in Smith, *World Come of Age*, 43. According to Bethge, the radicals (he calls them "liberals") find "in the late Bonhoeffer a great confirmation for their cause by overlooking the Christology which leads to Bonhoeffer's 'new liberalism'" (44). More recently, Georg Huntemann has argued that there was no radical break in Bonhoeffer's theology during the spring of 1944; rather, it is "a seamless whole with no dramatic breaks," whose great theme was a "Christ-mystical understanding of this God-forsaken modern world"—in the tradition of Luther and H. E. Kohlbrügge. See Georg Huntemann, *The Other Bonhoeffer: An Evangelical Reassessment of Dietrich Bonhoeffer*, tr. Todd Huizinga (Grand Rapids, Mich.: Baker, 1993), 65, 212.

46. See, Arthur W. Hoogstrate, "Dietrich Bonhoeffer: Who Was He?" *The Banner* (August 22, 1969): 4. Hoogstrate writes that *The Cost of Discipleship* contains "many inspiring things about the nature of our life for Christ" but that in prison Bonhoeffer "wrote certain provocative things which did not seem consistent with his earlier affirmations." In *Moody Monthly*, Charles Horne lamented that although Bonhoeffer had much to say that is "refreshing and helpful to Christian life," his prison writings seemed to "cut away a true vital approach to the Christian walk." See "What Is Bonhoeffer Theology?" *Moody Monthly* 66:9 (May 1966): 40–42; 41.

47. In 1966 Hodgson observed that "a single, basic theme runs through [Bonhoeffer's] theological work from the Christology lectures of 1933, to the *Ethics* of 1940–43, to the last prison letters of 1944: God is present as the center of the reality of the world in *Christ*" (Hodgson, "The Death of God and the Crisis in Christology," 455). According to Gibbs, "All [Bonhoeffer's] thinking stemmed from one centre, the revelation of God in Jesus Christ, and every utterance is in the end a Christocentric utterance." See John Gibbs, "Dietrich Bonhoeffer," in T. G. A. Baker, John Gibbs, B. S. Moss, and Martin Jarrett-Kerr, *The New Theologians:*

Bultmann, Bonhoeffer, Tillich, Teilhard de Chardin (London: A. R. Mowbray, 1964), 11–25; 17–18. Rasmussen writes that Bonhoeffer's resistance activity "was his Christology enacted with utter seriousness . . . To seek Jesus Christ among new claims . . . is the *cantus firmus* that winds through the polyphony of Bonhoeffer's abbreviated life." See Larry L. Rasmussen, *Dietrich Bonhoeffer: Reality and Resistance* Studies in Christian Ethics (Nashville: Abingdon, 1972), 15, 94.

See also Thomas N. Ogletree, "The Church's Mission to the World in the Theology of Dietrich Bonhoeffer," *Encounter* 25 (autumn 1964): 457–69; and Paul L. Lehmann, "Faith and Worldliness in Bonhoeffer's Thought," in Vorkink, *Bonhoeffer in a World Come of Age*, 33. On Phillips, Ott, Dumas, and Feil, see Hopper, *A Dissent on Bonhoeffer*, ch. 2. Clifford Green complains of a "teleological bias" which favors the prison letters as the hermeneutical key for unlocking Bonhoeffer's theology. In contrast, Green contends that ". . . the Christology and anthropology presented in terms of sociality in the early theology is indispensable for understanding the content and method of Bonhoeffer's prison theology." See *Bonhoeffer: A Theology of Sociality*, rev. ed. (Grand Rapids, Mich.: Eerdmans, 1999), 4, 7.

More recently, Godsey has identified "suffering" as the theme that unties Bonhoeffer's theology. See John D. Godsey, "Dietrich Bonhoeffer on Suffering," *Stauros Notebook* 14:2 (summer 1995), http://www.stauros.org/notebooks/v14n2901.html. In *Remembered Voices*, Douglas John Hall sees discipleship as "the constant that runs throughout all of [Bonhoeffer's] works" (73). And Andreas Pangritz writes that "the question 'Who Is Jesus Christ?' forms the *cantus firmus* of Bonhoeffer's theological development from the beginning to the end." See "Who Is Jesus Christ for Us Today?" in *The Cambridge Companion to Dietrich Bonhoeffer*, ed. John W. de Gruchy (Cambridge: Cambridge University Press, 1999), 134–53; 134.

As James Patrick Kelley has noted, the publication order of Bonhoeffer's works in English—with *Letters and Papers from Prison* preceding earlier texts such as *Life Together, Ethics*, and *Creation and Fall*—contributed to a tendency to read Bonhoeffer in reverse, thus making it "virtually impossible to discern any possibility of genetic development in the thought of Bonhoeffer." See "Bonhoeffer Studies in English: How Theologians Become Popular," *Lexington Theological Quarterly* 3:1 (1968): 12–19.

48. Robinson, *Honest to God*, 36.

49. Paul van Buren, "Bonhoeffer's Paradox: Living with God without God," in Vorkink, *Bonhoeffer in a World Come of Age*, 4.

50. Altizer and Hamilton, *Radical Theology and the Death of God*, 93.

51. Bethge, *Bonhoeffer: Exile and Martyr*, 15.

52. E. H. Miscall, *The Secularization of Christianity: An Analysis and a Critique* (New York: Holt, Rinehart & Winston, 1965), 41: "It would be perhaps unfair to Bonhoeffer to take *au pied de la lettre* words written from a Nazi prison camp under conditions of grave physical and emotional distress; the spiritual experience of feeling forsaken by God has been common to many of the greatest saints and can claim even more august authority in the Fourth Word from the Cross." Similarly, Alisdair McIntyre argues that Bonhoeffer's Christianity is only intelligible in the context of helplessness in a Nazi prison camp (cited in Miscall, *The Secularization of Christianity*, 180).

53. Miscall notes that Tillich, Bultmann, and Bonhoeffer—who provide Robinson's theological inspiration—"represent the reaction within German Protestantism from the extreme revelationism and supernaturalism of the school of Barth, Brunner, and Heim" (ibid., 120).

54. Ibid., viii.

55. David E. Jenkins, *Guide to the Debate about God* (Philadelphia: Westminster, 1966), 100.

56. Paul L. Lehmann, review of *The Communion of Saints* and *No Rusty Swords*, *Union Seminary Quarterly Review* 21:3 (March 1966): 364–69; 365.

57. John A. Phillips, "The Killing of Brother Dietrich," *Christianity and Crisis* 29 (February 16, 1969): 24–26; 26. Phillips was critical of the *Union Seminary Quarterly Review*, a recent issue of which had been dedicated to protecting Bonhoeffer from radical expropriation: "Those who have been really comforted and disturbed and freed by reading the prison letters will only be saddened by the Siegfried Line [one essay in the journal] constructs around the tomb, with continual admonitions against 'distortion,' 'expropriation for alien purposes,' 'capricious dissemination of half truths,' and 'carelessness,' written by a disciple who apparently believes that the best offense against the radical is a defense based upon what Bonhoeffer Really Said" (ibid., 24).

58. John Macquarrie, *New Directions in Theology Today, Volume III: God and Secularity* (Philadelphia: Westminster, 1967), 38.

59. Robinson, *Honest to God*, 25; Hamilton, "Bonhoeffer: Christology and Ethic United," 195.

60. Bonhoeffer's use of the term "world come of age" (beginning in a letter of June 8, 1944) was a self-conscious allusion to the celebrated passage in which Immanuel Kant takes cognizance of the new age to which he was a witness. See Gustavo Gutiérrez, "The Limitations of Modern Theology: On a Letter of Dietrich Bonhoeffer," in *Gustavo Gutiérrez: Essential Writings*, ed. James B. Nickoloff (Minneapolis: Fortress Press, 1996), 35–42; 37. See also J. Sperna Weiland, *New Ways in Theology*, tr. N. D. Smith (New York: Newman), 69.

61. Douglas John Hall, "Ecclesia Crucis: The Disciple Community and the Future of the Church in North America," in *Theology and the Practice of Responsibility: Essays on Dietrich Bonhoeffer*, ed. Wayne Whitson Floyd Jr. and Charles Marsh (Valley Forge, Pa.: Trinity Press International, 1994), 59–73; 60. See also Barry Harvey, "The Wound of History: Reading Bonhoeffer after Christendom," in *Bonhoeffer for a New Day: Theology in a Time of Transition*, ed. John W. de Gruchy (Grand Rapids, Mich.: Eerdmans, 1997), 72–93.

62. Hans D. van Hoogstraten, "Ethics and the Problem of Metaphysics," in Floyd and Marsh, *Theology and the Practice of Responsibility*, 223–37.

63. Barry Harvey, "A Post-Critical Approach to 'Religionless Christianity,'" in Floyd and Marsh, *Theology and the Practice of Responsibility*, 39–58. Harvey writes that "Bonhoeffer's deconstruction of religion as a viable theological category is also an invitation to, and an opportunity for, the church to reexamine and reclaim its non-religious (i.e., its political and social) existence and vocation as the body of Christ. In short, religionless Christianity is both a subversive act of noncompliance with the hegemonic ordering of the (post)modern world (i.e., the church's refusal to be confined to the margins, where it had been assigned in a world come of age), and a summons to return to the center of the human village . . ." (55).

64. Walter Lowe, "Bonhoeffer and Deconstruction: Toward a Theology of the Crucified Logos," in Floyd and Marsh, *Theology and the Practice of Responsibility*, 207–22; 207, 208, 213. Lowe notes that "Bonhoeffer's rejection of metaphysics presses in the same direction as [Mark] Taylor's repudiation of ontotheology" and observes in *Ethics* a critique of partiality that might have been penned by a deconstructionist.

65. Wayne Whitson Floyd Jr., "Style and the Critique of Metaphysics: The Letter as Form in Bonhoeffer and Adorno," in Floyd and Marsh, *Theology and the Practice of Responsibility*, 239–51.

66. Ibid., 248. In protesting against system, the essay and letter "retain their power to keep in play the diversity of themes, which the metaphysical system would feel compelled to weave into a totality, or choose among—discarding some, retaining others" (247).

67. Ronald Thiemann, unpublished paper shared with the author, subsequently published as "Waiting for God's Own Time: Dietrich Bonhoeffer as Public Intellectual," *Die Gehalt des Christentums im 21. Jahrhundert*, ed. Christian Gremmels and Wolfgang Huber (Gütersloh, Germany: Güertersloher Verlagshaus, 2002), 88–107.

68. Ibid., 8 (manuscript pagination for this and subsequent notes).

69. Ibid., 15–16.

70. Ibid., 17.

71. Harvey Cox, "Using and Misusing Bonhoeffer," *Christianity and Crisis* 24 (October 19, 1964): 199–201; 200. See also Paulose Mar Paulose, *Encounter in Humanization: Insights for Christian-Marxist Dialogue and Cooperation* (at http://www.religion-online.org/cgi-bin/researchd.dll/showbook?item_id=1572, April 2003), in which the author offers a corrective to Marx's critique of religion based on an analysis of Bonhoeffer's theology.

72. Hanfried Müller, "Concerning the Reception and Interpretation of Dietrich Bonhoeffer," in Smith, *World Come of Age*, 182–214; 182.

73. As John A. Moses writes: "Precisely why it was legitimate to remember Bonhoeffer, whose bourgeois origins could not have been more apparent, is only explainable within the framework of Marxist-Leninist casuistry." See "Bonhoeffer's Reception in East Germany," in de Gruchy, *Bonhoeffer for a New Day*, 278–97; 281.

74. Ibid., 282.

75. According to Müller, Bonhoeffer was able to free himself from Lutheran clericalism and in his prison writings point "the way to a new orientation toward Marxism-Leninism as the revolutionary world movement" (ibid., 285).

76. Müller, "Concerning the Reception and Interpretation of Dietrich Bonhoeffer," 184; 213.

77. Ibid., 212.

78. Ibid., 189–90.

79. Ibid., 205.

80. Ibid., 207.

81. Ibid., 283.

82. Ibid., 286.

83. Wayne Whitson Floyd Jr. writes: "The time of most of Dietrich Bonhoeffer's adult life, between this century's two world wars and amidst the failed experiment of the Weimar Republic, was, despite its unarguable uniqueness—a time sharing many characteristics with our own. See "Bonhoeffer, Democracy, and the Public Tasks of Theology," in *Reflections on Bonhoeffer: Essays in Honor of F. Burton Nelson*, ed. Geffrey B. Kelly and C. John Weborg (Chicago: Covenant, 1999), 279–89; 279.

84. Vahanian, *No Other Name*, 14.

85. Harvey Cox, "Beyond Bonhoeffer? The Future of Religionless Christianity," *Commonweal* (September 17, 1965): 653–57; 654. See also Weiland, *New Ways in Theology*, 73. Jamie S. Scott takes a similar approach to understanding Bonhoeffer in *Christians and Tyrants: The Prison Testimonies of Boethius, Thomas More, and Dietrich Bonhoeffer*, Toronto Studies in Religion 19 (New York: Peter

Lang, 1995). Boethius, More, and Bonhoeffer, Scott writes, "lived and died during major shifts in Christian self-consciousness" (1).

86. Thus, William Hamilton regarded Bonhoeffer's statement that "there is no longer any need for God as a working hypothesis" as implying a rejection of "religion as salvation," his Christology as a "striking protest against all God-language that uses imagery of sovereignty, lordship, power, strength, holiness" ("Bonhoeffer: Christology and Ethic United," 199).

87. Keith W. Clements, *A Patriotism for Today: Love of Country in Dialogue with the Witness of Dietrich Bonhoeffer* (London: Collins Liturgical, 1984), 28.

88. Robert E. Huldschiner, "A Review Article—The Quest for the Historical Bonhoeffer," *Lutheran Forum* 3 (September 1969): 12–13.

89. Cited in Ice and Carey, *The Death of God Debate*, 22.

90. Altizer and Hamilton, *Radical Theology and the Death of God*, 158.

91. Ice and Carey, *The Death of God Debate*, 5. Hamilton's publication of an article on "the death of God" in *Playboy* is probably indicative of this attitude toward traditional sexual ethics. See Rev. William Hamilton, "The Death of God," *Playboy* (August 1966).

92. Hodgson, "The Death of God and the Crisis in Christology," 453: "His theology by no means represents an uncritical endorsement of human vitality, power, and strength. Man, to be sure, is virile, but his virility has destructive and demonic as well as creative potential; what is required is a 'form' by which the virility of man can be rightly shaped. That form, however, is given precisely by the presence of God at the center of life; it is the form of the cross."

93. See Stephen R. Haynes and John K. Roth, *The Death of God and the Holocaust: Radical Theology Encounters the Shoah* (New York: Greenwood, 1997).

94. Paul L. Holmer, "Contra the New Theologies," in Ice and Carey, *The Death of God Debate*, 133, 134.

95. The church that seeks to follow Bonhoeffer's lead will emphasize prayer (the "arcane discipline") and doing justice among men ("costly worldly solidarity"). It will focus on small groups of committed Christians with intense loyalty to Christ ("base Christian communities"). It will begin, as Bonhoeffer once said, by giving up its property for the sake of the needy. See Larry L. Rasmussen with Renate Bethge, *Dietrich Bonhoeffer: His Significance for North Americans* (Minneapolis: Fortress Press, 1990), 65, 66.

96. Macquarrie, *New Directions in Theology*, 84.

97. Cited in Ice and Carey, *The Death of God Debate*, 17, 224.

98. The citation is from a 1967 article published in *Saturday Review*. Cited in Hopper, *A Dissent on Bonhoeffer*, 20. The same year John Macquarrie commented

on Bonhoeffer's "special fascination for students . . . Here was a man who really lived out his faith." See Macquarrie, *New Directions in Theology Today*, 37–38. Cf. Thomas W. Ogletree, "The Church's Mission to the World in the Theology of Dietrich Bonhoeffer," 457–69, 457: "Few of the younger theologians of our time have excited as much attention in seminaries and student groups . . . "

99. Ice and Carey, *The Death of God Debate*, 13.

100. Bethge, *Bonhoeffer: Exile and Martyr*, 24.

101. Weiland, *New Ways in Theology*, 67.

102. Ralf K. Wüstenberg, "Bonhoeffer's Tegel Theology," in de Gruchy, *Bonhoeffer for a New Day*, 57–71; 58.

103. Ibid., 58, 59.

CHAPTER 3: Prophet

1. See Carl-Jürgen Kaltenborn, "Adolf von Harnack and Bonhoeffer," in *A Bonhoeffer Legacy: Essays in Understanding*, ed. A. J. Klassen (Grand Rapids, Mich.: Eerdmans, 1981), 48–57.

2. Eckard Minthe, "Bonhoeffer's Influence on the Younger Generation of Ministers in Germany," *Andover Newton Quarterly* 2 (September 1961): 13–45; 18.

3. Reinhold Niebuhr, "The Death of a Martyr," *Christianity and Crisis* 5:11 (June 25, 1945): 6–7; William Hamilton, "Bonhoeffer: Christology and Ethic United," *Christianity and Crisis* 24 (October 19, 1964): 195–201; Leroy S. Rouner, "Bonhoeffer and the Seventies," *Christianity and Crisis* 29 (April 14, 1969): 104–5; and Stephen C. Rose, "Bethge's Monument," *Christianity and Crisis* 30:13 (July 20, 1970): 154–55. For a history of the magazine, see Mark Hulsether, *Building a Protestant Left: Christianity and Crisis Magazine, 1941–1993* (Knoxville: University of Tennessee Press, 1999).

4. These articles vary in length and content, from movie and book reviews to news stories to articles dealing with ecumenicity and the campaign to have Bonhoeffer recognized as a "Righteous Gentile."

5. Geffrey B. Kelly, *Liberating Faith: Bonhoeffer's Message for Today* (Minneapolis: Augsburg Publishing House, 1984), 154, 98.

6. Ibid., 161–62.

7. Ibid., 154, 155.

8. Larry L. Rasmussen with Renate Bethge, *Dietrich Bonhoeffer: His Significance for North Americans* (Minneapolis: Fortress Press, 1990), 74.

9. Ibid., 78, 85, 87.

10. Rasmussen writes: "The theology of the cross, then, is this: that God happens for us in the humanity of Jesus of Nazareth; that everything we know of God and

God's purposes, or of ours and the world's nature and destiny, is buried in the details and drama of that life, death, and resurrection; and that Christian faith is a participation in the *Sein Jesu*, in messianic suffering, where cosmic joy and victory are both hidden and passed along" (ibid., 155).

11. Ibid., 147.

12. Ibid., 161, 173.

13. Geffrey B. Kelly, "The Idolatrous Enchainment of Church and State: Bonhoeffer's Critique of Freedom in the United States," in John W. de Gruchy, ed., *Bonhoeffer for a New Day: Theology in a Time of Transition* (Grand Rapids, Mich.: Eerdmans, 1997), 298–318; 309. See also Wayne Whitson Floyd Jr., "'These People I Have Loved Now Live': Commemorating Bonhoeffer after Fifty Years," unpublished paper graciously shared with the author. Floyd compares the American elections of 1994 with those in Germany in 1932.

14. Ibid., 311.

15. Robert McAfee Brown, "ABC—Assy, Bonhoeffer, Carswell," *Christian Century* 88 (March 24, 1971): 369–71; 369.

16. Keith W. Clements, *A Patriotism for Today: Love of Country in Dialogue with the Witness of Dietrich Bonhoeffer* (London: Collins Liturgical, 1984), 20.

17. Ibid., 31. Clements writes: "Typical of Bonhoeffer is this paradox, that while no-one was more committed to the cause of the Confessing church, in the end no one was more critical of that Church than he" (32).

18. Ibid., 54.

19. Ibid., 98.

20. Ibid., 105.

21. Donald W. Shriver Jr., "Faith, Politics, and Secular Society: The Legacy of Bonhoeffer for Americans," in *Ethical Responsibility: Bonhoeffer's Legacy to the Churches*, ed. John D. Godsey and Geffrey B. Kelly (Lewiston, N. Y.: Edwin Mellen, 1981), 197–229.

22. Ibid., 209, 213.

23. Rasmussen, *Dietrich Bonhoeffer: His Significance for North Americans*, 34, 35.

24. Ibid., 39.

25. Ibid., 42.

26. Daniel Berrigan, "The Passion of Dietrich Bonhoeffer," *Saturday Review* (May 30, 1970): 17–22; 17.

27. Ibid., 22.

28. Ibid.

29. Rasmussen, *Dietrich Bonhoeffer: His Significance for North Americans*, 124.

30. G. Clarke Chapman, "What Would Bonhoeffer Say to Christian Peace-makers Today?" in *Theology, Politics and Peace*, ed. Theodore Runyan (Maryknoll, N.Y.: Orbis, 1989), 167–75. See also "What Would Bonhoeffer Say Today to Christian Peacemakers?" in *Bonhoeffer's Ethics: Old Europe and New Frontiers*, ed. Guy Carter, René van Eyden, Hans-Dirk van Hoogstraten, and Jurjen Wiersma (Kampen: Kok Pharos, 1991), 226–29; and Daniel Berrigan, "A Hymn for Resisters," *The Other Side* 37:3 (May–June 2001), http://www.theotherside.org/archive/may-june01/berrigan.html.

31. Geffrey B. Kelly and F. Burton Nelson, *The Cost of Moral Leadership: The Spirituality of Dietrich Bonhoeffer* (Grand Rapids, Mich.: Eerdmans, 2003), 120.

32. Ibid., 121.

33. Rasmussen, *Dietrich Bonhoeffer: His Significance for North Americans*, 37.

34. Clements, *A Patriotism for Today*, 155.

35. Victoria J. Barnett, "Dietrich Bonhoeffer's Ecumenical Vision," *Christian Century* 112 (April 26, 1995): 454–57.

36. Clements, *A Patriotism for Today*, 199.

37. Letter to Bishop Ammundsen, chairman of the Executive Committee of the World Alliance for Promoting Friendship through the Churches, cited in W. A. Visser 't Hooft, "Dietrich Bonhoeffer and the Self-Understanding of the Ecumenical Movement," *Ecumenical Review* 27:2 (April 1976): 198–203; 199.

38. Ibid., 201.

39. Keith Clements, "Ecumenical Witness for Peace," in *The Cambridge Companion to Dietrich Bonhoeffer*, ed. John W. de Gruchy (Cambridge: Cambridge University Press, 1999), 154–72; 167.

40. Konrad Reiser, "Bonhoeffer and the Ecumenical Movement," in de Gruchy, *Bonhoeffer for a New Day*, 319–39; 319. The enduring significance of Bonhoeffer's ecumenism among mainline Protestants was evident in 2001 when the Evangelical Lutheran Church in America sponsored An Ecumenical Bonhoeffer Journey. This "journey of prayer, study, reflection, discussion and action informed by Bonhoeffer's life, ministry, prayers and writings" involved teams from the Reformed Church in America, the Presbyterian Church (USA), the United Church of Christ, the Episcopal Church, and the Moravian Church. This ecumenical journey sought to relate Bonhoeffer's context to the "current situation," particularly the problems of racism and economic imperialism (at http://www.elca.org).

41. Cited in Rasmussen, *Dietrich Bonhoeffer: His Significance for North Americans*, 35–36.

42. See John D. Godsey, "Bonhoeffer and the Third World: West Africa, Cuba, Korea," in Godsey and Kelly, *Ethical Responsibility*, 257–65. Godsey summarizes

several presentations made at the 1980 International Bonhoeffer Conference at Oxford that explored Bonhoeffer's contributions to third-world theology.

43. Ibid., 261. The reference is to Bonhoeffer's role in Korea.

44. Beatriz Melano, "The Influence of Dietrich Bonhoeffer, Paul Lehmann, and Richard Shaull in Latin America," *Princeton Seminary Bulletin* 22:1 (2001): 65–84; 64.

45. Ibid., 65.

46. Ibid., 80.

47. Julio de Santa Ana, "The Influence of Bonhoeffer on the Theology of Liberation," *Ecumenical Review* 27:2 (April 1976): 189–97; 190. According to Santa Ana, ISAL included liberation theologians José Miguez Bonino, Rubem Alves, Mauricio López, Jovelino Ramos, Gonzalo Castillo Cárdenas, and Hiber Conteris.

48. Santa Ana writes: "On the one hand, they knew how he had died, his part in German resistance to Nazism, his complicity in the plot against Hitler in July 1944 when Bonhoeffer was already in prison. Some people saw all this as an indication that the use of violence and participation in subversive activities against oppressive regimes were possible for Christians. On the other hand, however, they also had to bear in mind the theologian who condemned war, who opposed all chauvinistic fanaticism (which is very similar to ideological fanaticism) and who was interested in the non-violent action of Gandhi. The tension between the different moments in Bonhoeffer's life did nothing to help solve the problem" ("The Influence of Bonhoeffer on the Theology of Liberation," 195).

49. Melano, "The Influence of Dietrich Bonhoeffer, Paul Lehmann, and Richard Shaull in Latin America," 83.

50. Ibid., 78.

51. Ibid., 66.

52. Ibid., 68.

53. Ibid., 67.

54. Melano perceives an emphasis on theological contextualization already in Bonhoeffer's dissertation *Sanctorum Communio*. Keith Clements notes that in that work Bonhoeffer wrote of a certain affinity between socialism and the Christian idea of community, which must not be neglected: "In *Sanctorum Communio* (of all places, one might say) there is a remarkable section on 'Church and Proletariat'— and so provocative did it appear to Bonhoeffer's teacher Reinhold Seeberg that the latter insisted it be excluded from the thesis as presented for examination" (Clements, *A Patriotism for Today*, 138).

55. John W. de Gruchy, *Bonhoeffer and South Africa: Theology in Dialogue* (Grand Rapids, Mich.: Eerdmans, 1984). See also, "Bonhoeffer in South Africa:

An Exploratory Essay by John W. de Gruchy," in Eberhard Bethge, *Bonhoeffer: Exile and Martyr* (New York: Seabury, 1975), 26–42.

56. De Gruchy, *Bonhoeffer and South Africa*, 132. De Gruchy wrote in 1975 that "ever since the failure of the Cottesloe Consultation in 1960, there has been talk about a confessing Church in South Africa. This discussion reached its peak in 1968 after the publication by the South African Council of Churches of 'The Message to the People of South Africa,' which was hailed as an equivalent to the Barmen Declaration" ("Bonhoeffer in South Africa" in Bethge, *Bonhoeffer: Exile and Martyr*, 36).

57. *Bonhoeffer and South Africa*, 3. Following his visit in 1973, Bethge wrote an essay titled "A Confessing Church in South Africa? Conclusions from a Visit," which appears in *Bonhoeffer: Exile and Martyr*.

58. *Bonhoeffer and South Africa*, 128. De Gruchy writes: "Barmen as both a confessing word and event has functioned as a 'liberating symbol' within the church struggle in South Africa and continues to do so. But Barmen cannot simply be repeated in a different context. To idolize Barmen is to deny its message. In each situation the church struggle is at once the same and yet different. The confession remains 'Jesus is Lord,' but the concrete implications differ. To know the implications requires listening, as did Bonhoeffer, to the cry of the victims that has brought the *status confessionis* into being" (130–31).

59. "A Confessing Church in South Africa: Conclusions from a Visit," in Bethge, *Bonhoeffer: Exile and Martyr*, 168. Bethge mentions banning and censorship, legal support for racial superiority, appeals to protection from communism, and oppression of the churches.

60. *Bonhoeffer and South Africa*, 42. De Gruchy also observes that "for those who experience the brunt of apartheid, who feel its daily pain, the discussion of its relationship to Nazism is academic" (39).

61. Alan Boesak, "What Dietrich Bonhoeffer Has Meant to Me," in Carter et al., *Bonhoeffer's Ethics*, 21–29; 22. At the same conference, John W. de Gruchy contributed an article titled "The Freedom of the Church and the Liberation of Society: Bonhoeffer on the Free Church, and the 'Confessing Church' in South Africa" (173–89).

62. Boesak, "What Dietrich Bonhoeffer Has Meant to Me," 23.

63. See John W. de Gruchy, "Bonhoeffer, Apartheid and Beyond: The Reception of Bonhoeffer in South Africa," in de Gruchy, *Bonhoeffer for a New Day*, 353–65; and "Christian Witness in South Africa in a Time of Transition," in *Theology and the Practice of Responsibility: Essays on Dietrich Bonhoeffer*, ed. Wayne Whitson Floyd Jr. and Charles Marsh (Philadelphia: Trinity Press International, 1994), 283–93.

64. Chung Hyun Kyung, "Dear Dietrich Bonhoeffer," in de Gruchy, *Bonhoeffer for a New Day*, 9–19; 10.

65. Poulose Mar Poulose, "The Understanding of Bonhoeffer in India," in Carter et al., *Bonhoeffer's Ethics*, 212–16; 212.

66. Ibid., 215.

67. Hiroshi Murakami, "What Has the Japanese Church Learned from Dietrich Bonhoeffer?" in Carter et al., *Bonhoeffer's Ethics*, 217–21; 217.

68. Ibid., 220.

69. See G. Clarke Chapman, "Hope and the Ethics of Formation: Moltmann as an Interpreter of Bonhoeffer," *Studies in Religion/Sciences Religieuses* 12:4 (Fall 1983): 449–60. Chapman contends there is "clear evidence of the early and persistent influence" of Bonhoeffer on Moltmann and claims that the latter's publications "manifest a wide knowledge and accurate usage of the range of Bonhoeffer's writings, rather than just a few favourite proof texts" (450). Yet despite obvious familiarity with Bonhoeffer (one of his earliest published works was a study of Bonhoeffer's theology) Moltmann refers directly to Bonhoeffer relatively rarely and generally in the form, "as Bonhoeffer once said . . ." As Chapman acknowledges, Moltmann's relationship with Bonhoeffer's theology has been a conflicted one. In an interview, Moltmann offered: "My relationship to Bonhoeffer was first very sympathetic . . . When later hope occupied my heart and eschatology my mind I left B[onhoeffer] behind, because of his incarnational starting point" (454).

In *Christ the Representative: An Essay after the 'Death of God,'* tr. David Lewis (Philadelphia: Fortress Press, 1967), Sölle devotes a brief chapter to analyzing the concepts of dependence and responsibility in Bonhoeffer's *Ethics* (92–97). Sara K. Pinnock, author of a study of Sölle's theology, writes that "when Sölle does engage Bonhoeffer, it is with respect and affirmation . . . She is not an exegete of Bonhoeffer, however, and explicit references to his work are brief and rare. There is no one essay focusing on him, to the best of my knowledge, and her intellectual autobiography mentions him only in passing" (e-mail message to author, June 11, 2003). See Sarah K. Pinnock, ed., *The Theology of Dorothy Sölle* (Harrisburg, Pa.: Trinity Press International, 2003).

70. Rebecca S. Chopp, *The Praxis of Suffering: An Interpretation of Liberation and Political Theologies* (Maryknoll, N.Y.: Orbis, 1986).

71. In Eberhard Bethge, *Bonhoeffer: Exile and Martyr*, 14.

72. See Josef Smolik, "The Church without Privileges," *Ecumenical Review* 28:2 (April 1976): 174–87.

73. Gregory Baum, *The Church for Others: Protestant Theology in Communist East Germany* (Grand Rapids, Mich.: Eerdmans, 1996), 88.

74. John A. Moses, "Bonhoeffer's Reception in East Germany," in de Gruchy, *Bonhoeffer for a New Day*, 278–97; 280. See also Eberhard Bethge's introduction in *Bonhoeffer: Exile and Martyr*.

75. Moses, "Bonhoeffer's Reception in East Germany," 291; and Albrecht Schoenherr, "Dietrich Bonhoeffer: The Message of a Life," *Christian Century* 102 (November 27, 1985): 1090–94; 1092.

76. Moses, "Bonhoeffer's Reception in East Germany," 296.

77. Ernst Feil, ed., *Glauben lernen in einer Kirche für andere: Der Beitrag Dietrich Bonhoeffers zum Christsein in der Deutschen Demokratischen Republik* (Gütersloh, Germany: Chr. Kaiser, 1993), tr. Elizabeth Enger.

78. This generalization ignores James H. Cone, a black liberation theologian who has been an important voice in relating Bonhoeffer to the American racial situation. Nevertheless, as in Western European political theology, the role of Bonhoeffer in Cone's theology is secondary. In general, he utilizes provocative quotes from Bonhoeffer's works to clarify his own arguments. See, e.g., "The White Church and Black Power," in *Black Theology: A Documentary History 1966–1979*, ed. Gayraud S. Wilmore and James H. Cone (Maryknoll, N.Y.: Orbis, 1979), 112–32.

79. Brown, *Theology in a New Key*, 50, 51.

80. In a later study Chapman noted that the socialist revolution in Cuba was supported by some student groups inspired by Bonhoeffer and that he influenced the 1977 Confession of Faith of the Presbyterian-Reformed Church in Cuba. Clarke also observed that a Spanish translation of *Letters and Papers from Prison* was the first book published by the state press of Nicaragua after the Sandinistas took power there. See G. Clarke Chapman, "Bonhoeffer, Liberation Theology and the 1990s," in *Reflections on Bonhoeffer: Essays in Honor of F. Burton Nelson*, ed. Geffrey B. Kelly and C. John Weborg (Chicago: Covenant Publications, 1999), 299–314.

81. G. Clarke Chapman, "Bonhoeffer: Source for Liberation Theology," *Union Seminary Quarterly Review* 36:4 (summer 1981): 225–42; 235. Chapman adds that perhaps "the occasional and sometimes enigmatic character of Bonhoeffer's writings have aided his popularity in the third world, where there is mistrust of comprehensive systems of ideas and a preference for experimentation with grass-roots theology." Chapman, "Bonhoeffer and Liberation Theology," 188. See also G. Clarke Chapman, "Bonhoeffer and Liberation Theology," in Godsey and Kelly, *Ethical Responsibility*, 147–96; 159, 160.

82. Geffrey B. Kelly, "Bonhoeffer's Theology of Liberation," *Dialog* 34:1 (winter 1995): 22–29. It is interesting that in a long footnote on the article's first page,

Kelly acknowledges that Bonhoeffer's life experience overlaps very little with that of the typical Latin American theologian of liberation. See also Kelly's article "Bonhoeffer and Romero: Prophets of Justice for the Oppressed," in Floyd and marsh, *Theology and the Practice of Responsibility*, 85–105.

83. Kelly, "Bonhoeffer's Theology of Liberation," 24. To underscore Bonhoeffer's reputation as a defender of the poor, Kelly analyzes a 1932 sermon on the Lucan story of Lazarus and the Rich Man in which the young vicar warned his congregation against "insolent and hypocritical spiritualizing of the gospel." Addressing rich Christians with the question of their personal responsibility in the distribution of the world's prosperity, Bonhoeffer refused to be drawn into interpretations that spiritualized and moralized the condition of the poor. The same refusal is reiterated in *Ethics*: "To allow the hungry to remain hungry would be blasphemy against God and one's neighbor, for what is nearest to God is precisely the need of one's neighbor." See Geffrey B. Kelly, "Dietrich Bonhoeffer on Justice for the Poor," *Weavings: A Journal of the Christian Spiritual Life* 17:6 (November–December 2002): 26–34; 31.

84. Ibid., 27.

85. Ibid., 25, 26.

86. Gustavo Gutiérrez, "The Limitations of Modern Theology: On a Letter of Dietrich Bonhoeffer," in *Gustavo Gutiérrez: Essential Writings*, ed. James B. Nickoloff, The Making of Modern Theology (Minneapolis: Fortress Press, 1996), 35–42.

87. Ibid., 37. Keith Clements concurs: For all his supposedly "radical" influence in post-war western Christianity, Bonhoeffer was "relatively naïve and partial in his social judgments and, lacking the sociological tools to analyse the structure of society, worked with unexamined bourgeois presuppositions" (*A Patriotism for Today*, 137). According to Thomas I. Day, Bonhoeffer's early writings make it clear that he was more interested in the fate of the church than the welfare of the poor: "Without analyzing their concrete needs, he purposed to impose upon them the structures of his own aristocratic family. To the masses crying out against their imposed alienation and disempowerment he would bring paternalism." See *Bonhoeffer on Christian Community and Common Sense*. Toronto Studies in Theology 11 (New York and Toronto: Edwin Mellen, 1975), 31.

88. Gutiérrez, "The Limitations of Modern Theology," 37–38.

89. René van Eyden, "Dietrich Bonhoeffer's Understanding of Male and Female," in Carter et al., *Bonhoeffer's Ethics*, 200–7. Van Eyden notes that a group of German women holding a "Bonhoeffer week" in 1986 found it "impossible just to adopt or apply [Bonhoeffer's] very masculine theology to women." Interestingly, Virginia Ramey Mollenkott, a lesbian theologian, cites Bonhoeffer's *Ethics*

as resonant with "the complexities of the world in which we who are lesbitransgay find ourselves." See "A Call to Subversion," *The Other Side* 35:4 (July–August 1999), http://www.theotherside.org/archive/jul-aug99/mollenkott.html.

90. These excerpts from Bonhoeffer's work are cited in van Eyden, "Dietrich Bonhoeffer's Understanding of Male and Female," 200–2. Renate Bethge is quite charitable in her interpretation of the wedding sermon Bonhoeffer wrote for her and Eberhard: "I explained this sermon to myself with the thought that Dietrich wanted to give his friend Eberhard, my husband, a better chance to make his voice audible in our big Berlin family, which was used to planning and deciding everything predominantly by women." Yet she concedes that "like the church, Bonhoeffer in his time did not notice that the biblical order, as it was seen then, was not in accordance with the attitude of Jesus toward women." See Renate Bethge, "Bonhoeffer and the Role of Women," in Kelly and Weborg, *Reflections on Bonhoeffer*, 169–84; 177, 180.

91. Van Eyden, "Dietrich Bonhoeffer's Understanding of Male and Female," 203. Karl Barth described Bonhoeffer's theory of the mandates as smacking of "North-Germanic patriarchalism."

92. Chung Hyun Kyung, "Dear Dietrich Bonhoeffer," in de Gruchy, *Bonhoeffer for a New Day*, 9–19; 15.

93. Ibid., 16.

94. Bethge, "Bonhoeffer and the Role of Women," 176. With regard to Bonhoeffer's interpretation of creation, Bethge cites the work of Leonore Siegele-Wenschkewitz.

95. Van Eyden, "Dietrich Bonhoeffer's Understanding of Male and Female," 205.

96. Not only was Union Theological Seminary (UTS) Bonhoeffer's academic home during 1930–31, but a series of UTS faculty—including Reinhold Niebuhr, Donald W. Shriver, and Larry Rasmussen—have written on Bonhoeffer's legacy.

97. Clements, *A Patriotism for Today*, 72, 73.

98. James Patrick Kelley, "Bonhoeffer Studies in English: How Theologians Become Popular," *Lexington Theological Quarterly* 3:1 (1968): 12–19; 15.

99. Hans J. Hillerbrand, "Dietrich Bonhoeffer and America," *Religion in Life* 30:4 (autumn 1961): 568–79. As Hillerbrand points out, Bonhoeffer noticed positive changes on the American theological scene during his short stay in 1939.

100. Thomas W. Ogletree, "The Church's Mission to the World in the Theology of Dietrich Bonhoeffer," *Encounter* 25 (autumn 1964): 457–69; 463.

101. Chapman, "Bonhoeffer and Liberation Theology," 175; "Bonhoeffer: Resource for Liberation Theology," 234.

102. Chapman, "Bonhoeffer: Resource for Liberation Theology," 228–29; 237. For a catalog of the problems associated with making Bonhoeffer a source for liberation theology, see ibid., 236ff. The Bonhoeffers' aristocratic impulses—and their influence on "the pattern of [Dietrich's] quest for faith"—have been well documented. See, e.g., David H. Hopper, A *Dissent on Bonhoeffer* (Philadelphia: Westminster, 1975), ch. 5.

103. De Gruchy, *Bonhoeffer and South Africa*, 76. See also Renate Wind, *Dietrich Bonhoeffer: A Spoke in the Wheel*, tr. John Bowden (Grand Rapids: Eerdmans, 1992), 162: "Imprisoned with himself and his history, Dietrich arrived at a critical assimilation and finally a 'conversion,' a re-orientation in his situation. Reading the gospel, the 'good news' of liberation for solidarity, once again led him anew and finally to go beyond the bounds of the background of his class. The man of law and order became a liberation theologian. And the liberation also changed Dietrich himself."

104. Young, *No Difference in the Fare*, 151 et passim. See also Elizabeth Raum, *Dietrich Bonhoeffer: Called by God* (New York: Continuum, 2002), 53. In Ernst Feil's view, Bonhoeffer's "leap of faith" is important mainly in terms of its effects on the a posteriori character of his theology, while David Hopper sees the real turning point in Bonhoeffer's life in his decision to return to Germany from America in 1939, after which he "became his own man" (Hopper, A *Dissent on Bonhoeffer*, 74, 117). Theodore A. Gill writes that "there is some evidence of an otherwise undocumentable personal crisis, a private turmoil which Dr. Bethge insists should not be called a 'conversion'—there is hardly a more un-Bonhoefferian word (if un Bonhoefferian is a word)." See *Memo for a Movie: A Short Life of Dietrich Bonhoeffer* (New York: Macmillan, 1971), 126–27.

105. Donald W. Shriver Jr., "Faith, Politics, and Secular Society: The Legacy of Bonhoeffer for Americans," in Godsey and Kelly, *Ethical Responsibility*, 197–229; 212–13.

106. Kelly, *Liberating Faith*, 156. Robert M. Brown adds that "the remarkable shift" undergone by Bonhoeffer under the force of historical circumstances "is not unfamiliar in Christian history; it is called conversion" (*Theology in a New Key*, 51).

107. Clifford J. Green, "Bonhoeffer in the Context of Ericksen's Luther Study," in Roger A. Johnson, *Psychohistory and Religion: The Case of Young Man Luther* (Philadelphia: Fortress Press, 1977), 162–96. Green judges that in the Sermon on the Mount Bonhoeffer heard "the authoritative word which spoke to his condition," while in the resistance Bonhoeffer won true freedom over narcissism by putting his life on the line. See also *Bonhoeffer: A Theology of Sociality* (Grand Rapids, Mich.: Eerdmans, 1999), 3.

108. Robin W. Lovin and Jonathan P. Gosser, "Dietrich Bonhoeffer: Witness in an Ambiguous World," in James W. Fowler and Robin W. Lovin with Katherina Ann Herzog, et al., *Trajectories in Faith: Five Life Stories* (Nashville: Abingdon, 1980), 147–84; 166.

109. Kelly, "Bonhoeffer's Critique of Freedom in the United States," 312. This summary of Bonhoeffer's ecumenical career is based on Visser 't Hooft, "Dietrich Bonhoeffer and the Self-Understanding of the Ecumenical Movement," 198–203.

110. A partial answer to this question may be found in "Terrorism and the War in Afghanistan" in Kelly and Nelson, *The Cost of Moral Leadership*, 115–20.

111. Melano, "The Influence of Dietrich Bonhoeffer, Paul Lehmann, and Richard Shaull in Latin America," 82. For a post-9/11 meditation on Bonhoeffer and nonviolence, see Stanley Hauerwas, *Performing the Faith: Bonhoeffer and the Practice of Nonviolence* (Grand Rapids, Mich.: Brazos, 2004).

112. In response to Tutu's sermon, the *Times* published an article by Paul Oestreicher titled "Dietrich Bonhoeffer: Assassin or Saint?" which explained the difference this way: Bonhoeffer did not baptize his decision to resort to violence, but rather "divorced his complicity in the bomb plot from his ministry." See David E. Jenkins, *The Contradiction of Christianity* (London: SCM, 1976), 134–35. Oestreicher's article appeared April 12, 1975.

CHAPTER 4: Apostle

1. Chief among these authors is Thomas I. Day, who writes (in *Bonhoeffer on Christian Community and Common Sense*, Toronto Studies in Theology 11 [New York and Toronto: Edwin Mellen, 1975]) that Bonhoeffer's upbringing made his style "elitist" and his ecclesiology "aristocratic" (11). Day links the emphasis on "community" in *Sanctorum Communio* to "19th century conservative reaction" (16), writes that Bonhoeffer embraced an "aristocratic 'noblesse oblige' Christianity" (26), and reminds us of Bonhoeffer's view that "the Christian community is based upon the innate inequality of persons" (31). Day perceives elitism also in the resistance writings where Bonhoeffer recorded his vision for postwar German society. On the aristocratic impulses in Bonhoeffer's thought, see also David H. Hopper, *A Dissent on Bonhoeffer* (Philadelphia: Westminster, 1975). Hopper writes that in *Letters and Papers from Prison* Bonhoeffer reached out "to an aristocratic ideal to combat what he feels is common and mean within the 'religious tradition,' The end result is that Bonhoeffer attempts to transpose the gospel into an aristocratic idiom even though the gospel cannot be read in this fashion" (143).

2. See, e.g., G. Clarke Chapman, "Bonhoeffer and Liberation Theology," in *Ethical Responsibility: Bonhoeffer's Legacy to the Churches*, ed. John D. Godsey

and Geffrey B. Kelly (Lewiston, N.Y.: Edwin Mellen, 1981), 147–96. Chapman writes that Bonhoeffer "was strongly predisposed toward conservatism. His family background, social class, education all converged with the Lutheran tradition of sharply separating law/coercion/public accountability for consequences, on the one hand, from gospel/nonresistance/personal justification before God on the other hand . . ." (154).

3. George A. Lindbeck, "The Demythologizing of Dietrich Bonhoeffer," *Commonweal* 96:22 (September 29, 1972): 527–28; 527.

4. Keith W. Clements, *A Patriotism for Today: Love of Country in Dialogue with the Witness of Dietrich Bonhoeffer* (London: Collins Liturgical Publications, 1984), 37. "Moreover," Clements writes, "it may be argued that Bonhoeffer's central ethical notion of responsible action or 'deputyship' reveals the bourgeois assumption that ethics is about *individual* action and ignores the corporate dimension" (ibid.).

5. James W. Woelfel, for instance, speaks of "conservative" interpreters of Bonhoeffer whose approaches are distinct from those of liberals and radicals. Woelfel has in mind "the loyal Barthian and Lutheran of the *Kirchenkampf* whose prison writings were penned under enormous physical and psychological strain and therefore taken with a large grain of salt" (*Bonhoeffer's Theology: Classical and Revolutionary* [Nashville: Abingdon, 1970], 291).

According to Eberhard Bethge, the reception of Bonhoeffer in West Germany has portrayed him as "a menace to Christian identity and a destroyer of the Lutheran doctrine of the two separate kingdoms of Church and State." Bethge goes on: "His 'non-religious interpretation' is looked upon as one of the causes of a dangerous second Enlightenment, and his underground activity against Hitler as overstepping the legitimate boundaries of the Church's domain. At the few ceremonies which took place in the churches of west Germany in commemoration of his death on 9 April 1945, churchmen and preachers avoided this embarrassing problem by saying: 'Do not worry, in spite of everything—that is, in spite of Bonhoeffer's participation in the conspiracy against Hitler, and in spite of his last theological utterances and formulations—he was a Christian and remained one'." See *Bonhoeffer: Exile and Martyr* (New York: Seabury, 1975), 11–12.

6. Georg Huntemann, *The Other Bonhoeffer: An Evangelical Reassessment of Dietrich Bonhoeffer*, tr. Todd Huizinga (Grand Rapids, Mich.: Baker, 1993). The book was originally published in German in 1989 as *Der andere Bonhoeffer*.

7. Ibid., 61.

8. Ibid., 18, 76. "That Bonhoeffer was a man of order and inner discipline is important. For it was precisely the lack of order and discipline that comprised the threat of the revolution in which he lived" (25).

9. Ibid., 265.

10. Ibid., 162.

11. Ibid., 163. According to Huntemann, Bonhoeffer possessed deep insight into the neo-pagan essence of National Socialism, in which he perceived the "dance around the golden calf, the worship of naturalism and vitalism" (49, 310). The "paternally minded Bonhoeffer" saw clearly that the struggle of Nazism against Judaism was "the struggle against the Father God of the Bible" (53). In places, Huntemann seems to regard modern feminism as the root of all evil in the Christian church. On the coattails of Christianity's feminization, he contends, ride cheap grace, emotionalization, and electronic evangelization (338).

12. Ibid., 225.

13. Ibid., 87, 50.

14. http://www.masterscommission.com, February 2003. The Christian Life School of Theology advertises "Spirit-filled teaching from the Word of God, and preparation for ministry to the body of Christ and the world."

15. Given my young friend's description of Bonhoeffer, it is very possible that he was exposed to the German theologian in a course called Great Christian Personalities. But this is speculation.

16. In August 2002, a search of the archives at http://www.christianitytoday.com (which includes items in *Christianity Today*, *Leadership Journal*, *Christian History*, and *Christian Reader*) produced 131 hits for Bonhoeffer, 87 for Barth, 20 for Bultmann, and 13 for Tillich.

17. "The Ten Most Influential Christians of the Twentieth Century," *Christian History*, http://www.ctlibrary.com/ch/2000/65/16.44.html, August 2002.

18. Milton D. Hunnex, "Religionless Christianity: Is It a New Form of Gnosticism?" *Christianity Today* 10 (January 7, 1966): 7–9.

19. Ibid., 8.

20. Harold B. Kuhn, "The Old New Worldliness," *Christianity Today* 12 (December 8, 1967): 56. The same year, *Moody Monthly* warned that Bonhoeffer's inspiring words in *The Cost of Discipleship* should not deceive Christians into thinking that he was a fundamentalist. Influenced by Leon Morris's interpretation of Bonhoeffer in *The Abolition of Religion* (Chicago: InterVarsity, 1964), the article warned that "the evangelical Protestant cannot forsake the biblical emphasis on the need for *true* religion." See Charles Horne, "What Is Bonhoeffer Theology?," *Moody Monthly* 66:9 (May 1966): 40–42; 42.

21. Harold B. Kuhn, "But Which Bonhoeffer?" *Christianity Today* 16 (April 14, 1972): 49–50; 49. In the late 1960s the magazine published reviews of William Kuhns's *In Pursuit of Dietrich Bonhoeffer* and Mary Bosanquet's *The Life and*

Death of Dietrich Bonhoeffer, both of which struck an approving tone. See "Quo Vadis Bonhoeffer?" *Christianity Today* 12 (March 15, 1968): 29–30; and "Bonhoeffer: The Man," *Christianity Today* 14 (October 20, 1969): 28–29. In an article appearing in 1970, Donald G. Bloesch called Bonhoeffer "an authentic evangelical ecumenist," who nevertheless at times "diverged from the scriptural norm, particularly in the belief expressed in his *Ethics* that all men are included in the kingdom of Christ." See Donald G. Bloesch, "True and False Ecumenism: Growing Disenchantment with the Ecumenical Movement," *Christianity Today* 14 (July 17, 1970): 3–5.

22. Ibid., 49. Also in 1972, Cornelius van Til reviewed Bethge's biography of Bonhoeffer in *Westminster Theological Journal*. Seeking to contribute to the debate over the orthodoxy of Bonhoeffer's theology, van Til concluded that "the theological positions of Bonhoeffer and Calvin are diametrically opposed to each other," that "the Christ of Bonhoeffer is not the Christ of the Scriptures," and that "Bonhoeffer's Christ existing as community differs only in detail from [the] Christ-Event of Barth." See Cornelius van Til, "Dietrich Bonhoeffer: A Review Article," *Westminster Theological Review* 34:2 (May 1972): 152–73; 167, 170.

23. Kevin A. Miller, "A Man for Others," review of *A Testament to Freedom: The Essential Writings of Dietrich Bonhoeffer*, ed. Geffrey B. Kelly and F. Burton Nelson, *Christianity Today* 35 (July 22, 1991): 58–59.

24. David P. Gushee, "Following Jesus to the Gallows," *Christianity Today* 39 (April 3, 1995): 26–32; 27.

25. The example of the Bonhoeffer family, Gushee observes, teaches us that Christians need an "offense-oriented" strategy for living in the world, "a way of life that advances the kingdom of God and hinders the work of the Evil One" (ibid., 28).

26. Ibid., 32.

27. Ibid., 29.

28. Philip Yancey, "The Bible Jesus Read," *Christianity Today* 43 (January 11, 1999), http://www.ctlibrary.com/ct/1999/jan11/9t1062.html; James R. Edwards, "What's In a Name: Why We Shouldn't Call the Old Testament the 'Hebrew Scriptures'," *Christianity Today* 43 (August 9, 1999), http://www.ctlibrary.com/ct/1999/aug9/9t9059.html; and Timothy George, "What I'd Like to Tell the Pope about the Church," *Christianity Today* 42 (June 15, 1998), http://www.ctlibrary.com/ct/1998/june15/8t7041.html.

29. The ministry was initiated by evangelical author Charles Colson, who himself cites Bonhoeffer as authority for his claim (following the 2000 presidential election) that "there are times when Christians must stand against an unjust regime." See Charles Colson, "Caesar and Christ: Should We Disobey Our Government?"

Break Point (November 28, 2000), at http://www.beliefnet.com/story/55/story _5541_1.html .

30. "The Best Devotional Books of All Time (Part 2)," *Christian Reader* (September–October 1997), at http://www.christianitytoday.com/tc/7r5/7r5366.html. *Christian Reader, Books and Culture, Christian History,* and *Leadership Journal,* are published by Christianity Today International.

31. David P. Gushee, "Rescue Those Being Led Away to Death," *Books and Culture* (March–April 2002), http://www.christianitytoday.com/bc/2002/11.22.html; and Betty Smartt Carter, "Bonhoeffer: Factual Fictions" *Books and Culture* (September–October 1998), http://www.christianitytoday.com/bc/2002/11.22.html. Carter notes in relation to Giardina's book that "evangelicals might bristle at the idea of a Christian hero carrying on an illicit affair."

32. Gordon MacDonald, "Speaking into Crisis," *Leadership Journal* (spring 2002), http://www.christianitytoday.com/lc/2002/001/10.62.html.

33. *Glimpses* 63, at http://www.gospelcom.net/chi/glimpsef/glimpses/g/mps063 .shtml.

34. See K. Runia, "Dietrich Bonhoeffer: The Man and His Beliefs," *Eternity* 16 (December 1965): 11–13; and C. Horne, "What Is Bonhoeffer Theology?" *Moody Monthly* (May 1966): 40ff.

35. Glen Stassen, "Incarnating Ethics: We're Called to Faithful Discipleship, Not Creedal Rigidity," *Sojourners* 28:2 (March–April 1999): 14; Michael Westmoreland-White, Glen Stassen, and David P. Gushee, "Disciples of the Incarnation: The Witness of Dietrich Bonhoeffer, Martin Luther King, Jr., and Christian Rescuers of Jews Informs Our Discipleship Today," *Sojourners* 23:4 (May 1994): 26–30; Walter Wink, "The Bonhoeffer Assumption," *Sojourners* 31:1 (January–February, 2002): 33; and Leon Howell, "A Time of Trials: The Tribulation of Dietrich Bonhoeffer," *Sojourners* 24:2 (May–June, 1995): 50–51.

The Other Side is another journal on the evangelical left in which Bonhoeffer's name regularly appears. See, e.g., Daniel Berrigan, "A Hymn for Resisters," *The Other Side* 37:3 (May–June 2001), http://www.theotherside.org/archive/ may-june01/berrigan.html; David Hilfiker, "Call and Conversion," *The Other Side* 37:5 (September–October 2001), http://www.theotherside.org/archive/may-june01/berrigan.html; and Virginia Ramey Mollenkott, "A Call to Subversion," *The Other Side* 35:4 (July–August 1999), http://www.theotherside.org/archive/ jul-aug99/mollenkott.htm.

36. Bill McCartney, "Which Legacy?" at http://www.ibelieve.com/ content.asp?CID-15505, April 2003. Similarly, *Breakaway,* a magazine for teen boys, incorporates a "truth quote" on costly grace from Bonhoeffer's *The Cost of*

Discipleship; and an evangelical Web site for Christian "over-fifties" cites Bon-hoeffer's advice on marriage as a "nugget of wisdom" for married couples. See Roberta Rand, "Pundits and Poets on the Rewards of Long-Term Marriage," at http://www.family.org/focusoverfifty/articles/a0019657.html; and Mark Hartwig, "Why Would God Do That?" *Teachers in Focus,* at http://www.family.org/cforum/teachersmag/firstwrites/a0005360.cfm.

37. Charles Colson, "Caesar and Christ."

38. James Dobson, "The New Cost of Discipleship," *Christianity Today* 43 (September 6, 1999), http://www.ctlibrary.com/ct/1999/sept6/9ta056.html. See also Dobson's editorial in *Focus on the Family Newsletter* (June 1999) where he explicitly attacks the "evangelical isolationism" represented by Cal Thomas and Ed Dobson's book *Blinded by Might: Can the Religious Right Save America?,* at http://www.family.org/docstudy/newsletters.

39. *Focus on the Family Newsletter* (May 2000), at http://www.family.org/docstudy/newsletters. Dobson follows this passage with a long quote from the church's confession of guilt in Bonhoeffer's *Ethics.*

40. *Focus on the Family Newsletter* (May 2000), at http://www.family.org/docstudy/newsletters, April 2003.

41. http://www.fuller.edu, March 2003. Christian Discipleship in a Secular Society is "a study of urgent ethical issues in the church's ministry to persons caught in the cross-pressures of secular society, with concentration on Bonhoeffer's *Cost of Discipleship* . . ." The "Ethics of Bonhoeffer" explores how Bonhoeffer's ethics and theology are "Christ-centered and mutually interwoven" and uses Bon-hoeffer's spirituality as a guide for "deepening our own spirituality and identity as Christians." "Bonhoeffer: Life and Thought" promises that "students will be enabled to develop a critical theological basis for addressing ethical issues such as advocacy for the oppressed, Christian discipleship in the secular sphere, and the church's ministry to the marginalized in society . . ."

42. Richard Weikart, *The Myth of Dietrich Bonhoeffer: Is His Theology Really Evangelical?* (San Francisco: International Scholars, 1997), 4, 6.

43. Ted Olsen, "Weblog: Evangelical Support of Israel Isn't Just about Premil-lennialism," *Christianity Today* 46 (April 22, 2002), http://www.christianitytoday.com/ct/2002/115/12.0.html. Roger J. Green of Gordon College confirms that evangelical admiration for Bonhoeffer is rooted partly in their own identification with the Jewish people (e-mail to the author, October 3, 2002).

44. David P. Gushee, "Following Jesus to the Gallows," 29.

45. Eberhard Bethge, *Bonhoeffer: Exile and Martyr,* 17. Bethge notes that among the thirty or so doctoral theses he knows of, only two are devoted to *The*

Cost of Discipleship, and these are by Roman Catholic Scholars. For a liberal Protestant gloss of *The Cost of Discipleship* and *Life Together*, see L. Gregory Jones, "The Cost of Forgiveness: Grace, Christian Community and the Politics of Worldly Discipleship," in *Theology and the Practice of Responsibility: Essays on Dietrich Bonhoeffer*, ed. Wayne Whitson Floyd Jr. and Charles Marsh (Valley Forge, Pa.: Trinity Press International, 1994), 149–69.

46. Rubel Shelly, "Biographers Needed! Please Apply," at http://www.ibelieve.com/content.asp?cid=16342.

47. Weikart, *The Myth of Dietrich Bonhoeffer*, 127.

48. "The Best Ten Devltional Books of All Time, Part 2," *Christian Reader* (September–October 1997), http://www.christianitytoday.com/tc/7r5/7r5366.html.

49. "Books of the Century," *Christianity Today* 46 (April 24, 2000), http://www.christianitytoday.com/ct/2000/005/5.92.html. *Letters and Papers from Prison* also made the top 100.

50. Dale Larsen and Sandy Larsen, *Dietrich Bonhoeffer: Costly Grace*, Christian Classics Bible Study Series (Downers Grove, Ill.: Intervarsity, 2002), 5. Five of eleven excerpts from Bonhoeffer's works in the Bible study are taken from *The Cost of Discipleship*, two from *Life Together*. The "Study Notes" supplement Bonhoeffer's writings with references to works by J. I. Packer, John Stott, and Corrie ten Boom. According to the Larsens, Bonhoeffer challenges contemporary Christians to think deeply about their faith; he dissolves the controversy between faith and works by insisting that belief and obedience to Christ are inseparable; he breaks the impasse between the historical Jesus and the abstract Christ by emphasizing the living Jesus who meets them here and now; and he reminds them that the church is more than an organization or institution, but a living body with Christ as head (11).

51. Beatriz Melano credits the development of Protestant liberation theology in the Southern Cone of Latin America to the introduction of *The Cost of Discipleship* to the Presbyterian Seminary in Campinas, Brazil, in 1952. See "The Influence of Dietrich Bonhoeffer, Paul Lehmann, and Richard Shaull in Latin America," *Princeton Seminary Bulletin* 22:1 (2001): 65–84; 80.

52. Publications that reflect discipleship's central role in evangelical piety include Leroy Eims, *The Lost Art of Disciple Making* (Grand Rapids, Mich.: Zondervan, 1978); Robert E. Coleman, *The Master Plan of Discipleship* (Grand Rapids, Mich.: Baker, 1998); Greg Ogden, *Discipleship Essentials: A Guide to Building Your Life in Christ* (Downers Grove, Ill.: Intervarsity, 1998); and *Discipleship Journal*, which is "full of advice about such topics as dating, the importance of prayer, being a believer in the workplace, and plans for Bible

reading—all articles that will help you to further deepen your faith" (http://www.ls.magazineagent.com, April 2003).

53. Richard Bliese writes that "In *The Cost of Discipleship* Bonhoeffer places the church squarely under the Great Commission's mandate of 'baptizing and teaching all that I have commanded you,'" and notes that "missionaries and mission-minded Christians from around the world have gravitated to Bonhoeffer's writings since the 1970s." See "Bonhoeffer and the Great Commission: Does Bonhoeffer Have a Theology of Mission?" in *Reflections on Bonhoeffer: Essays in Honor of F. Burton Nelson*, ed. Geffrey B. Kelly and C. John Weborg (Chicago: Covenant, 1999), 253–66; 263, 253. Erwin Lutzer demonstrates the transitive form of "discipleship" with reference to Bonhoeffer: "To illustrate Bonhoeffer's point, I will add a story I heard from a fellow pastor who was discipling a group of men." See Erwin W. Lutzer, *Hitler's Cross: The Revealing Story of How the Cross of Christ Was Used as a Symbol of the Nazi Agenda* (Chicago: Moody, 1995), 184.

54. Eberhard Bethge, *Dietrich Bonhoeffer: Man of Vision, Man of Courage* (New York: Harper & Row, 1977), 153.

55. Ibid., 154–55.

56. Eberhard Bethge, "Turning Points in Bonhoeffer's Life and Thought," in *Bonhoeffer in a World Come of Age*, ed. Peter Vorkink II (Philadelphia: Fortress Press, 1968), 80.

57. Theodore J. Kleinhans, *Till the Night Be Past: The Life and Times of Dietrich Bonhoeffer* (St. Louis: Concordia, 2002), 36.

58. The Bethany House "Men of Faith" biography of Bonhoeffer is just one popular evangelical work that emphasizes his transformation from academic to believer: "Dietrich had gone to New York as a theologian. His experiences there turned him in the direction of exploring what it meant to be a Christian as well. He found himself turning away from academic theological language. The Bible was no longer simply sermon material. As he learned to read the Bible in a meditative way, he discovered that it was a practical guide to living the Christian life." See Susan Martins Miller, *Dietrich Bonhoeffer*, Men of Faith Series (Minneapolis: Bethany House, 2002), 25–26. The time line at the book's end lists "experiences personal conversion" next to 1930 (133).

59. Don B. Harbuck, "Bonhoeffer Speaks to Baptists," *The Baptist* (October 1966): 28–29; 28.

60. Gary Wearne, "Perspectives: A Dialogue with Bonhoeffer," http://www.members.ozone.com.au/~seccomn/dbonhl.htm.

61. Gene Edward Veith Jr., *Modern Fascism: Liquidating the Judeo-Christian Worldview* (St. Louis: Concordia, 1993), 65. See also David A. Rausch, A *Legacy of*

Hatred: Why Christians Must Not Forget the Holocaust, 2d ed. (Grand Rapids, Mich.: Baker, 1984), 65–66.

62. Lutzer, *Hitler's Cross,* 96. Nazism warns us, according to Lutzer, of "the lie that Christianity can be combined with the esoteric mysticism of other religions . . ." (65). Abortionists argue, "just as Hitler's emissaries had done, that they could not be murderers because they were not breaking any laws" (119).

63. Ibid., 50, 64. "The voices he heard and the powers from which he drew his strength were not from God but from Satan . . . perhaps no man in history was so clearly indwelt by dark, cruel demons." Similarly, Houston Stewart Chamberlain was "driven by demons" (89) and Richard Wagner's ideas constituted "worship of Lucifer under the guise of an Aryan Christ" (80). Like Hitler, Antichrist will be "indwelt by demonic forces, most likely by Satan himself" (73).

64. Ibid., 174, 122, 192.

65. Ibid., 143, 29, 30.

66. Ibid., 178.

67. Ibid., 134, 204, 160. Italics in the original.

68. Ibid., 188.

69. Ibid., 11.

70. Ibid., 338.

71. Ibid., 87.

72. Michael van Dyke, *Dietrich Bonhoeffer: Opponent of the Nazi Regime,* Heroes of the Faith Series (Ulrichsville, Ohio: Barbour, 2001). Most of the excerpts from Bonhoeffer's writings are taken from his sermons and more pious letters from prison. Bonhoeffer sees himself "primarily as a pastor" (127), a fact that is clearest while he is imprisoned. Viewing his fellow prisoners as parishioners, Bonhoeffer prays "over each patient on a daily basis, repeating fairly standard prayers that would cover a multitude of sins and sicknesses" (165). As a result, "many of his fellow prisoners who survived the war would later recall Dietrich's peaceful demeanor during this time and remark on how calm he was. They would remember how encouraging he was to those who were better off than he, and how resolute he was in his simple faith toward God. In the worst of all possible circumstances, it seemed that he had resigned himself to God's will and had found an inward contentment" (188).

73. Ibid., 67. "He spent more time reading the Bible, especially the Sermon on the Mount, and his prayer life was growing deeper, too. Dietrich had never had a sudden and dramatic 'conversion' experience like the ones testified about at the Abyssinian Baptist Church in Harlem. Yet as he gradually learned how to recognize God's grace in his life, he endeavored to respond to that grace with faith. And he took every new step of faith very seriously."

74. Ibid., 32. Van Dyke highlights the contrast between the German university (where students were taught "to read the Bible as if it were an academic textbook") and Finkenwalde (where they were asked to "read it in order to find out what God might be saying to them *individually*") (ibid., 104).

75. Ibid., 50, 53. Although Bonhoeffer's April essay is excerpted and the "Bethel Confession's" section on the Jews is summarized, there is no critique of the problematic elements in either. We are told that "in his *Ethics*, Dietrich also went beyond *The Cost of Discipleship* in his statements about the treatment of the Jews. His concern for German Jews "developed in the late 1920s when segregation first began" (179). But two pages later van Dyke notes Dietrich's declaration that "the Church had too long been only interested in maintaining a righteousness like that of the Pharisees" (181).

76. Ibid., 77, 83, 92, 91.

77. Ibid., 85, 205.

78. Ibid., 129.

79. Ibid., 131–32.

80. It is interesting to observe that one may link to "The C. S. Lewis Web Site" directly from "Bonhoeffer's Cell."

81. *Christian History* 10:4 (issue 32, 1991). "Some Christians have compared America's treatment of the unborn to Nazi Germany's treatment of the Jews. Would you agree with this comparison? Why or why not?" (42).

82. *Bonhoeffer: The Cost of Freedom*, written and directed by Paul McCusker (Colorado Springs: Focus on the Family, 1997, 1999). Focus on the Family Radio Theatre has produced pieces on Luke/Acts, *The Chronicles of Narnia, Ben Hur, Silas Marner* and *The Christmas Carol*, but *Bonhoeffer: The Cost of Freedom* is the only radio theater biography dealing with a historical figure after the first century.

83. Exceptions are the positive portrayal of Bonhoeffer's ecumenical work and the narrated excerpts from his prison letters, though we are led to believe that it is the "religionless world," not "religionless Christianity," with which Bonhoeffer is concerned.

84. "A Martyr's Death," at http://www.radiotheatre.org/products/bonhoeffer/.

85. Michael Phillips, *The Eleventh Hour* (Wheaton, Ill.: Tyndale, 1993), 461.

86. Ibid., 462.

87. Ibid., 120.

88. Ibid., 154.

89. Ibid., 193, 195.

90. Ibid., 360, 418.

91. Ibid., 363.

92. Ibid., 384.

93. Ibid., 387, 365, 344, 424. On their final night together, the rabbi and baron organize a service—part Communion and part Passover—to celebrate their "common Hebrew heritage." The narrator relates that at the climactic moment when the communion bread is shared, "the lips of both men broke into smiles, neither able to contain the exhilaration of feeling the walls of division being shattered at such a wonderful moment" (ibid., 428, 434). The service concludes with the singing of a Christian hymn and a selection from the Psalter.

94. Ibid., 449, 452.

95. At one point Bonhoeffer and the baron pray aloud for one another. Other evangelical trademarks include repeated references to God as Father (e.g., 188), the baron's tendency to ask "What would Jesus do" in any situation, and his act of "witnessing" to an American diplomat and his son.

96. These three elements of Christian praxis are combined in a single passage. As the Nazi assault on the Jews intensifies, the baron is deep in prayer, asking for guidance. He reads from the book of Revelation and is led to see that "Satan's synagogue" refers to the Nazis, while God's "beloved people" are "*true* Jews . . . the *true* church . . . the *true* people of God!" (305). He becomes convicted that he must open his home to those who are persecuted.

97. In *Ethics*, Bonhoeffer argued that in such instances it may be acceptable, even necessary, to lie. But von Dortmann is no theologian and his piety is not amenable to theological rationalization.

98. Phillips, *The Eleventh Hour*, 428, 207, 54, 209, 303.

99. Gary Wearne, "Perspectives: A Dialogue with Bonhoeffer."

100. Miller, *Dietrich Bonhoeffer*, 130. In an appendix, Miller includes this innocuous description of *Letters and Papers from Prison*: "In the letters and other papers he wrote while in prison, Bonhoeffer identified the evils of his times, especially evils that arose from the war. He warned against being deceived by evil that is disguised as good" (139).

101. Todd Kappelman, "Dietrich Bonhoeffer, The Man and His Mission," at http://www.probe.org/docs/bonhoeffer.html.

102. Runia, "Dietrich Bonhoeffer: The Man and His Beliefs," 13. The article offers a surprisingly positive evangelical assessment of Bonhoeffer at a time when he was associated with the death-of-God movement.

103. Georg Huntemann characterizes Bonhoeffer's "coming of age" as an aristocratic state that "affirms the Christian-Occidental order against the uncouth uprising from below." It would be a "maniacal misunderstanding of that which Bonhoeffer meant," in fact, "if one were to misuse this concept in order to give

one's theological blessing to the cultural and moral revolution and its 'emancipation' from the created order and commandments of God." Bonhoeffer "endorsed the notion of humanity come of age because he had gotten to know it in men and women of conservative values who with mind and heart stood on the side of the rule of law" (*The Other Bonhoeffer*, 87, 279, 70).

104. Gushee, "Following Jesus to the Gallows," 28, 32. Michael van Dyke quotes Bonhoeffer's statement from prison that "I'm not religious by nature. But I have to think continually of God and Christ." (*Dietrich Bonhoeffer*, 142).

105. Kenneth Hamilton, *Life in One's Stride: A Short Study in Dietrich Bonhoeffer* (Grand Rapids, Mich.: Eerdmans, 1968).

106. Ibid., 64. On Bonhoeffer's request that Bethge should not "forget to pray for me . . . I am so sure of God's guiding hand, and I hope I shall never lose that certainty" (July 21, 1944), Hamilton comments: "The completely unselfconscious use of the language of traditional piety is as typical of Bonhoeffer as is his boldness in thrusting aside accepted opinions and conventional valuations . . . The simple believer, the sophisticated student of culture, and the acute theologian were, however, one man" (ibid., 76).

107. Ibid., 85, 87.

108. See Donald G. Bloesch, *The Christian Witness in a Secular Age: An Evaluation of Nine Contemporary Theologians* (Minneapolis: Augsburg Publishing House, 1968).

109. Ibid., 27. He did so, reputedly, on the basis of an epistemological dualism that allowed him to distinguish between religious and empirical truth.

110. Ibid., 48.

111. It is interesting that while Georg Huntemann attempts to make Bonhoeffer palatable for conservatives, his "other Bonhoeffer" seems quite neoorthodox. He evinces a pronounced affinity for dialectic and paradox and wields a Barthian critique of "religion."

112. Bonhoeffer believed, in fact, that Bultmann had not gone far enough: "Not only the 'mythological' concepts, such as miracle, ascension, etc. . . . but 'religious' concepts generally are problematic," he wrote in *Letters and Papers from Prison* (cited in Weikart, *The Myth of Dietrich Bonhoeffer*, 45).

113. Ibid., 56.

114. Ibid., 43.

115. Ibid., 42. Weikart also observes that Bonhoeffer's christological equation of Jesus Christ with reality is "curiously similar to Hegel's dictum" that the real is rational and the rational is the real (65).

116. Weikart also sees in *The Cost of Discipleship* evidence of Bonhoeffer's view of the "unhistorical character of the Bible" ("We cannot and may not go behind

the word of Scripture to the real events," Bonhoeffer writes) and claims that in a footnote to this book so adored by evangelicals, Bonhoeffer effectively denies the resurrection as a literal, historical event. Ibid., 38.

117. Ibid., 77, 28. On this point Huntemann and Weikart are in essential agreement. While Bonhoeffer was purportedly "a theologian of rebirth," Huntemann describes Bonhoeffer's own religious experience in terms that defy evangelical convention. Asking "how pious was Bonhoeffer," Huntemann answers that while he did love Jesus, talk of "personal dealings" with God were repulsive to him, as was "the readiness to pray, to use religious phrases, to reveal oneself in communal prayers or reports of conversion experiences." Bonhoeffer probably experienced "conversion," Huntemann concludes, as a change of direction to the Christian faith that occurred gradually. Ibid., 39, 102, 179, 283.

118. Ibid., 86.

119. Ibid., 105. Weikart also argues that "Bonhoeffer's shift from pacifism to advocacy of tyrannicide points up some fundamental weaknesses of his ethical thought . . ." (124).

120. Ibid., 146.

121. Ibid., 119, 125.

122. Ibid., 139. Weikart does "not believe there are many churches committed to evangelical doctrines that would want to hire a pastor upholding the tenets Bonhoeffer taught" (148).

123. "Dietrich Bonhoeffer: General Teachings/Activities," http://www.rapid-net.com/~jbeard/bam/exposes/bonhoeffer/general.htm. See also Wearne, "Perspectives: A Dialogue with Bonhoeffer": "Is it surprising [given his rather late conversion] that Bonhoeffer was so dedicated to ecumenicalism without understanding the Bible's stress on the importance of Truth and separation from false teachers? 2 Cor 6:17-18; Eph 5:11; 2 John 11-12; 1 Kings 12, 2 Chron 19:2; Rom 16:17, 2 Thess 3:6 and 1 Tim 6:3-5."

124. Burton Nelson relates that one day before he was to be interviewed by the radio network of the Moody Bible Institute, he was informed that the interview had been canceled. When he asked why, Nelson was told by the Institute's representative that further research had revealed Bonhoeffer was not a Christian. This conclusion was based on the fact that he was a smoker, that he had positive things to say about the Catholic church, and that he had once commented that he had not been to church in a while and did not miss it (interview with the author, October 7, 2002).

125. In 1972, Cornelius van Til dismissed Bonhoeffer's nonorthodox Christology with these words: "The Christ of Bonhoeffer, Christ as man for others, may well be taken as the motto for the ecumenical movement." See "Dietrich Bonhoeffer: A Review Article," 173.

126. Bethge, *Bonhoeffer: Exile and Martyr*, 82. See also W. A. Visser 't Hooft, "Dietrich Bonhoeffer, 1945–1965," *Ecumenical Review* 17 (July 1965): 224–31; 226: ". . . the attitude of the national-socialists was quite clear. They regarded the ecumenical movement as a form of decadent internationalism, and as a negation of nationhood . . ." Keith Clements adds that "neither Bonhoeffer the pacifist nor Bonhoeffer the conspirator wear the normal patriotic colours, a fact which still makes him *persona non grata* for many Germans today, whatever their views on the Nazi period" (A *Patriotism for Today*, 110).

127. According to Georg Huntemann, the ecumenical movement of Bonhoeffer's time cannot be compared to the movement of today: "The ecumenical Bonhoeffer was not a World Council of Churches-type bureaucrat like we often see nowadays, the result of an unpleasant synthesis of pragmatism and socialism." Further, the radical pacifism Bonhoeffer expressed at Fanö in 1934 was a "lonely exception" in his life (*The Other Bonhoeffer*, 55, 326).

128. *Dietrich Bonhoeffer: Memories and Perspectives*, directed by Bain Boehlke, Trinity Films (1983).

129. Cited in Larry Rasmussen, *Dietrich Bonhoeffer: Reality and Resistance*, Studies in Christian Ethics (Nashville: Abingdon, 1972), 116.

130. Bethge, *Bonhoeffer: Exile and Martyr*, 122–23. In "The Church and the Resistance Movement," Bell writes: "When he visited England in the spring of 1939 he came to see me in Chichester about two questions in particular. The first was by what means the Confessional church could be kept in touch with the churches abroad . . . The second was a question personal to himself. 'I am thinking of leaving Germany sometime. The main reason is the compulsory military service to which men of my age (1906) will be called up this year. It seems conscientiously impossible to join in a war under present circumstances. On the other hand the Confessional Church as such has not taken any definite attitude in this respect and probably cannot take it as things are. So I should cause a tremendous damage to my brethren if I were to make a stand on this point which would be regarded by the regime as typical of the hostility of our Church towards the State . . . Perhaps the worst thing of all is the military oath which I should have to swear.'" See *I Knew Dietrich Bonhoeffer*, ed. Ronald Gregor Smith and Wolf-Dieter Zimmerman, tr. Käthe Gregor Smith (New York: Harper & Row, 1966), 197.

131. Rasmussen, *Dietrich Bonhoeffer: Reality and Resistance*, 124. For a discussion of Bonhoeffer's "selective conscientious objection" and its relation to pacifism, see ibid. 94ff., especially 116. See also Renate Wind, *Dietrich Bonhoeffer: A Spoke in the Wheel*, tr. John Bowden (Grand Rapids, Mich.: Eerdmans, 1992), 133–34. Bonhoeffer, Hellmut Traub confirms, "was sure to find no mercy

[in post-Nazi Germany], as he was bound to be a conscientious objector." See Hellmut Traub, "Two Recollections," in Smith and Zimmerman, *I Knew Dietrich Bonhoeffer*, 159.

132. According to Walter Wink, "Americans who have used Bonhoeffer as a way of justifying the just war theory overlook his clear statement that he does not regard this as a justifiable action—that it's a sin—and that he throws himself on the mercy of God. He does not use this act as a legitimization of war" (Wink, "The Bonhoeffer Assumption," 31:1 [January–February 2002]: 33 at http://www.sojourners.net/index.cfm?action=magazine.article&issue=soj0201&article=020113c).

133. Eberhard Bethge, "The Challenge of Bonhoeffer's Life and Theology," in *World Come of Age*, ed. Ronald Gregor Smith (Philadelphia: Fortress Press, 1967), 59, 61.

134. Bethge, "Turning Points in Bonhoeffer's Life and Thought," 62. Bethge writes of Bonhoeffer's attitude toward visitors from the Oxford Movement: "Interestingly enough, it was he who worried about their insistence on the 'change.' The man of discipleship, of the first step, of engagement, was repelled by their replacement of the testimony of scripture by the testimony of personal change. He passionately disliked being led into the circle of reflecting about one's own beginnings." The letter cited is dated July 21, 1944.

135. Bethge, *Bonhoeffer: Exile and Martyr*, 48-49. Larry Rasmussen cites evidence that Bonhoeffer was a self-proclaimed pacifist as late as mid-1939. See *Dietrich Bonhoeffer: Reality and Resistance*, 58.

136. Cited in Bethge, *Bonhoeffer: Exile and Martyr*, 46.

137. Even non-evangelical commentators have recognized how rare among contemporary theologians are Bonhoeffer's concerns with prayer and devotional Scripture reading. See William E. Hull, "A Changing Mind," review of *The Way to Freedom* and *I Knew Dietrich Bonhoeffer* in *Christian Century* (July 12, 1967): 920–21; and Ed L. Miller and Stanley J. Grenz, *Fortress Introduction to Contemporary Theologies* (Minneapolis: Fortress Press, 1998), 77.

138. In the May 2002 issue of the newsletter, Dobson wrote: "What if today were 1943 and you were in Nazi Germany and knew that Hitler and his henchmen were killing Jews and Poles and Gypsies and homosexuals and the mentally handicapped, among other 'undesirables'? You knew these helpless people were being gassed, and that little children were standing all day, on one occasion in a freezing rain, for their turn to die in the gas chambers. Would you have said if you were there, 'We're not going to get political in my church! That's somebody else's problem. I'm not called to address controversial issues!' Would you try to make a case for silence in the church? I thank God that Dietrich Bonhoeffer did not

shrink in timidity when he saw unmitigated wickedness being perpetrated by the Nazis. He spoke out boldly, even though he had to know it would cost him his life. Bonhoeffer was hanged in 1945, naked and alone, because he called evil by its name." See *Focus on the Family Newsletter* (May 2002), at http://www .family.org/docstudy/newsletters.

CHAPTER 5: Bridge

1. Cited in Elizabeth Raum, *Dietrich Bonhoeffer: Called by God* (New York: Continuum, 2002), 14.

2. According to Thomas I. Day, Bonhoeffer's imprisonment has been "unduly romanticized, despite his warnings against this. Its beginning was harsh indeed. The sensitive esthete was thrown into solitary confinement in the Tegel jail, where he could not bring himself to use the urine-reeking blanket and received dried bread tossed in onto the floor for breakfast. For ten days in April he did experience the 'view from below' of whose advantages he had written a few months earlier. However, word soon got round of his family connections. He was moved to a better cell and began to enjoy a swelling stream of privileges." See *Bonhoeffer on Christian Community and Common Sense*, Toronto Studies in Theology 11 (New York: Edwin Mellen, 1975), 180.

3. Ruth Zerner regards Bonhoeffer and Hans von Dohnanyi as "forerunners of contemporary human-rights activists, providing paradigms for people of conscience struggling to find words and ways to express their concern for those caught in the grip of oppressive political systems." See Zerner, "Church, State and the 'Jewish Question,'" in *The Cambridge Companion to Dietrich Bonhoeffer*, ed. John W. de Gruchy (Cambridge: Cambridge University Press, 1999), 190–205; 197.

4. Reinhold Niebuhr, "The Death of a Martyr," *Christianity and Crisis* 5:11 (June 25, 1945): 6–7. In a letter to Eberhard Bethge written in October 1968, Karl Barth referred to Bonhoeffer as a martyr. See Bethge, *Bonhoeffer: Exile and Martyr* (New York: Seabury, 1975), 118.

5. Cited in Raum, *Dietrich Bonhoeffer*, 14.

6. Keith W. Clements, *A Patriotism for Today: Love of Country in Dialogue with the Witness of Dietrich Bonhoeffer* (London: Collins Liturgical Publications, 1984), 18. See also Benjamin A. Reist, *The Promise of Bonhoeffer* (Philadelphia: J. B. Lippincott, 1969), 39: "Bonhoeffer has had an astonishing impact on Americans, both because of his martyrdom and because of his ideas."

7. Clemens, *A Patriotism for Today*, 18. The 1963 Macmillan edition of *The Cost of Discipleship* included a "memoir" by Gerhard Leibholz, in which Bonhoeffer's

brother-in-law asserted that his "life and death belong to the annals of Christian martyrdom."

8. John Gibbs, "Dietrich Bonhoeffer," in *The New Theologians: Bultmann, Bonhoeffer, Tillich, Teilhard de Chardin*, ed. R. R. Acheson (London: Mowbray, 1964), 11–25; 11. Around the same time, David E. Jenkins wrote, "Bonhoeffer is a martyr of the Christian Faith in the old and original sense of that term, viz. one who witnessed to the reality of his faith in conditions of great stress, culminating in suffering and death." See David A. Jenkins, *Guide to the Debate about God* (Philadelphia: Westminster, 1966), 99. See also Franklin Sherman, "Death of a Modern Martyr: The Witness of Dietrich Bonhoeffer," *Expository Times* 76 (April 1965): 204–7.

9. Charles E. Lange, "Bonhoeffer: Modern Martyr," *The Episcopalian* (May 1966): 48–49. According to Lange, Bonhoeffer felt compelled to stand with the apostles in saying, "We must obey God rather than men" (Acts 5:29 RSV). Like St. Paul awaiting trial in Rome, he "spent his last two years pondering the Christian faith and its implications for living" (ibid.).

10. Don B. Harbuck, "Bonhoeffer Speaks to Baptists," *The Baptist* (October 1966): 28–29; 28: "The martyrdom of a seminarian for resisting the Nazis has strong implications for Baptist life."

11. Fabian von Schlabrendorff, "In Prison with Dietrich Bonhoeffer," in *I Knew Dietrich Bonhoeffer*, ed. Ronald Gregor Smith and Wolf-Dieter Zimmerman, tr. Käthe Gregor Smith (New York: Harper & Row, 1966), 226. See also Wilhelm Rott, "Something Always Occurred to Him," ibid., 137: "But then we experienced in this very camp [Moosburg] that the blood of the martyrs is the seed of the Church; not if we adorn the prophets' graves, but if by their witness we are called to him whose community our brother Dietrich sought 'in discipline and in action and in suffering,' and in which he has found eternal freedom."

12. Eberhard Bethge, "Turning Points in Bonhoeffer's Life and Thought," in *Bonhoeffer in a World Come of Age*, ed. Peter Vorkink II (Philadelphia: Fortress Press, 1968), 74.

13. Detlev Dädelow, *Evangelische Sammlung*, Berlin (January 5, 1986), cited in Georg Huntemann, *The Other Bonhoeffer: An Evangelical Reassessment of Dietrich Bonhoeffer*, tr. Todd Huizinga (Grand Rapids, Mich.: Baker, 1993), 270.

14. John W. de Gruchy, *Bonhoeffer and South Africa: Theology in Dialogue* (Grand Rapids, Mich.: Eerdmans, 1984), 16. Similarly, Helmut Gollwitzer recalls that in 1951 in the vicinity of Flossenbürg "a commemorative tablet was being discussed, and the question was raised whether Bonhoeffer had really died as a martyr of his faith or only for his political convictions." See Gollwitzer, "The Way

of Obedience," in *I Knew Dietrich Bonhoeffer*, ed. Ronald Gregor Smith and Wolf-Dieter Zimmerman, tr. Käthe Gregor Smith (New York: Harper & Row, 1966)143.

15. Bethge, *Bonhoeffer: Exile and Martyr*, 159ff. Contemporary Christian martyrs, Bethge asserts, die by choice, undergo the agony of universal rejection, and become "dishonored witnesses" on behalf of humanity. One of the few scholars to qualify the term "martyr" in reference to Bonhoeffer is Wolfgang Huber: "By martyrs I mean the people who in their efforts to help their persecuted fellow beings risked or actually forfeited their own lives . . . Dietrich Bonhoeffer is one of those martyrs." See "Answering for the Past, Shaping the Future," photocopy of English translation in Bonhoeffer archive, Union Theological Seminary, New York. The original German version was published in *Ökumenische Rundschau* (April 1995): 147–64.

16. Cited in de Gruchy, *Bonhoeffer and South Africa*, 16.

17. Alistair Kee, "I Did Not Know Dietrich Bonhoeffer," *Christian Century* 89 (October 25, 1972): 1064–68; 1065. In 1969 Benjamin A. Reist referred to Bonhoeffer as a "guilty martyr" (*The Promise of Bonhoeffer*, 40).

18. "Beatification and Coronization," http://www.newadvent.org/cathen/02364.htm, September 2002.

19. Klemens von Klemperer calls Bonhoeffer "one of the few German clergymen to suffer martyrdom for his faith." Bonhoeffer's whole life, von Klemperer writes, "was in a way a preparation for martyrdom." See Klemens von Klemperer, "Totalitarianism and Resistance in Germany: Dietrich Bonhoeffer," in *The Terrible Alternative: Christian Martyrdom in the Twentieth Century*, ed. Andrew Chandler (New York: Cassell, 1998), 81–101. Von Klemperer acknowledges that the meaning of Bonhoeffer's sacrifice is contested among German Protestants, but he attributes this to their difficulty in believing that "the saintliest of their martyrs suffered for his faith, preferring to identify his sacrifice with his political convictions." The book's title appears to be taken from Bonhoeffer's letter to Reinhold Niebuhr upon his departure from New York in 1939, in which he wrote that "Christians in Germany will face the terrible alternative of either willing the defeat of their nation in order that Christian civilization may survive, or willing the victory of their nation and thereby destroying our civilization" (cited in ibid., 93). See also the book by Craig J. Slane, *Bonhoeffer as Martyr: Social Responsibility and Modern Christian Commitment* (Grand Rapids, Mich.: Brazos, 2003).

20. Eberhard Bethge, "My Friend Dietrich," *Christian History* 10:4 (issue 32, 1991): 41. Similarly, Dale Larsen and Sandy Larsen promise that Bonhoeffer's words, "like the man himself, are bound to inspire anyone who encounters them." See *Dietrich Bonhoeffer: Costly Grace*, Christian Classics Bible Study Series

(Downers Grove, Ill.: Intervarsity, 2002), 12. The authors observe that through his writings and the example of his life Bonhoeffer "has spoken and will continue to speak to generations of believers" (11). Furthermore, "sorting through Bonhoeffer's questions and the answers he found will profoundly enrich your Christian life" (back cover).

21. According to E. H. Robertson, Bonhoeffer "so analysed the means by which he lived that we can see our own faith more clearly and more honestly . . . There is much in Bonhoeffer to help us discover ourselves. Perhaps the greatest contribution of Bonhoeffer however is his firm call to us to be men." See *Dietrich Bonhoeffer*, Makers of Contemporary Theology (Philadelphia: John Knox, 1966), 53–54. An early assessment of Bonhoeffer as spiritual guide may be found in Martin Thornton, *The Rock and the River: An Encounter between Traditional Spirituality and Modern Thought* (New York: Morehouse-Barlow, 1965), 49–64. Thornton found Bonhoeffer to be "a key figure" in the search for "a synthesis of orthodox spirituality and modern thought" (49), paying particular attention to Bonhoeffer's doctrine and practice of prayer.

22. The first authors to use the term "spirituality" in connection with Bonhoeffer were Geffrey B. Kelly and F. Burton Nelson. See Kelly, *Liberating Faith* (Minneapolis: Augsburg Publishing House, 1984), especially chapter 5, "Freedom and Discipline: Rhythms of a Christocentric Spirituality"; and Nelson, "Bonhoeffer and the Spiritual Life: Some Reflections," *Journal of Theology for Southern Africa* 30 (March 1980): 34–38. According to John Godsey, spirituality has to do "with the formation of the self by the Spirit of God into the likeness of Jesus Christ." But it can also be described more generically, as having to do with "our identity, with who we are at the deepest level of our being, with that self that we call 'spirit' or 'soul.'" See John D. Godsey, "Dietrich Bonhoeffer and Christian Spirituality," in *Reflections on Bonhoeffer: Essays in Honor of F. Burton Nelson*, ed. Geffrey B. Kelly and C. John Weborg (Chicago: Covenant, 1999), 77–86; 79.

23. Mary Glazener, "On Being a Christian Today: Dietrich Bonhoeffer's Personal Faith," in Kelly and Weborg, *Reflections on Bonhoeffer*, 87–99. The quotation is from a letter Bonhoeffer wrote on August 21, 1944.

24. Gregory Baum, *The Church for Others: Protestant Theology in Communist East Germany* (Grand Rapids, Mich.: Eerdmans, 1996), 94.

25. Godsey, "Dietrich Bonhoeffer and Christian Spirituality," 85.

26. Robert L. Hunter, "Dietrich Bonhoeffer: A Vision and a Voice for Our Times," *Saturday Evening Post* (September–October 1997): 50–51; 50.

27. Geffrey B. Kelly and F. Burton Nelson, *The Cost of Moral Leadership: The Spirituality of Dietrich Bonhoeffer* (Grand Rapids, Mich.: Eerdmans, 2003), 40, 42, 129, 152.

28. Robert Coles, *Dietrich Bonhoeffer*, Modern Spiritual Masters (Maryknoll, N.Y.: Orbis, 1998), 31.

29. "The Best Devotional Books of All Time (Part 2)," *Christian Reader* (September–October 1997), at http://www.christianitytoday.com/tc/7r5/7r5366.html.

30. "The 100 Best Spiritual Books of the Century," at http://www.harpercollins.com, September 2002.

31. "Books of the Century," *Christianity Today* 117 (April 24, 2000), at http://www.christianitytoday.com/ct/2000/005/5.92.html.

32. Franklin Sherman sees in Bonhoeffer's death "a deeply personal testimony, which can serve to inspire any Christian, however he may come to his last hour, to face it with serenity and courage." See "Death of a Modern Martyr," 207.

33. http://www.wce.wwu.edu/nwche/bonhoeffer.html, April 2003; and James C. Howell, *Servants, Misfits, and Martyrs: Saints and Their Stories* (Nashville: Upper Room, 1999), 146.

34. Hunter, "Dietrich Bonhoeffer: A Vision and a Voice for Our Times," 51. "There may be many forms of expression of one's faith in the concrete realities of this world, but the integrating power of the central core of belief and faith holds that person on a clear course" (ibid.).

35. Otto Dudzus, ed., *Bonhoeffer Brevier* (Munich: Chr. Kaiser, 1963); idem, ed., *Bonhoeffer for a New Generation*, ET of *Dietrich Bonhoeffer Lesebuch* (London: SCM, 1986). The most recent German edition appeared in 1998. The book begins with and is structured by Bonhoeffer's poem "Stations on the Road to Freedom."

36. Richard J. Foster and James Bryan Smith, *Devotional Classics: Selected Readings for Individuals and Groups*, A Renovaré Resource for Spiritual Renewal (San Francisco: Harper, 1990). The texts anthologized here "aim at the transformation of the human personality. They seek to touch the heart, to address the will, to mold the mind. They call for radical character formation. They instill holy habits" (1).

37. Charles Ringma, *Seize the Day with Dietrich Bonhoeffer* (Colorado Springs: Piñon, 2000); Manfred Weber, ed., *Dietrich Bonhoeffer: Meditations on the Cross*, tr. Douglas W. Stott (Louisville, Ky.: Westminster John Knox, 1998); Edwin Robertson, ed. and tr., *My Soul Finds Rest: Reflections on the Psalms by Dietrich Bonhoeffer* (Grand Rapids, Mich.: Zondervan, 2002); idem, ed. and tr., *Voices in the Night: The Prison Poems of Dietrich Bonhoeffer* (Grand Rapids, Mich.: Zondervan, 1999); and Wayne Whitson Floyd Jr., *The Wisdom and Witness of Dietrich Bonhoeffer* (Minneapolis: Fortress Press, 2000).

38. J. Martin Bailey and Douglas Gilbert, *The Steps of Bonhoeffer: A Pictorial Album* (Philadelphia: Pilgrim, 1969), 15.

39. Godsey, "Dietrich Bonhoeffer and Christian Spirituality," 77. Godsey writes that Bonhoeffer's "powerful testimony to what it means to be a disciple of Jesus Christ challenged me to think more deeply about my own spiritual journey . . ." (ibid.).

40. Kelly and Nelson, *The Cost of Moral Leadership*, xii, 2.

41. Coles, *Dietrich Bonhoeffer*, 41.

42. Ibid.

43. Thomas C. Oden, "Theology and Therapy: A New Look at Bonhoeffer," *Dialogue* 5 (spring 1966): 98–111.

44. Uwe Siemon-Netto, *The Acquittal of God: A Theology for Vietnam Veterans* (New York: Pilgrim, 1990).

45. Ibid., 13.

46. Ibid., 18.

47. Ibid., 21, 22.

48. Ibid., 81.

49. Ibid., 40.

50. Ibid., 28, 80.

51. For example, Siemon-Netto writes that "the causes for which North Vietnam claimed to fight would have been recognized by Germans of Bonhoeffer's generation. There was the cause of national pride and unity; there was also the alleged cause of social justice" (ibid., 33).

52. James W. Fowler, *Stages of Faith: The Psychology of Human Development and the Quest for Meaning* (New York: Harper & Row, 1981).

53. Ibid., 201.

54. Bonhoeffer first considered traveling to India in 1928 while he was living in Spain. In a letter to his grandmother in the early 1930s he announced his plan to study with Gandhi at the university of Rabindranath Tagore, writing: "At any rate it sometimes seems to me that 'paganism' contains more Christian elements than our whole *Reich* Church" (Smith and Zimmerman, *I Knew Dietrich Bonhoeffer*, 73). For a comparison of the two men and their approaches to nonviolent resistance, see Dena Davis, "Gandhi and Bonhoeffer," *Manchester College Bulletin of the Peace Studies Institute* 11:1 (June 1981): 44–49. See also Larry L. Rasmussen, *Dietrich Bonhoeffer: Reality and Resistance*, Studies in Christian Ethics (Nashville: Abingdon, 1972), 213–17.

55. Robin W. Lovin and Jonathan P. Gosser, "Dietrich Bonhoeffer: Witness in an Ambiguous World," in James W. Fowler and Robin Lovin with Katherine Herzog, et al., *Trajectories in Faith: Five Life Stories* (Nashville: Abingdon, 1980), 147–84.

56. Ibid., 150, 164.

57. Ibid., 180. "Bonhoeffer's love of life, balanced against his sense that its meaning is hidden in death, is surely an example of some of the agony that accompanies this final stage of faith development" (181).

58. Ibid., 83.

59. Fowler, *Stages of Faith*, 200.

60. Ibid., 201. For a similar view of mature faith, applied explicitly to Bonhoeffer, see Fritz de Lange, "Saint bonhoeffer? Dietrich Bonhoeffer and the Paradox of Sainthood," where the author writes that saints are "virtuosos of receptivity that surrender to an endless source of divine goodness . . . 'Saints' are those people that relocate the center of their self in God and want to allow their lives to be completely and without reservation determined by the influence of this formative vision of their identity." http://www.home.netnet.nl/~fritz.lange/artsaintbonhoeffer.htm.

61. Ibid., 204.

62. Ibid., 210–11.

63. Robert L. Hunter, "Dietrich Bonhoeffer: A Vision and a Voice for Our Times," *Saturday Evening Post* (September–October 1997): 50–51; "Hitler's Would-Be Assassin," *Saturday Evening Post* (November–December 1997): 44–47; http://www.bonhoeffer.com/thefilm.htm; and Kelly and Nelson, *The Cost of Moral Leadership*, 173.

64. Robert Coles, *Lives of Moral Leadership: Men and Women Who Made a Difference* (New York: Random House, 2000); idem, *Dietrich Bonhoeffer*. The "modern spiritual masters" treated in the series in which Coles's *Dietrich Bonhoeffer* appears "have engaged in a spiritual journey shaped by the influences and concerns of our age. Such concerns include the challenges of modern science, religious pluralism, secularism, and the quest for social justice" (page facing title page in *Dietrich Bonhoeffer*).

65. Clifford Green, "Bonhoeffer's Legacy," at http://www.pbs.org/opb/bonhoeffer/legacy/index.html.

66. Foreword to Josiah Ulysses Young III, *No Difference in the Fare: Dietrich Bonhoeffer and the Problem of Racism* (Grand Rapids, Mich.: Eerdmans, 1998), x.

67. As Geffrey B. Kelly writes, "Bonhoeffer's belief in Christ's centrality to brotherhood and sisterhood in a world community freed to transcend racial, religious, and national divisions led him into the anti-Hitler conspiracy and to his eventual execution." See *Liberating Faith*, 15.

68. Eberhard Bethge, "Friends," in Smith and Zimmerman, *I Knew Dietrich Bonhoeffer*, 49.

69. Paul Lehmann, "Paradox of Discipleship," in Smith and Zimmerman, *I Knew Dietrich Bonhoeffer*, 41.

70. Ibid.

71. Victoria Barnett, "Theology or Politics: The Development of Bonhoeffer's Critique of Racial Ideology," unpublished paper graciously shared with the author, 4.

72. Ibid., 5, 6.

73. Ibid., 11.

74. *No Difference in the Fare*, 6, 65.

75. Scott Holland, "First We Take Manhattan, Then We Take Berlin: Bonhoeffer's New York," *Cross Currents* 50:3 (Fall 2000), excerpted at http://www.crosscurrents.org/hollandf20.htm. Holland examines the course on "Ethical Viewpoints in Modern Literature" Bonhoeffer took with Reinhold Niebuhr, a course that taught Bonhoeffer to do theology "in conversation with James Weldon Johnson's *Autobiography of an Ex-Colored Man*, W. E. B. Du Bois's *The Souls of Black Folks*, and the collected poetry of Langston Hughes and Countee Cullen, poets of the Harlem Renaissance." These connections are explored in Ralph Garlin Clingan, "Against Cheap Grace in a World Come of Age: A Study in the Hermeneutics of Adam Clayton Powell, 1865–1953, in His Intellectual Context," Ph.D. dissertation, Drew University, 1997.

76. Cheryl Heckler-Feltz, "Agent of Grace Gains Prestige," *Christianity Today* 44 (August 7, 2000), http://www.christianitytoday.com/ct/2000/132/44.0.html. According to the article, "for many Lutherans, another important element of Bonhoeffer's life is his opposition to Christian prejudice against Jews. He became an advocate for the rights of Jews in Nazi Germany, and helped save many Jewish lives."

77. *Glimpses* 63, at http://www.rapidnet.com/~jbeard/bdm/exposes/bonhoeffer/general.htm.

78. "Dietrich Bonhoeffer: General Teachings/Activities," at http://www.rapidnet.com/~jbeard/bdm/exposes/bonhoeffer/general.htm, August 2002.

79. Denise Giardina, *Saints and Villains* (New York: Fawcett, 1998), 12. See also pages 33, 96, 100, 112, 115, 116, 119, 124, 132, 135, 139, 142f., 157, 170, 173, 177f., 182, 213, 225, 234, 238, 241, 252, 255, 256, 268, 270, 276, 287, 291, 292, 294, 295, 302, 310, 321, 349, 398, 409, 418, 427, 435, 436, 438, 446, 451, 454–56, and 479.

80. Ibid., 216, 225, 270, 301, 272, 297, 298.

81. Ibid., 480.

82. Mary Glazener, *The Cup of Wrath: A Novel Based on Dietrich Bonhoeffer's Resistance to Hitler* (Macon, Ga.: Smith & Helwys, 1992). See, e.g., part one, chapters 3 and 4; part two, chapters 14 and 23; part three, chapter 31.

83. Ibid., 140. In another episode some Nazi agents in search of a "Herr Libowitz" come to Bonhoeffer's door by mistake. After their departure, Bonhoeffer attempts to contact and warn his neighbor Mordecai Libowitz (175–76).

84. Giardina is careful not to overplay the success of Bonhoeffer's efforts to protect Jews from the Nazis. During his imprisonment, Dietrich's evil Doppelgänger Alois Bauer taunts him with the claim, "I've saved more Jews than you have" (456).

85. Harry James Cargas, "'Protestant Martyr' Canonization Fitting," *National Catholic Reporter* 19 (October 22, 1982): 21. Cargas writes: "He was among the very few to understand early the threat of Adolf Hitler. In 1933, a full six years before the Germans marched on Poland to begin World War II, Bonhoeffer publicly warned citizens of his country of what was happening in a radio broadcast which was cut off the air before completion . . . Bonhoeffer understood his Christianity to be rooted in Judaism. He had a great love for the Old Testament and cautioned against an exclusive emphasis on the New Testament . . ."

86. The main page of the World Wide Web site http://www.holocaust-heroes.com reads simply "Bonhoeffer Deserves to be Named 'Righteous among the Nations.'" The site features background on the designation "Righteous among the Nations" as bestowed by Yad Vashem's Commission for the Designation of the Righteous, summarizes the argument made by Bonhoeffer's petitioners that he "clearly risked his life in numerous ways to save Jews," and claims that he was never really a member of German counterintelligence. The site also includes excerpts from Eberhard Bethge's affidavit in support of Bonhoeffer's candidacy http://www.holocaust-heroes.com/bonhoeffer.html, April 2003. See also Ruth Zerner's "Chronicle of Compassion and Courage," in "Church, State and the 'Jewish Question'," in *The Cambridge Companion to Dietrich Bonhoeffer*, ed. John W. de Gruchy (Cambridge: Cambridge University Press, 1999), 190–205; 197.

87. Stephen A. Wise, "Why Isn't Bonhoeffer Honored at Yad Vashem?" *Christian Century* 115 (February 25, 1998): 202–4.

88. Ibid., 203.

89. Ibid., 202.

90. For a strong critique of Paldiel's arguments as "self-serving, tendentious and biased," see Geffrey B. Kelly, "Bonhoeffer and the Jews: Implications for Jewish-Christian Relations," in Kelly and Weborg, *Reflections on Bonhoeffer*, 133–66.

91. Marilyn Henry, "Who, Exactly, Is a 'Righteous Gentile'?" *Jerusalem Post* (April 22, 1998), http://www.jpost.com/com/Archive/29.April/1998/Features/Article-6.html. Victoria Barnett agrees with Hoffman's assessment of the matter: "I suspect that the real reason for Yad Vashem's decision is based upon Bonhoeffer's connections to the *Abwehr* resistance circles operating out of Wilhelm Canaris'

office. This is also probably why a petition (submitted during the 1980s) to recognize Hans von Dohnanyi was turned down as well . . . Whatever their innermost thoughts or convictions may have been, these individuals continued to be high-ranking members of the Nazi machine well into the war" (Victoria A. Barnett, "Response to Richard L. Rubenstein," American Academy of Religion/Society of Biblical Literature Annual Meeting, Nashville, November 20, 2000).

92. Cited in Richard Rubenstein, "Was Dietrich Bonhoeffer a 'Righteous Gentile,'" paper presented at the AAR/SBL Annual Meeting, Nashville, November 20, 2000, and graciously shared with the author.

93. Ibid., 7; 10. Responses to Rubenstein's presentation were offered by Robert Ericksen and Victoria Barnet, scholars possessing both interest and expertise in this matter. Ericksen admitted that in the aftermath of the Holocaust "we feel a special need for heroes. But we must balance our desire for heroes with some sense of the magnitude of the disaster." With respect to Bonhoeffer, he concluded that while he may have been good at opposing Hitler and National Socialism, "it is less certain that he was good on the 'Jewish Question'" ("Response to Richard L. Rubenstein," AAR/SBL Annual Meeting, Nashville, November 20, 2000).

94. From Lawrence L. Langer, *Versions of Survival: The Holocaust and the Human Spirit* (Albany: SUNY Press, 1982).

95. Eberhard Bethge, *Dietrich Bonhoeffer: Man of Vision, Man of Courage* (New York: Harper & Row, 1977), 559.

96. Coles, *Dietrich Bonhoeffer*, 41.

97. Similarly, novelist Marilynne Robinson finds inspiration in Bonhoeffer's resistance: "If being modern means having the understanding and will to oppose the passions of collective life that can at any time emerge to disgrace us, and now even to destroy us, then one great type of modern man is surely Dietrich Bonhoeffer—more particularly, Pastor Bonhoeffer in his pulpit, Pastor Bonhoeffer at his prayers." See *The Death of Adam: Essays on Modern Thought* (Boston: Houghton Mifflin, 1998), 113.

98. In January 2003, the on-line journal *Chickenbones: A Journal for Literary and Artistic African American Themes* featured a section titled "Dietrich Bonhoeffer in New York (1930–1931): The Black Connection." In January, 2003, the site had links to Bonhoeffer's writings, including "The Negro Church," and excerpts from a recent article on "Bonhoeffer's New York" by Scott Holland.

99. Rubenstein, "Was Dietrich Bonhoeffer a 'Righteous Gentile,'" 8.

100. Young, *No Difference in the Fare*, 127; 86. Young acknowledges that very little of what we know of Bonhoeffer's Harlem sojourn is helpful in tracing his subsequent theological development. Yet he is not deterred by this paucity of evidence:

"Frank Fisher left no record of his friendship with Bonhoeffer, and virtually nothing substantial has been written on Bonhoeffer and African-Americans. Anyway, the presence of more information would not have changed what I have to say" (ibid., 89).

101. E. Hardwick, "The Place of Bonhoeffer," *Heythrop Journal* 5:3 (July 1964): 297–99.

102. For a review of the issues and the combatants, see Carol Rittner and John K. Roth, eds. *Pope Pius XII and the Holocaust* (New York: Leicester University Press, 2002).

103. Richard L. Rubenstein, "Dietrich Bonhoeffer and Pope Pius XII," in *The Century of Genocide: Selected Papers from the 30th Anniversary Conference of the Annual Scholars' Conference on the Holocaust and the Churches*, ed. Daniel J. Curran Jr., Richard Libowitz, and Marcia Sachs Littell (Merion Station, Pa.: Merion Westfield, 2002), 193–218.

104. Published in March 1998 by the Holy See's Commission for Religious Relations with the Jews and available at http://www.vatican.va/roman_curia/ pontifical_councils/chrstuni/documents/rc_pc_chrstuni_doc_16031998_shoah _en.html.

CHAPER 6: Saint

1. William Kuhns, "A Catholic Looks at Bonhoeffer," *Christian Century* 84 (June 28, 1967): 830–33; 832.

2. Harry James Cargas, "'Protestant Martyr' Canonization Fitting," *National Catholic Reporter* (October 22, 1982): 21.

3. Leo Zanchettin and Patricia Mitchell, *A Great Cloud of Witnesses: Sixteen Saints and Christian Heroes* (Ijamsville, Md.: The Word Among Us, 1998).

4. Howard V. Harper, *Profiles of Protestant Saints* (New York: Fleet, 1968). In 1969, Robert E. Huldschiner referred unabashedly to Bonhoeffer as a saint. See "A Review Article—The Quest for the Historical Bonhoeffer," *Lutheran Forum* 3 (September 1969): 12–13.

5. Robert Ellsberg, *All Saints: Daily Reflections on Saints, Prophets, and Witnesses for Our Time* (New York: Crossroad, 1997).

6. James C. Howell, *Servants, Misfits, and Martyrs: Saints and Their Stories* (Nashville: Upper Room, 1999), 144–45. See also, Frits de Lange, "Saint Bonhoeffer? Dietrich Bonhoeffer and the Paradox of Sainthood," http:// www.home.hetnet.nl/~Frits.lang/artsaintbonhoeffer.htm.

7. http://www.beliefnet.com, August 2002. A Web site dedicated to "noteworthy people" features Bonhoeffer, along with the Dalai Lama, Gandhi, Mother Teresa,

Martin Luther King Jr., and Morris Dees (http://www.perryland.com, April 2003); and the *Das Ökumenische Heiligenlexikon* (Ecumenical Encyclopedia of the Saints) project in Germany, which collects biographies, maps, and calendars for "holy," "blessed," and "memorable" persons in the Catholic, Orthodox, and Protestant traditions, includes Bonhoeffer as well (http://www.heilegenlexikon.de, April 2003).

8. This section is based on "Beatification and Canonization," *Catholic Encyclopedia* at http://www.newadvent.org/cathen/01264b.htm.

9. The ceremonies that developed around the early Christian martyrs resembled pagan ceremonies in some respects. Two differences from pagan practice revealed themselves early on, however. One was that the saint's anniversary was not the birthday, but the death-day (the *natalis* or birthday in heaven of the martyr, reunited with Christ by his death), the other that in the case of martyrs not only the family but the whole Christian community took part in the burial and anniversary.

10. "Beatification and Canonization," *Catholic Encyclopedia* at http://www.newadvent.org/cathen/01264b.htm.

11. Ibid., 17.

12. Ibid., 44.

13. Ibid., xvi. "The rise of romance in the age of chivalry deeply influenced the production of these beautiful but unreal *vitae*, in which imagination and elegance were more evident than the majesty and power emphasized by earlier European taste. This can be seen above all in the *Golden Legend* of James of Voragine, archbishop of Genoa (d. 1298), an elegantly written collection of legends of the saints that became immensely popular. The *Golden Legend* was translated and adapted by William Caxton, was printed in many editions and much read up to the Reformation" (ibid., xvii).

14. "Saints: A Universal Concept," at http://www.beliefnet.com, August 2002.

15. For a calendar of saints created for Anglicans, see http://www.justus.anglican.org/resources/bio/.

16. The Saint John Coltrane African Orthodox Church of San Francisco indicates that the phenomenon of sainthood exists even among the sects. See the church's website at http://www.saintjohncoltrane.org.

17. Cunningham, *The Meaning of Saints*, 44.

18. Robert Ellsberg, "The Mystery of Holiness: Taking Saints Seriously for the Needs of Our Time," *Sojourners* (September–October 1997): http://www.sojo.net/index.dfm?action=magazine.article&issue=soj9709&article970921.

19. Lawrence S. Cunningham, *The Meaning of Saints* (San Francisco: Harper & Row, 1980).

20. Ibid., 57.

21. Ibid., 49.

22. Ibid., 65.

23. Ibid., 6.

24. Ibid., 77.

25. Ibid., 174.

26. Ibid., 58.

27. Ibid., 146.

28. Ibid., 171–72.

29. Ibid., 173; 167–68. Only Mother Theresa and Thomas Merton are cited more often than Bonhoeffer as examples of modern heroic sanctity.

30. Ibid., 88.

31. Ibid., 73. For an analysis of sainthood from the perspective of ethical theory, see Edith Wyschogrod, *Saints and Postmodernism: Revising Moral Philosophy* (Chicago: Univ. of Chicago Press, 1990).

32. Alison Goddard Elliott, *Roads to Paradise: Reading the Lives of the Early Saints* (Hanover, N.H.: University of New England Press, 1987), 3.

33. Ibid., 11.

34. Ibid., 25, 19.

35. Ibid., 45.

36. Ibid., 42–43.

37. The way in which these subgenres can merge is evident in Northrop Frye's definition of "hagiographic romance," in which "heroism comes increasingly to be thought of in terms of suffering, endurance, and patience . . ." Cited in Elliott, *Roads to Paradise*, 14.

38. Michael Walsh, ed.. *Butler's Lives of the Saints, Concise Edition* (San Francisco: Harper & Row, 1985). The concise edition of *Butler's Lives* is especially appropriate for our purposes, since the briefer these saints' "lives," the more apparent are the common motifs that identify them as hagiography.

39. E.g., St. Elizabeth Bayley Seton (19th century foundress), was born "of a very distinguished family"; St. John De Ribera (seventeenth century, Archbishop of Valencia) was son of "one of the highest grandees of Spain"; St. Benedict (seventh century, Abbot of Wearmouth) was "a man of noble birth at the court of Oswy, king of the Northumbrians . . ."; St. Hilary's (fourth century, Bishop of Poitiers) "family was illustrious in Gaul"; St. Ita (sixth century, Virgin) "is said to have been of royal descent"; St. Meinrad (ninth century, Martyr) "is supposed to have been connected with the family of the Hohenzollerns"; St. John the Almsgiver (seventh century, Patriarch of Alexandria) was of noble family; St. Thomas Aquinas, (thirteenth

century, Doctor of the Church) was of "the family of the counts of Aquino [which] was of noble lineage . . ."; St. John Joseph-of-the-Cross's (eighteenth century) parents "were a well-to-do and most exemplary couple" (Walsh, *Butler's Lives*, passim). Alexander Murray confirms that in medieval hagiography the saints more often than not come from the "upper classes," though they transcend class to be accepted at all social levels (Cunningham, *The Meaning of Saints*, 168).

40. Elliott, *Roads to Paradise*, 80–81. These first two aspects of the template accord with what Elliott calls the theme of the hero's "prior life," which includes descriptions of the saint as from a noble family and as a *puer-senex* (that is, a youth with the wisdom of an old man). "From birth, or even before, the saintly hero of legend, like his secular counterpart, is often marked as a man or woman set apart, extraordinary." See Elliott, *Roads to Paradise*, 59, 77.

41. "Bede: Life of Cuthbert," in *Lives of the Saints: The Voyage of St. Brendan; Bede: Life of Cuthbert; Eddius Stephanus: Life of Wilfrid*, ed. J. F. Webb (Baltimore: Penguin, 1964), 73. See also the biographies of these saints: St. Honoratus (fifth century, Bishop of Arles): "In his youth he renounced the worship of idols . . ."; St. Scholastica (sixth century, Virgin) "consecrated herself to God from her earliest years"; St. Theotonius (twelfth century) "was destined for the priesthood from his earliest years"; St. Frances of Rome (fifteenth century, Widow): "Frances was a precocious little girl, and when she was eleven she asked her parents to allow her to become a nun, only to be met by a point-blank refusal. Her parents had quite different plans for their quite attractive little daughter." Typical of hagiography is this description of St. Peter of Atroa (ninth century, Abbot): "Nobody was surprised when, at the age of eighteen, he decided to be a monk." Of St. Gabriel Possenti (nineteenth century), we read that "as a youth he read novels, he was fond of gaiety and of the theatre . . . and on account of his cheerfulness and good looks he was a universal favourite" (Walsh, *Butler's Lives*, passim).

42. Walsh, *Butler's Lives*, 40. See also the descriptions of St. John the Almsgiver, who "employed his income in the relief of the poor"; St. Angela Merici (sixteenth century, Virgin and Foundress): "As she went about amongst her neighbours, she was appalled by the ignorance which prevailed amongst the poorer children . . . "; St. Peter Damian (eleventh century, Cardinal-Bishop of Ostia): "Not only did he give away much in alms, but he was seldom without some poor persons at his table, and took pleasure in serving them with his own hands"; and St. Frances of Rome, who visited the poor of Rome, "ministering to their wants and relieving their distress . . ." (Walsh, *Butler's Lives*, passim).

43. Ibid., 12; 23.

44. "Bede: Life of Cuthbert," 105. See also descriptions in *Butler's Lives* of the following saints: St Sava (thirteenth century, Archbishop of the Serbs) signed a copy of the psalter he translated into Serbian, "I, the unworthy lazy monk, Sava"; St. Honoratus "was by compulsion consecrated archbishop of Arles . . ."; St. Antony (fourth century, Abbot) "became a model of humility, charity, prayerfulness and many more virtues"; St. Wulfstan (eleventh century, Bishop of Worcester) "caused young gentlemen who were brought up under his care to carry in the dishes and wait on the poor at table, to teach them the true spirit of humility, in which he himself set an example"; St. Thomas Aquinas, after receiving a revelation while celebrating Mass, wrote that "all that I have written appears to be as so much straw after the things that have been revealed to me"; in 927 St. Meinrad was "forced, much against his inclination, to accept the archbishopric of Metz . . ."; the queen of Portugal "repeatedly urged [St. Theotonius] to accept a bishopric, but he always refused" (Walsh, *Butler's Lives*, passim).

45. For instance, it is written of St. Frances of Rome that "in all the forty years that she lived with her husband there was never the slightest dispute or misunderstanding between them" (Walsh, *Butler's Lives*, 72).

46. Of St. Cunegund (eleventh century, Empress and Widow) it is written that she and her husband, St. Henry, Duke of Bavaria, took a vow of virginity on their wedding day; St. Theophanes the Chronicler (ninth century, Abbot) "was induced to marry, but by mutual agreement his wife became a nun."

47. "Preserved chastity has its own martyrdom" (Jerome). Elliott, *Roads to Paradise*, 64, 86, 144, 206. Cunningham notes that the saint's calendar gives short shrift to married Christians, "as if that less-perfect state somehow disqualifies [them] from public recognition of sanctity." The exaggeration of celibate values, he says, "is familiar to anyone who has looked at a good deal of traditional hagiography" (53). See also Sebastian P. Brock and Susan Ashbrook Harvey, *Holy Women of the Syrian Orient* (Berkeley: University of California Press, 1987), 17: "The Christian lives as if spiritually dead to the world—indifferent to secular luxuries and unwilling to participate in society's perpetuating institutions of family (marriage) and state (sacrificing to the patron deities). The martyrs underscored the consequences of this life-style by physically dying for it—not forcing their own deaths but holding to a mode of life whose consequences could be fatal, both for the individual and for society."

48. Ellsberg, "The Mystery of Holiness."

49. St. Hilary (fourth century) was exiled when the Arians began to persecute the orthodox; St. Methodius (ninth century, Archbishop of Sirmium) was accused of heresy by the Holy See and persecuted by an ecclesiastical enemy who forged

pontifical documents; St. Boniface (thirteenth century, Bishop of Lausanne) "found himself continually opposed and misunderstood throughout the eight years of his episcopate" (Walsh, *Butler's Lives,* passim).

50. Elliott, *Roads to Paradise,* 206. The desert saint is the antithesis of Aristotle's political animal. He is "basically a 'loner,' isolated from a larger social context, even though his peers, whether parents or monastic brethren, desire his presence and often seek either to keep him with them or to join him in the solitude" (90–91).

51. Ibid., 174.

52. Walsh, *Butler's Lives,* 14; 24. See "Bede: Life of Cuthbert," ch. 28, "How He Predicted His Own Death to Hereberht the Hermit." According to *Butler's Lives,* St. John the Almsgiver "was admonished from Heaven that his death was near at hand . . ."

53. "Bede: Life of Cuthbert," ch. 39. See *Butler's Lives* on St. Peer of Atroa ("In the church of St. Zachary's, while the monks were singing the night office with their abbot on a bed of sickness in the choir, death came to [him] after he had lovingly addressed his brethren for the last time"); and St. Frances of Rome ("'The angel has finished his task: he beckons me to follow him' were his last words").

54. Theodore J. Kleinhans, *Till the Night Be Past: The Life and Times of Dietrich Bonhoeffer* (St. Louis: Concordia, 2002), 20–21.

55. Renate Wind, *Dietrich Bonhoeffer: A Spoke in the Wheel,* tr. John Bowden (Grand Rapids, Mich.: Eerdmans, 1992), 15.

56. Helmut Goes, cited in Michael F. Moeller, "The Child, the Fool, the Sufferer: Dietrich Bonhoeffer: A Reflection on His Life and Ministry," at http://www.luther95.org/NELCA/internos/moeller.htm. Bonhoeffer's teaching assistant recalls a visit to Dietrich's mountain cabin in 1933 in which Bonhoeffer described each constellation in the night sky in exquisite detail. "How do you know this?" he asked. One knows," was the reply. See Elizabeth Raum, *Dietrich Bonhoeffer: Called by God* (New York: Continuum, 2002), 21.

57. See Geffrey B. Kelly, "Bonhoeffer's Theology of Liberation," *Dialog* 34:1 (winter 1995): 22–29; 23.

58. Eberhard Bethge, *Dietrich Bonhoeffer: Man of Vision, Man of Courage* (New York: Harper & Row, 1977), 22.

59. Kleinhans, *Till the Night Be Past,* 100; Wind, *A Spoke in the Wheel,* 108. These judgments are based on Bonhoeffer's admission in a letter from prison that he had once been "in love with a girl . . . [but] being totally committed to my work for the Church in the ensuing years, I thought it not only inevitable but right that I should forgo marriage altogether." Cited in F. Burton Nelson, "The Life of Dietrich

Bonhoeffer," in *The Cambridge Companion to Dietrich Bonhoeffer*, ed. John W. de Gruchy (Cambridge: Cambridge University Press, 1999), 22–49; 41. Mary Glazener identifies the woman in question as Elisabeth Zinn, who confirmed to Glazener that she and Bonhoeffer had been "unofficially engaged." See "On Being a Christian Today: Dietrich Bonhoeffer's Personal Faith," in *Reflections on Bonhoeffer: Essays in Honor of F. Burton Nelson*, ed. Geffrey B. Kelly and C. John Weborg (Chicago: Covenant, 1999), 87–99; 87.

60. In Geffrey B. Kelly and F. Burton Nelson, *The Cost of Moral Leadership: The Spirituality of Dietrich Bonhoeffer* (Grand Rapids, Mich.: Eerdmans, 2003), 31.

61. Bonhoeffer wrote to Bethge from prison: "We have been engaged for nearly a year and have never been alone together for one hour! Isn't it absurd . . ." (cited in Raum, *Dietrich Bonhoeffer: Called by God*, 142).

62. Michael van Dyke, *Dietrich Bonhoeffer: Opponent of the Nazi Regime*, Heroes of the Faith Series (Ulrichsville, Ohio: Barbour, 2001), 144; Mary Glazener, *The Cup of Wrath: A Novel Based on Dietrich Bonhoeffer's Resistance to Hitler* (Macon, Ga.: Smith & Helwys, 1992), 258, 302; Kleinhans, *Till the Night Be Past*, 149.

63. Georg Huntemann, *The Other Bonhoeffer: An Evangelical Reassessment of Dietrich Bonhoeffer*, tr. Todd Huizinga (Grand Rapids, Mich.: Baker, 1993), 267.

64. Eberhard Bethge, "The Challenge of Dietrich Bonhoeffer's Life and Theology," in *World Come of Age*, ed. Ronald Gregor Smith (Philadelphia: Fortress Press, 1967), 22.

65. Bethge argues that Bonhoeffer's experience of exile was reflected in his theology as he incorporated "the exilic element in Christian faith, the alienation of discipleship." See Bethge, *Bonhoeffer: Exile and Martyr* (New York: Seabury, 1975), 105, 107, 109, 111, 113, 121, 130, 132.

66. Eberhard Bethge, "Turning Points in Bonhoeffer's Life and Thought," in *Bonhoeffer in a World Come of Age*, ed. Peter Vorkink II (Philadelphia: Fortress Press, 1968), 73.

67. "Disguise is yet another form of surrogate or displaced death in which the hero, having shed an old identity, assumes an interim one prior to the final moment of revelation with which comes the integration of past and present" (Elliott, *Roads to Paradise*, 120). Symbolic death, burial, and rebirth, are also topoi in saints' lives. "This emblematic death prefigures his real death and resurrection into Paradise, but even more it serves as a *rite de passage*, a purificatory ritual in which the saint sheds his cultural existence in preparation for his new way of life" (ibid., 110). Cf. Bonhoeffer's time in an "underground" seminary and his belowground cell at Tegel prison.

68. Cited in Ed L. Miller and Stanley J. Grenz, *Fortress Introduction to Contemporary Theologies* (Minneapolis: Fortress Press, 1998), 76.

69. *Glimpses* 63 at http://www.gospelcom.net/chi/GLIMPSEF/Glimpses/glmps063.shtml.

70. See Helmut Gollwitzer, Käthe Kuhn, and Reinhold Schnider, eds., *Dying We Live: The Final Messages and Records of the Resistance*, tr. Reinhard C. Kuhn (New York: Pantheon, 1956), 213–18, where excerpts from Bonhoeffer's prison writings are gathered and presented as his final testament.

71. Cunningham, *The Meaning of Saints*, 75; 115. Alison Goddard Elliott adds that the martyr's passion is an image of the fight between good and evil that is fought by Christians everywhere (Elliott, *Roads to Paradise*, 29).

72. Brock and Harvey, *Holy Women of the Syrian Orient*, 14, 18.

73. Ibid., 13. Ellsberg, "The Mystery of Holiness."

74. Brock and Harvey, *Holy Women of the Syrian Orient*, 14.

75. Harper, *Profiles in Protestant Sainthood*, 196–97.

76. Huldschiner, "A Review Article—The Quest for the Historical Bonhoeffer," 13. See also Dan Caldwell, "Bonhoeffer's *Life Together* and the Christian University," *Faculty Dialogue* (spring 1992): 27–38; 27, where the author compares Bonhoeffer and Jesus.

77. Van Dyke, *Dietrich Bonhoeffer: Opponent of the Nazi Regime*, 161.

78. Ibid.

79. In J. Martin Bailey and Douglas Gilbert, *The Steps of Bonhoeffer: A Pictorial Album* (Philadelphia: Pilgrim, 1969), 14. Geffrey B. Kelly and F. Burton Nelson speak of Bonhoeffer's "personal Calvary," his "death-resurrection on a Nazi gallows," the "Christic parallels" in his decision to break with his church and join the conspiracy against Hitler, and his poem "By the Powers for Good" as "reminiscent of Jesus' Gethsemane prayer of resignation to God's will." See *The Cost of Moral Leadership*, xv, 41, 248.

80. Elizabeth Berryhill, *The Cup of Trembling: A Play in Two Acts* (Greenwich, Conn.: Seabury, 1958). Berryhill's thinly veiled Bonhoeffer (Erich Friedhoffer) tells Bishop Hale: "When we look at Adolf Hitler, we come as near as we ever shall to seeing the Antichrist. He is evil incarnate" (57). To Keppler, the Tegel interrogation officer, he says: "Satan is truly at work in the world. And he has men to help him; not only to help him but *happy* to help him. And thus you are not men at all, but fiends!" (75).

81. Glazener, *The Cup of Wrath*, 433, 435.

82. Ibid., 436–41. Cf. Gordon Houser, "An Uncommon Cup: The Challenge of a Historical Novel," review of Mary Glazener, *The Cup of Wrath*, *Sojourners*

23:7 (August 1994): 45–46: "At times the book reads like hagiography, especially in the recounting of Bonhoeffer's last hours before being hung by the Nazis on April 9, 1945."

83. Van Dyke, *Dietrich Bonhoeffer: Opponent of the Nazi Regime*, 47, 55.

84. Kleinhans, *Till the Night Be Past*, 17. "He kept himself trim in a way that would have shocked the typically reserved professors in Germany—by swimming and playing tennis with his students" (ibid.).

85. Zanchettin and Mitchell, *Great Cloud of Witnesses*, 57. "With his blond hair, strong brow, and sharp blue eyes, his outward appearance and actions corresponded with the inner intensity with which he worked" (ibid.).

86. Harper, *Profiles in Protestant Sainthood*, 192.

87. Ibid., 196. Huntemann, *The Other Bonhoeffer*, 26. See also John D. Godsey, *The Theology of Dietrich Bonhoeffer* (Philadelphia: Westminster, 1960), 13: "Bonhoeffer was the sort of person who, by his very demeanor, stood out in a crowd. There was a certain aura about this powerfully built man with aristocratic features and gentle eyes, which attracted people to him. He was a man among men . . ."

88. An official report of Bonhoeffer's vicarage in Barcelona included this passage: "He has been able in particular to attract children who are very fond of him." See Kelly and Nelson, *The Cost of Moral Leadership*, 15.

89. Sabine Leibholz, "Childhood and Home," in *I Knew Dietrich Bonhoeffer*, ed. Ronald Gregor Smith and Wolf-Dieter Zimmerman, tr. Käthe Gregor Smith (New York: Harper & Row, 1966), 33.

90. Raum, *Dietrich Bonhoeffer: Called by God*, 126; Eberhard Bethge, "Aftermath of Flossenburg: Bonhoeffer, 1945–1970," *Christian Century* 87 (May 27, 1970): 656–89; 656.

91. Michael Novak, "Bonhoeffer's Way," *Book Week* 4 (February 19, 1967): 5–6; 5.

92. Other members of Bonhoeffer's extended family, including Sabine Leibholz-Bonhoeffer, Renate Bethge and Dorothee Bracher, have played a similar role in endorsing books on Bonhoeffer.

CHAPTER 7: Cult

1. Jeff Favre, "Remembering Bonhoeffer," *The Lutheran* (April 2002), http://www.thelutheran.org/0204/page23/html. See also http://www.dbmintrav.com. In their promotional material, the Johnsons note that "the subject can be dealt with in a variety of ways, e.g., sermons (each 15 minutes), adult forums including youth beginning with age 12, family nights, seminars, clergy gatherings, etc."

2. J. Martin Bailey and Douglas Gilbert, *The Steps of Bonhoeffer: A Pictorial Album* (Philadelphia: Pilgrim, 1969).

3. Ibid., 16.

4. Jane Pejsa, *To Pomerania in Search of Dietrich Bonhoeffer: A Traveler's Companion and Guide for Those Who Venture East of the Oder River, Seeking Markers of Bonhoeffer's Life and Ministry—1935 through 1943* (Minneapolis: Kenwood, 1996), v.

5. Ibid., 43. In another place, Pejsa writes that "a veritable memorial-frenzy is now underway to mark those places of Bonhoeffer's life that now lie in Poland. The first memorial was mounted in 1995—a major bronze plaque in the church at Slawno (Schlawe) near the sites of the Gross Schlonwitz and Sigurdshof Collective Pastorates. Then, in May of 1996, a group of Americans erected plastic markers at Szczecin Zdroje (Finkenwalde), at Koszalin (Koslin), and at Tychowo (Sigurds-hof). Later in the year a joint committee of Germans and Poles, amid great fanfare, erected a bronze plaque to mark Bonhoeffer's birthplace in Wraclaw (Breslau)." See Jane Pejsa, ". . . they burned all the meeting places of God in the land," in *Reflections on Bonhoeffer: Essays in Honor of F. Burton Nelson*, ed. Geffrey B. Kelly and C. John Weborg (Chicago: Covenant, 1999), 129–32; 131.

6. Keith Clements, "Bonhoeffer's Last Days: A Pilgrimage," *International Bonhoeffer Society (English Language Section) Newsletter* 80 (fall 2002): 1, 4–7.

7. Ibid., 5.

8. Ibid.

9. Ibid., 7. Another sort of pilgrimage guide is provided by James H. Burtness's "Reading Bonhoeffer: A Map to the Literature," which begins with Bethge's "illustrated introduction" to Bonhoeffer. See *Shaping the Future: The Ethics of Dietrich Bonhoeffer* (Philadelphia: Fortress Press, 1985), 171–79.

10. Donald Goddard, *The Last Days of Dietrich Bonhoeffer* (New York: Harper & Row, 1976). Goddard acknowledges "taking many liberties in fleshing out the bare bones of what is known, inventing the substance (though not the fact) of his interrogations, as well as conversation, incident, and even some minor characters in the story. . . ."

11. Ibid., 244.

12. Ibid.

13. Mary Glazener, *The Cup of Wrath: A Novel Based on Dietrich Bonhoeffer's Resistance to Hitler* (Macon, Ga.: Smith & Helwys, 1992), 1. Glazener writes: "I cannot claim that you are about to meet the real Dietrich Bonhoeffer. I can only say that in these pages you will meet the Dietrich Bonhoeffer who over the years has become real to me" (ibid.). The book does possess unique features, including

its attention to the inner states of Bonhoeffer's fiancée Maria and his mother Paula, who endures so much as her children and their spouses undergo persecution by the Nazis.

14. Theodore J. Kleinhans, *Till the Night Be Past: The Life and Times of Dietrich Bonhoeffer* (St. Louis: Concordia, 2002), 15.

15. According to F. Burton Nelson, who has served as a consultant on the project, *Hitler and the Pastor*, a documentary film by New York filmmaker Bea Rothenbuecher, has run into financial troubles. In addition, Hans Joachim Dörger has produced a German documentary called *Dietrich Bonhoeffer: Nachfolge und Kreuz, Widerstand und Galgen* (Matthias Film/GmbH, 1983).

16. *Dietrich Bonhoeffer: Memories and Perspectives*, dir. Bain Boehlke (Trinity Films, 1983).

17. *Hanged on a Twisted Cross*, dir. T. N Mahan (Gateway Films, 1996).

18. *Bonhoeffer*, dir. Martin Doblmeier (Journey Films, 2003). See http://www.bonhoeffer.com/news; and Elvis Mitchell, "Film in Review: 'Bonhoeffer'," *New York Times* (July 20, 2003): 14.

19. The film received 3 1/2 stars (out of 4) from the *Chicago Tribune*, which called it "a mesmerizing U.S. documentary" (http://www.bonhoeffer.com, April 2003); and the *Santa Fe New Mexican* gave *Bonhoeffer* four jalapeño peppers (out of five), calling the film a "stirring documentary" about a man "who remains a lightning rod for this century's ethical quandaries regarding war, capital punishment and terrorism." See the *Santa Fe New Mexican* (July 11–17, 2003): 76.

20. Lawrence S. Cunningham, *The Meaning of Saints* (San Francisco: Harper & Row, 1980), 5, 8, 16, 21.

21. Kleinhans, *Till the Night Be Past*, 18.

22. Ibid., 58: "Like Ernest Hemingway, who was roaming Spain about the same time, Dietrich became an aficionado of bullfighting." Michael van Dyke emphasizes Bonhoeffer's early military training: "Soon, Dietrich found himself spending a couple of evenings during the week practicing his shooting and sword fighting. Once a month, the Hedgehogs held mock battles on the fields that surrounded the campus and Dietrich, to his surprise, found himself enjoying the strenuous, physical part of these exercises. He was stronger than many of the fraternity brothers and could hold his own on the field. He also entertained notions that he wouldn't be half-bad as a real soldier if given the chance." See Michael van Dyke, *Dietrich Bonhoeffer: Opponent of the Nazi Regime*, Heroes of the Faith Series (Ulrichsville, Oh.: Barbour, 2001), 27–28.

23. Elizabeth Berryhill, *The Cup of Trembling* (New York: Seabury, 1958), 9. In addition to those discussed here, there are at least two other plays on Bonhoeffer in

English: *Testament — The Life and Death of Dietrich Bonhoeffer*, by Steve Pederson of Northwestern College in Orange City, Iowa. (see Burtness, *Shaping the Future*, 173) and *The End: The Beginning of Life: The Prison Experiences of Dietrich Bonhoeffer*, which I received from a friend of the author, whose name has been lost to me. Not described here is the one-man dramatic interpretation of Bonhoeffer's life by Al Staggs, titled *A View from the Underside: The Legacy of Dietrich Bonhoeffer*. Staggs has been staging this dramatization of Bonhoeffer's life since the late 1980s, averaging twenty-five to thirty performances a year at venues ranging from churches of the major Christian denominations to synagogues, Holocaust conferences, and colleges (e-mail correspondence with Al Staggs, April 8, 2003).

24. Berryhill, *The Cup of Trembling*, 50.

25. Ibid., 52, 53. While meeting with Bishop Hale (Bell), Erich says "I will throw myself in the arms of God — and pray to watch with Christ in Gethsemane" (64).

26. Ibid., 14.

27. Wilfred Harrison, *Coming of Age: A Play* (Trotten, U.K.: Fernhurst, 1973), 1, 2.

28. Ibid., 15.

29. Ibid., 49.

30. Marsh seeks to demonstrate his argument by playing "rousing, passionate, martial" Spanish music, arguing that "you can trace much of his later and mature philosophy right back to things he said in Barcelona when he was only 22" (Ibid, 25).

31. Douglas Anderson, *The Beams Are Creaking* (Boston: Baker's Plays, 1982), 20.

32. Ibid., 32–33.

33. Ibid., 29.

34. Ibid., 40. Cf. Johann (Hans) in *The Cup of Trembling*, who expresses the resisters' "intent to repeal the Nürnberg Laws and restore all stolen property to the Jews" (60).

35. Ibid., 69.

36. *Bonhoeffer: Agent of Grace*, dir. Eric Till (Gateway Films, 1999).

37. John Matthews, review of *Bonhoeffer: Agent of Grace*, *Association of Contemporary Church Historians Newsletter* 6:7/8 (July–August 2000). Matthews objects that "the perceived 'essence' of his life and witness seems to be that of heroism, a descriptive image Bonhoeffer would have vehemently opposed." See also the promotional material at http://www.pbs.org/opb/bonhoeffer, August 2002.

38. Theodore A. Gill, *Memo for a Movie: A Short Life of Dietrich Bonhoeffer* (New York: Macmillan, 1971), 1, 2.

39. Ibid., 4–5.

40. Ibid., 5.

41. Ibid., 64, 98, 58–59, 203, 217.

42. Ibid., 191.

43. Ibid., 195.

44. Ibid., 239.

45. Ibid., 8, 91. Gill writes of the Bonhoeffer who "one generation ago anticipated our presently active generation and its whole habit of thought." In another place Gill claims that done right, a discussion between Bonhoeffer and Moltke about the morality of using force against Hitler "can be a major contribution to current national and international affairs" (ibid., 155, 180).

46. Ibid., 18.

47. Renate Wind, *Dietrich Bonhoeffer: A Spoke in the Wheel*, tr. John Bowden (Grand Rapids, Mich.: Eerdmans, 1992), 176. The last verse of this poem has become a popular motto on calendars and postcards.

48. Herman Berlinski, Heinz Werner Zimmermann, and Robert M. Helmschrott, *Bonhoeffer Triptychon*. See John W. de Gruchy, "The Reception of Bonhoeffer's Theology," in *The Cambridge Companion to Dietrich Bonhoeffer*, ed. John W. de Gruchy (Cambridge: Cambridge University Press, 1999), 93–109; 93.

49. *International Bonhoeffer Society (English-Language Section) Newsletter* 81 (spring 2003): 19.

50. The play was written by Timothy Stoller, pastor of Moriah and Bethany Lutheran churches.

51. Douglas K. Huneke, *The Stones Will Cry Out: Pastoral Reflections on the Shoah (with Liturgical Resources)* (Westport, Ct.: Greenwood, 1995), 175ff. As an alternative to the sermon, Huneke suggests a dramatic reading of Elizabeth Berryhill's *The Cup of Trembling* or that a group of congregants select Bonhoeffer quotations and prepare five-minute personal reflections upon them. Another order of worship commemorating Bonhoeffer can be obtained from the New England Lutheran Clergy Association.

52. See http://www.bonhoeffer-berlin.de/e_bonhoeffer-haus.htm. There is also a Dietrich Bonhoeffer Haus Hotel in Berlin that caters to visitors.

53. Karen L. Mulder, "Martyrs Carved in Stone," *Christianity Today* 43 (September 7, 1998), http://www.ctlibrary.com/ct/1998/sept7/8ta27c.html; Stephen Johnson, "Classical: Music for Martyrs," *Independent* (London: July 14, 1998) For a comparison of Bonhoeffer with King and Romero, see Geffrey B. Kelly and F. Burton Nelson, *The Cost of Moral Leadership: The Spirituality of Dietrich Bonhoeffer* (Grand Rapids, Mich.: Eerdmans, 2003), 182ff.

54. John W. de Gruchy, "Bonhoeffer's Legacy: A New Generation," Christian Century 114 (April 2, 1997): 343–45.

Chapter 8: Domestication

1. Dietrich Bonhoeffer, *Ethics*, ed. Eberhard Bethge (New York: Macmillan, 1955), 175–76.

2. Erwin Lutzer, *Hitler's Cross: The Revealing Story of How the Cross of Christ Was Used as a Symbol of the Nazi Agenda* (Chicago: Moody, 1995), 96, 134, 204, 160.

3. *Focus on the Family Newsletter* (May 2000), at http://www.family.org/doc-study/newsletters, April 2003.

4. Amanda Ripley, "Terrorists and Saints," *Washington City Paper* (February 5–11, 1999), http://www.washingtoncitypaper.com/archives/cover/1999/cover0205 .html; and John Yewell, "Straight Shooters," *Independent Online* (January 24, 2001), www.indyweek.com/durham/2001-01-24/cover.htm. The American Coalition of Life Activists was successfully sued in 1999 over their "Nuremberg Files Project," a web site identifying abortion doctors. The project's goal, according to ACLA national director David Crane, was "to gather all available information on abortionists and their accomplices for the day when they may be formally charged and tried at Nuremberg-type trials for their crimes." See Skipp Porteous, "Banquet of the White Rose," *Albion Monitor* (at http://www.monitor.net/monitor/abor-tion/whiterose.html).

5. The Web site, titled American-Nazi War Memorial, pairs photos of aborted fetuses with scenes from Nazi camps under several themes ("body parts," "experimentation," "killers," "final solution," "waste management," and "trophies"). The site asks: "Do you feel upset about what happened to Jewish people in Nazi Germany? Why don't you feel the same outrage at what is happening to unborn children? See the evidence. It is the same thing" (at http://www.mttu.com/memorial, December 2003).

6. Paul J. Hill, "Should We Defend Born and Unborn Children with Force?" (July 1993), at http://www.webcom.com/~pinknoiz/right/knowenemy.html.

7. http://www.acidink.org/200309archive001.asp

8. Joe Pavone, "Men of Courage: Paul Hill and Dietrich Bonhoeffer," at http://www.mttu.com/Articles/Men%20of%20Courage%20-%20Paul%20Hill%20 and%20Dietrich%20Bonhoeffer.htm. On another site, Pavone calls Hill "truly the American Dietrich Bonhoeffer" ("Paul Hill Message Board" at http://www .armyofgod.com/PhillMessageBoard.html, December 2003).

9. Ripley, "Terrorists and Saints."

10. Mark Juergensmeyer, *Terror in the Mind of God: The Global Rise of Religious Violence* (Berkeley: University of California Press, 2000), 21–22. Shelley Shannon is another antiabortion activist who refers to Bonhoeffer's role in her awakening to the necessity of violence in the struggle. See Shelley Shannon, "Toward the Use of Force," at http://www.armyofgod.com/ShelleyForce.html, January 2003.

11. Juergensmeyer, *Terror in the Mind of God*, 23.

12. *The Brockhoeft Report* 1:4 (December 1993), http://www.saltshaker.us/br-4.htm. According to http://www.armyofgod.com/BrockSelect.html (January 2003), "John Brockhoeft, a defender of the unborn, has completed serving several years in prison for closing down abortuaries by means of fire. While he was incarcerated, he wrote what has become known as *The Brockhoeft Report*. The *Brockhoeft Report* was originally in newsletter format and edited by Shelley Shannon until her subsequent arrest and conviction for shooting late term abortionist George Tiller. After Shelley's trial *The Brockhoeft Report* was published in the *Prayer & Action News*, edited by Dave and Dorothy Leach. John Brockhoeft is a signer of Paul Hill's Defensive Action statement. He was released from prison under severe restrictions placed on his personal liberties."

13. An author at http://www.lifeadvocate.org makes a similar observation: "I seem to recall everyone from Christian Action Coalition to Operation Rescue making a big deal out of Dietrich Bonhoeffer some years ago. They used his statements on the evil of abortion, the necessity for activism, and the justifiability of civil disobedience to bolster their speeches and literature. He was all the rage. Most of these people simply passed over the fact that Bonhoeffer had participated in an attempt to assassinate the lawfully elected leader, Chancellor Adolf Hitler, of the German Republic. Suddenly, now that a couple of serial child-killers have been shot, there is a mysterious dearth of Bonhoeffer references from these prolife leaders. Maybe they didn't like his reasoning and philosophy as much as they previously thought. Is it just because the full implications are now present—and uncomfortable—that they abandon their former hero?" (at http://www.lifeadvocate.org/bio/paul/95041a.htm).

14. In a reference to fellow activist Mike Griffin, Brockhoeft argued that since Bonhoeffer's approach was to use lethal force against a killer and Griffin's approach "was exactly the same and for exactly the same reason," Mike Griffin is "exactly the Dietrich Bonhoeffer figure for our generation."

15. See, e.g., Albert Mohler, "The Execution of Justice: The Real Meaning of Paul Hill," http://www.clarkprosecutor.org/html/death/us/hill873.htm (September 4, 2003): "Those who defend Hill's killing of the two men have compared him to

Dietrich Bonhoeffer, the German Lutheran pastor who was executed for his part in a conspiracy against Adolf Hitler. Bonhoeffer did join the conspiracy to kill Hitler, but only after it was clear that no legal or political process could lead to the recovery of the nation and the end of Hitler's death machine. Even then, Bonhoeffer was not certain that his actions were fully right. He called for Christians to act humbly, acknowledging that moral questions on what he called 'the borderland' could not be settled with absolute certainty. In the end, he believed that joining the conspiracy against Hitler was more right than wrong. When it failed, he paid for his complicity with his life. Paul Hill is no Dietrich Bonhoeffer."

16. Lutzer, *Hitler's Cross*, 119.

17. See Clifford J. Green, "Bonhoeffer: 'No!' to Paul Hill," *International Bonhoeffer Society (English-Language Section) Newsletter* 83 (fall 2003), 10. In response to an August 2003 media report that Missionaries to the Unborn regarded Hill's murder of an abortion doctor as morally equivalent to Bonhoeffer's involvement in the plot to assassinate Hitler, Green pointed out that Bonhoeffer was involved in tryannicide, not assassination.

18. William Kuhns, "A Catholic Looks at Bonhoeffer," *Christian Century* 84 (June 28, 1967): 830–33; 832. Similarly, Dan Caldwell writes that Bonhoeffer's integrity between thought and deed recalls the life of Christ, "the combined effect of [whose] words and actions is what made him one of history's most influential figures." See "Bonhoeffer's *Life Together* and the Christian University," *Faculty Dialogue* (spring 1992): 27–38; 27.

19. Alison Goddard Elliott, *Roads to Paradise: Reading the Lives of the Early Saints* (Hanover, N. H.: University of New England Press, 1987), 35–36.

20. Renate Wind, *Dietrich Bonhoeffer: A Spoke in the Wheel*, tr. John Bowden (Grand Rapids, Mich.: Eerdmans, 1992), 70.

BIBLIOGRAPHY

English Language Bonhoeffer Web Sites

Dietrich Bonhoeffer Home Page (http://www.dbonhoeffer.org)

United States Holocaust Memorial Museum (http://www.ushmm.org/bonhoeffer/)

Public Broadcasting System (http://www.pbs.org/opb/bonhoeffer/)

Bonhoeffer's Cell (http://www.thesumners.com/bonhoeffer/)

Holocaust Heroes (http://www.holocaust-heroes.com/bonhoeffer.html)

Online Bonhoeffer Bibliography: Secondary Sources (pdf file available at http://www.uts.columbia.edu/burke_library/Sources.html)

Acheson R., *The New Theologians*. London: Mowbray, 1964.

Altizer, Thomas J. J,. and William Hamilton. *Radical Theology and the Death of God*. Indianapolis: Bobbs-Merrill, 1966.

Anderson, Douglas. *The Beams Are Creaking*. Boston: Baker's Plays, 1982.

Andrews, A. R. "Bonhoeffer's Psychology: Humanistic Ally or Christian Corrective?" *Christian Scholars Review* 4:1 (1974): 16–25.

Arnold, E. R. "Who's Afraid of Dietrich Bonhoeffer? *Journal of Reformed Theology* 29:1 (1972): 57–75.

Bailey, J. Martin and Douglas Gilbert. *The Steps of Bonhoeffer: A Pictorial Album*. Philadelphia: Pilgrim Press, 1969.

Baker, T. G. A., John Gibbs, B. S. Moss, and Martin Jarrett-Kerr. *The New Theologians: Bultmann, Bonhoeffer, Tillich, Teilhard de Chardin*. London: Mowbray, 1964.

Barnett, Victoria. "Dietrich Bonhoeffer's Ecumenical Vision." *Christian Century* 112 (April 26, 1995): 454–57.

Barnett, Victoria. "Response to Richard L. Rubenstein." Paper presented at the AAR/SBL Annual Meeting, Nashville, November 20, 2000.

Barnett, Victoria. "Theology or Politics: The Development of Bonhoeffer's Critique of Racial Ideology." Unpublished Paper.

Bartley, W. W., III. "The Bonhoeffer Revival." *New York Review of Books* 3 (August 26, 1965): 14–17.

Baum, Gregory. *The Church for Others: Protestant Theology in Communist East Germany.* Grand Rapids, Mich.: Eerdmans, 1996.

"Beatification and Coronization." *The Catholic Encyclopedia,* http://www.newadvent.org/cathen/02364b.htm.

Beaudoin, Tom. *Virtual Faith: The Irreverent Spiritual Quest of Generation X.* San Francisco: Jossey-Bass, 1998.

Berger, P. L., "Camus, Bonhoeffer and the World Come of Age." *Christian Century* 76 (April 8, 1959): 417–18; (April 15, 1959): 450–52; reply by W. H. Hudnut (May 20, 1959): 618–19.

Berrigan, Daniel. "A Hymn for Resisters." *The Other Side* 37:3 (May–June, 2001), http://www.theotherside.org/archive/may-june01/berrigan.html.

Berrigan, Daniel. "The Passion of Dietrich Bonhoeffer." *Saturday Review* (May 30, 1970): 17–22.

Berryhill, Elizabeth. *The Cup of Trembling, A Play in Two Acts, Suggested by and with Material Derived from the Life of Dietrich Bonhoeffer.* New York: Seabury, 1958.

"The Best Devotional Books of All Time, Part 2," *Christian Reader* (September–October 1997), http://www.christianitytoday.com/tc/7r5/7r5366.html.

Bethge, Eberhard. "Aftermath of Flossenburg: Bonhoeffer, 1945–1970." *Christian Century* 87 (May 27, 1970): 656–59.

Bethge, Eberhard. *Bonhoeffer: Exile and Martyr.* New York: Seabury, 1975.

Bethge, Eberhard. *Dietrich Bonhoeffer: A Biography.* Revised and edited by Victoria J. Barnett. Philadelphia: Fortress Press, 2000.

Bethge, Eberhard. *Dietrich Bonhoeffer: Man of Vision, Man of Courage.* New York: Harper & Row, 1977.

Bethge, Eberhard. "Dietrich Bonhoeffer 1906–1945." *Christianity and Crisis* 25 (April 19, 1965): 75.

Bethge, Eberhard. *Friendship and Resistance: Essays on Dietrich Bonhoeffer.* Grand Rapids, Mich.: Eerdmans, 1995.

Bethge, Eberhard. "My Friend Dietrich." *Christian History* 10:4 (issue 32, 1991): 41.

Bethge, Eberhard. "Unfulfilled Tasks." *Dialog* 34:1 (Winter 1995): 30–31.

Bianchi, E. C. "Bonhoeffer and the Church's Prophetic Mission." *Theological Studies* 28:4 (December 1967): 801–11.

Bloesch, Donald G. *The Christian Witness in a Secular Age: An Evaluation of Nine Contemporary Theologians.* Minneapolis: Augsburg, 1968.

Bloesch, Donald G. "True and False Ecumenism." *Christianity Today* 14:2 (July 17, 1970): 3–5.

Bonhoeffer, Dietrich, *Ethics.* Edited by Eberhard Bethge. New York: Macmillan, 1955.

Bonhoeffer, Dietrich. *Letters and Papers from Prison.* Edited by Eberhard Bethge. New York: Macmillan, 1972.

Bonhoeffer, Dietrich. *Who Is Christ for Us?* Edited and translated by Craig Nessan and Renate Wind. Minneapolis: Fortress Press, 2002.

Bonhoeffer. Directed by Martin Doblmeier. Journey Films, 2003.

Bonhoeffer: Agent of Grace. Directed by Eric Till. Gateway Films, 1999.

Bonhoeffer: The Cost of Freedom. Written and directed by Paul McCusker. Colorado Springs: Focus on the Family, 1997.

"Bonhoeffer: Representative Christian," *Christian Century* 82 (April 7, 1965): 420–21.

"Bonhoeffer's Love Letters." *Time* 90 (December 1, 1967): 100.

"Books of the Century." *Christianity Today* 117 (April 24, 2000), http://www.christianitytoday.com/ct/2000/005/5.92.html.

Bosanquet, Mary. *The Life and Death of Dietrich Bonhoeffer.* New York: Harper & Row, 1968.

Brock, Sebastian P., and Susan Ashbrook Harvey. *Holy Women of the Syrian Orient.* Berkeley: University of California Press, 1987.

Brown, Robert. M. "ABC: Assy, Bonhoeffer, Carswell." *Christian Century* 88 (March 24, 1971): 369–70.

Brown, Robert M. *Theology in a New Key: Responding to Liberation Themes.* Philadelphia: Fortress Press, 1978.

Burtness, James H. *Shaping the Future: The Ethics of Dietrich Bonhoeffer.* Philadelphia: Fortress Press, 1985.

Busing, P. F. "Reminiscences of Finkenwalde." *Christian Century* 77 (September 20, 1961): 1108–11.

Caldwell, Dan. "Bonhoeffer's *Life Together* and the Christian University." *Faculty Dialogue* (spring 1992): 27–38.

Cargas, Harry James. "'Protestant Martyr' Canonization Fitting." *National Catholic Reporter* 19 (October 22, 1982): 21.

Carter, Betty Smartt. "Bonhoeffer: Factual Fictions." *Books and Culture* (September–October 1998), http://www.ctlibrary.com/bc/1998/scptoct/865024.html.

Carter, Guy, René van Eyden, Hans–Dirk van Hoogstraten, and Jurjen Wiersma, eds. *Bonhoeffer's Ethics: Old Europe and New Frontiers.* Kampen: Kok Pharos, 1991.

Chandler, Andrew, ed. *The Terrible Alternative: Christian Martyrdom in the Twentieth Century*. New York: Cassell, 1998.

Chapman, G. Clarke. "Bonhoeffer: Source for Liberation Theology." *Union Seminary Quarterly Review* 36:4 (summer 1981): 225–42.

Chapman, G. Clarke. "Hope and the Ethics of Formation: Moltmann as an Interpreter of Bonhoeffer." *Studies in Religion/Sciences Religieuses* 12:4 (fall 1983): 449–60.

Chapman, G. Clarke. "What Would Bonhoeffer Say to Christian Peacemakers Today?," 167–175. In *Theology, Politics and Peace*, Edited by Theodore Runyan. Maryknoll, N.Y.: Orbis, 1989.

Chopp, Rebecca S. *The Praxis of Suffering: An Interpretation of Liberation and Political Theologies*. Maryknoll, N.Y.: Orbis, 1986.

Clements, Keith W. "Bonhoeffer's Last Days: A Pilgrimage." *International Bonhoeffer Society (English-Language Section) Newsletter* 80 (Fall 2002): 1, 4–7.

Clements, Keith W. *A Patriotism for Today: Love of Country in Dialogue with the Witness of Dietrich Bonhoeffer*. London: Collins Liturgical Publications, 1984.

Cleverly, Paul. "An Overview of Dietrich Bonhoeffer's Theology: Interpretations and Possibilities of 'Religionless Christianity' and Other Principle Themes," http://www.thesumners.com/bonhoeffer/essay03.html.

Clingan, Ralph Garlin. "Against Cheap Grace in a World Come of Age: A Study in the Hermeneutics of Adam Clayton Powell, 1865–1953, in His Intellectual Context." Ph. D. dissertation, Drew University, 1997.

Coleman, Robert E. *The Master Plan of Discipleship*. Grand Rapids, Mich.: Baker, 1998.

Coles, Robert. *Dietrich Bonhoeffer*. Modern Spiritual Masters Series. Maryknoll, N.Y.: Orbis, 1998.

Coles, Robert. *Lives of Moral Leadership: Men and Women Who Made a Difference*. New York: Random House, 2000.

Colson, Charles. "Caesar and Christ: Should We Disobey Our Government?" *Break Point* (November 28, 2000).

Cox, Harvey. "Beyond Bonhoeffer? The Future of Religionless Christianity." *Commonweal* (September 17, 1965): 653–57.

Cox, Harvey. *The Secular City: Secularization and Urbanization in Theological Perspective*. Revised edition. New York: Macmillan, 1966.

Cox, Harvey. "Using and Misusing Bonhoeffer." *Christianity and Crisis* 24 (October 19, 1964): 199–201.

"'Creative Misuse' of Bonhoeffer." *Christianity Today* 11:8 (January 20, 1967): 39–40.

Cunningham, Lawrence S. *The Meaning of Saints*. San Francisco: Harper & Row, 1980.

Das Ökumenische Heiligenlexikon (Ecumenical Encyclopedia of the Saints), http://www.heiligenlexicon.de.

Davis, Dena. "Gandhi and Bonhoeffer." *Manchester College Bulletin of the Peace Studies Institute* 11:1 (June 1981): 44–49.

Day, Thomas I. *Bonhoeffer on Christian Community and Common Sense*. Toronto Studies in Theology 11. Toronto: Edwin Mellen, 1975.

de Gruchy, John W. *Bonhoeffer and South Africa: Theology in Dialogue*. Grand Rapids, Mich.: Eerdmans, 1984.

de Gruchy, John W. "Bonhoeffer's Legacy: A New Generation." *Christian Century* 114 (April 2, 1997): 343–45.

de Gruchy, John W., ed. *Bonhoeffer for a New Day: Theology in a Time of Transition*. Grand Rapids, Mich.: Eerdmans, 1997.

de Gruchy, John W., ed. *The Cambridge Companion to Dietrich Bonhoeffer*. Cambridge: Cambridge University Press, 1999.

de Gruchy, John W., ed. *Dietrich Bonhoeffer: Witness to Jesus Christ*. The Making of Modern Theology: Nineteenth- and Twentieth-Century Texts. Minneapolis: Fortress Press, 1991.

de Lange, Frits. "Saint Bonhoeffer? Dietrich Bonhoeffer and the Paradox of Sainthood." http://www.home.hetnet.nl/~frits.lange/artsaintbonhoeffer.htm.

de Santa Ana, Julio. "The Influence of Bonhoeffer on the Theology of Liberation." *Ecumenical Review* 27:2 (April 1976): 189–97.

"Dietrich Bonhoeffer: General Teachings/Activities". http://www.rapidnet.com/~jbeard/bdm/exposes/bonhoeffer/general.htm.

Dietrich Bonhoeffer: Memories and Perspectives. Directed by Bain Boehlke. Trinity Films, 1983.

Dietrich Bonhoeffer: Nachfolge und Kreuz, Widerstand und Galgen. Matthias Film, 1983.

"Dietrich Bonhoeffer: Religionless Christianity: Maturity, Transcendence, and Freedom." In Roger A. Johnson and Ernest Wallwork, *Critical Issues in Modern Religion*. Englewood Cliffs, N. J: Prentice–Hall, 1973.

Dobson, James. "The New Cost of Discipleship." *Christianity Today* 43 (September 6, 1999), http://www.ctlibrary.com/ct/1999/sept6/9ta056.html..

Douglas, J. W. "From Bonhoeffer to Gandhi: God as Truth." *New Blackfriars Review* 48 (September 1967): 625–40.

Drewett, A. J. "Dietrich Bonhoeffer: Prophet and Martyr." *Modern Churchman* NS 11 (April 1968): 137–43.

Dudzus, Otto, "Discipleship and Worldliness in the Theology of Dietrich Bonhoeffer." *Religion in Life* 35 (spring 1966): 230–40.

Dudzus, Otto, ed. *Bonhoeffer Brevier.* München: Chr. Kaiser, 1963.

Dudzus, Otto, ed. *Bonhoeffer for a New Generation.* English Translation of *Dietrich Bonhoeffer Lesebuch.* London: SCM Press, 1986.

Dumas, André. *Dietrich Bonhoeffer: Theologian of Reality.* New York: Macmillan, 1971.

Edwards, James R. "What's in a Name: Why We Shouldn't Call the Old Testament the 'Hebrew Scriptures.'" *Christianity Today* 43 (August 9, 1999), http://www.ctlibrary.com/ct/1999/aug9/9t9059.html.

Eims, Leroy. *The Lost Art of Disciple Making.* Grand Rapids, Mich.: Zondervan, 1978.

Elliott, Alison Goddard. *Roads to Paradise: Reading the Lives of the Early Saints.* Hanover, N.H.: University of New England Press, 1987.

Ellsberg, Robert. *All Saints: Daily Reflections on Saints, Prophets, and Witnesses for Our Time.* New York: Crossroad, 1997.

Ellsberg, Robert. "The Mystery of Holiness: Taking Saints Seriously for the Needs of Our Time." *Sojourners* (September–October, 1997), http://www.sojo.net/index.cfm?action=magazine.article&issue=soj9709&article=970921.

Elson, J. T. "Man for Others." *Life* 58 (May 7, 1965): 108–9.

Ericksen, Robert. "Response to Richard L. Rubenstein." Paper presented at the AAR/SBL Annual Meeting, Nashville, November 20, 2000.

Farnham, Suzanne G., Joseph P. Gill, R. Taylor McLean, and Susan M. Ward. *Listening Hearts: Discerning Call in Community.* Harrisburg, Pa.: Morehouse Publishing, 1991.

Favre, Jeff. "Remembering Bonhoeffer." *The Lutheran* (April 2002), http://www.thelutheran.org/0204/page23.html.

Feil, Ernst. *Bonhoeffer Studies in Germany: A Survey of Recent Literature.* Edited by James H. Burtness. Translated by Jonathan Sorum. Philadelphia: Bonhoeffer Center, 1997.

Feil, Ernst, ed. *Glauben lernen in einer Kirche für andere: der Beitrag Dietrich Bonhoeffers zum Christsein in der Deutschen Demokratischen Republik.* Gütersloh: Chr. Kaiser, Gütersloher Verlagshaus, 1993.

Floyd, Wayne Whitson, Jr. "Bonhoeffer's Many Faces." *Christian Century* 112 (April 26, 1995): 444–45.

Floyd, Wayne Whitson, Jr. "Re-visioning Bonhoeffer for the Coming Generation: Challenges in Translating the Dietrich Bonhoeffer Works." *Dialog* 34 (Winter, 1995): 32–38.

Floyd, Wayne Whitson, Jr. "'These People I Have Loved Now Live': Commemorating Bonhoeffer After Fifty Years." Unpublished manuscript.

Floyd, Wayne Whitson, Jr., and Charles Marsh, eds. *Theology and the Practice of Responsibility: Essays on Dietrich Bonhoeffer.* Philadelphia: Trinity Press International, 1994.

Foster, Richard J., and James Bryan Smith. *Devotional Classics: Selected Readings for Individuals and Groups.* A Renovaré Resource for Spiritual Renewal. San Francisco: Harper, 1990.

Fowler, James W. *Stages of Faith: The Psychology of Human Development and the Quest for Meaning.* New York: Harper & Row, 1981.

Fowler, James W. and Robin W. Lovin with Katherine Ann Herzog et. al. *Trajectories in Faith: Five Life Stories.* Nashville: Abingdon, 1980.

George, Timothy. "What I'd Like to Tell the Pope about the Church." *Christianity Today* 42 (June 15, 1998), http://www.ctlibrary.com/ct/1998/june15/8t7041.html.

Giardina, Denise. *Saints and Villains.* New York: Fawcett, 1998.

Gill, Theodore A. *Memo for a Movie: A Short Life of Dietrich Bonhoeffer.* New York: Macmillan, 1971.

Gilmour, S. M. "Seven on Bonhoeffer." *Christian Century* 79 (October 17, 1962): 1260.

Glazener, Mary. *The Cup of Wrath: A Novel Based on Dietrich Bonhoeffer's Resistance to Hitler.* Macon, Ga.: Smith & Helwys, 1992.

Glimpses 63, http://gospelcom.net/chi/GLIMPSEF/Glimpses/glmps063.shtml.

Goddard, Donald. *The Last Days of Dietrich Bonhoeffer.* New York: Harper & Row, 1976.

Godsey, John D. "Dietrich Bonhoeffer on Suffering." *Stauros Notebook* 14:2 (Summer 1995), http://www.stauros.org/notebooks/v14n2901.html.

Godsey, John D. *Preface to Bonhoeffer: The Man and Two of His Shorter Writings.* Philadelphia: Fortress Press, 1965.

Godsey, John D. *The Theology of Dietrich Bonhoeffer.* Philadelphia: Westminster Press, 1960.

Godsey, John D. and Geffrey B. Kelly, eds. *Ethical Responsibility: Bonhoeffer's Legacy to the Churches.* Lewiston, N. Y.: Edwin Mellen, 1981.

Gollwitzer, Helmut, Käthe Kuhn, and Reinhold Schnider, eds. *Dying We Live: The Final Messages and Records of the Resistance.* Translated by Reinhard C. Kuhn. New York: Pantheon, 1956.

Gould, William Blair. *The Worldly Christian: Bonhoeffer on Discipleship.* Philadelphia: Fortress Press, 1967.

Green, Clifford J. "Bethge's Bonhoeffer." *Christian Century* 87 (July 1, 1970): 822–25.

Green, Clifford J. *Bonhoeffer: A Theology of Sociality.* Revised Edition. Grand Rapids, Mich.: Eerdmans, 1999.

Green, Clifford J. "Bonhoeffer in the Context of Ericksen's Luther Study," 162–96. In *Psychohistory and Religion: The Case of Young Man Luther,* edited by Roger A. Johnson. Philadelphia: Fortress Press, 1977.

Green, Clifford J. "Bonhoeffer's Legacy," www.pbs.org/opb/bonhoeffer/legacy/.

Grounds, V. C. "Pacesetters for the Radical Theologians of the '60s and '70s." *Journal of the Evangelical Theological Society* 18 (summer 1975): 151–71.

Gushee, David P. "Following Jesus to the Gallows." *Christianity Today* 39 (April 3, 1995): 26–32.

Gushee, David P. "Rescue Those Being Led Away to Death." *Books and Culture* (March–April 2002), http://www.christianitytoday.com/bc/2002/002/11.22.html

Gutiérrez, Gustavo. "The Limitations of Modern Theology: On a Letter of Dietrich Bonhoeffer," 35–42. In James B. Nickoloff, ed., *Gustavo Gutiérrez: Essential Writings.* Minneapolis: Fortress Press, 1996.

Hall, Douglas John. *Remembered Voices: Reclaiming the Legacy of "Neo-orthodoxy."* Louisville: Westminster John Knox, 1998.

Hamilton, Kenneth. *Life in One's Stride: A Short Study in Dietrich Bonhoeffer.* Grand Rapids, Mich.: Eerdmans, 1968.

Hamilton, William. "Bonhoeffer: Christology and Ethic United." *Christianity and Crisis* 23 (October 19, 1964): 195–98.

Hamilton, William. "Faith and the Facts of Life." *Christian Century* 82 (April 19, 1965): 424–26.

Hamilton, William. "A Secular Theology for a World Come of Age." *Theology Today* 18 (January 1962): 435–59.

Hanged on a Twisted Cross. Directed by T. N. Mahan. Gateway Films, 1996.

Harbuck, Don B. "Bonhoeffer Speaks to Baptists." *The Baptist* (October 1966): 28–29.

Hardwick, E. "The Place of Bonhoeffer." *Heythrop Journal* 5:3 (July 1964): 297–99.

Harper, H. V. *Profiles of Protestant Saints.* New York: Fleet Press, 1968.

Harrison, Wilfred. *Coming of Age: A Play.* TrottenU.K.: Fernhurst Press, 1973.

Hartwig, Mark. "Why Would God Do That?" *Teachers in Focus,* (1999), www.family.org/cforum/teachersmag/firstwrites/a0005360.cfm.

Hauerwas, Stanley. *Performing the Faith: Bonhoeffer and the Practice of Nonviolence.* Grand Rapids, Mich.: Brazos, 2004.

Haynes, Stephen R., and John K. Roth, eds. *The Death of God and the Holocaust: Radical Theology Encounters the Shoah.* New York: Greenwood, 1997.

Heckler–Feltz, Cheryl. "Agent of Grace Gains Prestige." *Christianity Today* 44 (August 7, 2000), http://www.christianitytoday.com/ct/2000/132/44.0.html.

Henry, Marilyn. "Who, Exactly, is a 'Righteous Gentile'?" *Jerusalem Post* (April 22, 1998), http://www.jpost.com/com/Archive/29.April.1998/Features/Article6.html.

Hilfiker, David. "Call and Conversion." *The Other Side* 37:5 (September–October 2001), http://www.theotherside.org/archive/sep-oct01/hilfiker.html..

Hillerbrand, H. J. "Dietrich Bonhoeffer and America." *Religion in Life* 30:4 (autumn 1961): 568–79.

Hodgson, Peter C. "The Death of God and the Crisis in Christology." *The Journal of Religion* 46 (October 1966): 446–62.

Holland, Scott. "First We Take Manhattan Then We Take Berlin: Bonhoeffer's New York." *Cross Currents* 50:3 (fall 2000), http://www.crosscurrents.org/hollandf20.htm.

Hoogstrate, A. "Dietrich Bonhoeffer—Who Was He?" *The Banner* (August 22, 1969): 4.

Hopper, David H. *A Dissent on Bonhoeffer.* Philadelphia: Westminster Press, 1975.

Horne, Charles. "What Is Bonhoeffer Theology?" *Moody Monthly* 66:9 (May 1966): 40–42.

Houser, Gordon. "An Uncommon Cup: The Challenge of a Historical Novel." Review of Mary Glazener, *The Cup of Wrath. Sojourners* 23:7 (August 1994): 45–46.

Howell, James C. *Servants, Misfits, and Martyrs: Saints and Their Stories.* Nashville: Upper Room Books, 1999.

Howell, Leon. "A Time of Trials: The Tribulation of Dietrich Bonhoeffer." *Sojourners* 24:2 (May–June 1995): 50–51.

Huber, Wolfgang. "Answering for the Past, Shaping the Future." Photocopy in Bonhoeffer archive, Union Theological Seminary, New York.

Hughes, Philip E. *Creative Minds in Contemporary Theology.* Grand Rapids, Mich.: Eerdmans, 1966.

Huldschiner, Robert E. "A Review Article—The Quest for the Historical Bonhoeffer." *Lutheran Forum* 3 (September 1969): 12–13.

Hull, William E. "Review of Dietrich Bonhoeffer, *The Way to Freedom: Lectures and Notes, 1935–1939,* and Wolf-Dieter Zimmerman and Ronald Gregor Smith, eds., *I Knew Dietrich Bonhoeffer.*" *Christian Century* 85 (July 12, 1967): 920–21.

Hulsether, Mark. *Building A Protestant Left: Christianity And Crisis Magazine, 1941–1993.* Knoxville: University of Tennessee Press, 1999.

Huneke, Douglas K. *The Stones Will Cry Out: Pastoral Reflections on the Shoah (with Liturgical Resources)*. Contributions to the Study of Religion 39. Westport, Conn.: Greenwood Press, 1995.

Hunnex, M. D. "Religionless Christianity: Is it a New form of Gnosticism?" *Christianity Today* 10 (January 7, 1966), 7–9.

Huntemann, Georg. *The Other Bonhoeffer: An Evangelical Reassessment of Dietrich Bonhoeffer*. Translated by Todd Huizinga. Grand Rapids, Mich.: Baker, 1993.

Hunter, Robert L. "Dietrich Bonhoeffer: A Vision and a Voice for Our Times." *Saturday Evening Post* (September–October 1997): 50–51.

Hunter, Robert L. "Hitler's Would-Be Assassin," *Saturday Evening Post* (November–December 1997): 44–47.

Ice, Jackson Lee and John J. Carey, eds. *The Death of God Debate*. Philadelphia: Westminster Press, 1967.

International Bonhoeffer Society (English-Language Section) Newsletter 81 (spring, 2003).

Jenkins, David E. *The Contradiction of Christianity*. London: SCM Press, 1976.

Jenkins, David E. *Guide to the Debate about God*. Philadelphia: Westminster Press, 1966.

Johnson, Stephen. "Classical: Music for Martyrs." *The Independent* (London), (July 14, 1998), 10.

Jones, L. Gregory. "Negotiating the Tensions of Vocation," 209–24. In *The Scope of Our Art: The Vocation of the Theological Teacher*, edited by Stephanie Paulsell and L. Gergory Jones. Grand Rapids, Mich.: Eerdmans, 2002.

Juergensmeyer, Mark. *Terror in the Mind of God: The Global Rise of Religious Violence*. Berkeley: University of California Press, 2000.

Kappelman, Todd. "Dietrich Bonhoeffer," http://www.probe.org/docs/bonhoeffer.html.

Kee, Alistair. "I Did Not Know Dietrich Bonhoeffer." *Christian Century* 89 (October 25, 1972): 1064–68.

Kelley, James Patrick. "Bonhoeffer Studies in English: How Theologians Become Popular." *Lexington Theological Quarterly* 3:1 (1968): 12–19.

Kelly, Geffrey B. "Bonhoeffer's Theology of Liberation." *Dialog* 34: 1 (Winter, 1995): 22–29.

Kelly, Geffrey B. "Dietrich Bonhoeffer on Justice for the Poor." *Weavings: A Journal of the Christian Spiritual Life* 17:6 (November–December 2002): 26–34.

Kelly, Geffrey B. *Liberating Faith: Bonhoeffer's Message for Today*. Minneapolis: Augsburg, 1984.

Kelly, Geffrey B., and C. John Weborg, eds. *Reflections on Bonhoeffer: Essays in Honor of F. Burton Nelson.* Chicago: Covenant, 1999.

Kelly, Geffrey B., and F. Burton Nelson. *The Cost of Moral Leadership: The Spirituality of Dietrich Bonhoeffer.* Grand Rapids, Mich.: Eerdmans, 2003.

Klassen, A. J., ed. *A Bonhoeffer Legacy: Essays in Understanding.* Grand Rapids, Mich.: Eerdmans, 1981.

Kleinhans, Theodore J. *Till the Night Be Past: The Life and Times of Dietrich Bonhoeffer.* St. Louis: Concordia, 2002.

Koonz, Claudia. "Ethical Dilemmas and Nazi Eugenics: Single Issue Dissent in Religious Contexts," 15–38. In *Resistance Against the Third Reich 1933–1990,* edited by Michael Geyer and John W. Boyer. Chicago: University of Chicago Press, 1992.

Koops, H. A. "The Ethics of Dietrich Bonhoeffer and the Crisis of Nuclear Power." *Review of Religion* 19:1 (September 1965): 25–39.

Kuhn, Harold B. "But Which Bonhoeffer?" *Christianity Today* 16 (April 14, 1972): 49–50.

Kuhn, Harold B. "The Old 'New Worldliness,'" *Christianity Today* 12:5 (December 8, 1967): 56.

Kuhns, William. "A Catholic Looks at Bonhoeffer." *Christian Century* 84 (June 28, 1967): 830–33.

Kuhns, William. *In Pursuit of Dietrich Bonhoeffer.* New York: Image Books, 1967.

Kuhns, William. "Who Is Dietrich Bonhoeffer?" *U.S. Catholic* (December 1967): 19–24.

Lange, Charles E. "Bonhoeffer: Modern Martyr." *The Episcopalian* (May, 1966): 48–49.

Langer, Lawrence L. *Versions of Survival: The Holocaust and the Human Spirit.* Albany: SUNY Press, 1982.

Larsen, Dale, and Sandy Larsen. *Dietrich Bonhoeffer: Costly Grace.* Christian Classics Bible Study Series. Downers Grove, Ill.: Intervarsity Press, 2002.

Lehmann, Paul. "Commentary: Dietrich Bonhoeffer in America." *Religion in Life* 30:4 (autumn 1961): 616–18.

Lehmann, Paul. Review of Dietrich Bonhoeffer, *The Communion of Saints* and *No Rusty Swords. Union Seminary Quarterly Review* 21:3 (March 1966): 364–69.

Leibholz, S. "Dietrich Bonhoeffer: A Glimpse into our Childhood." *Union Seminary Quarterly Review* 20 (May 1965): 319–31.

Lindbeck, George A. "De–mythologizing of Dietrich Bonhoeffer." *Commonweal* 96 (September 1972): 527–28.

Lutzer, Erwin W. *Hitler's Cross: The Revealing Story of How the Cross of Christ Was Used as a Symbol of the Nazi Agenda.* Chicago: Moody, 1995.

MacDonald, Gordon. "Speaking into Crisis." *Leadership Journal* (spring 2002),http://www.christianitytoday.com/le/2002/001/10.62.html.

Macquarrie, John. *New Directions in Theology Today, Volume III: God and Secularity.* Philadelphia: Westminster Press, 1967.

Maple, D. F. "Bonhoeffer, D. 1906–1945: Accepting the Paradox of Bonhoeffer." *Christian Century* 90 (January 10, 1973): 49–50.

Mark, J. "Bonhoeffer Reconsidered." *Theology* 76 (November 1973): 586–93.

Marshall, J. M. "Bonhoeffer: The Man." *Christianity Today* 14:1 (October 20, 1969): 28–29.

Marty, Martin E. "Bonhoeffer: Seminarians' Theologian." *Christian Century* 77 (April 20, 1960): 467–69.

Marty, Martin E., ed. *The Place of Bonhoeffer: Problems and Possibilities in His Thought.* New York: Association Press, 1962.

Marty, Martin E. and Dean Peerman, eds. *New Theology, #2.* New York: Macmillan, 1964.

"Martyr's Love: Bonhoeffer." *Newsweek* 70 (December 4, 1967): 84.

Mascall, E. *The Secularization of Christianity.* London: Darton, Longman & Todd, 1955.

Matthews, John. Review of "Bonhoeffer: Agent of Grace." *Association of Contemporary Church Historians Newsletter* 6:7/8 (July–August 2000).

McCartney, Bill. "Which Legacy?" http://www.ibelieve.com/content.asp?cid=15505

Mehta, V. "Profiles: Bonhoeffer." *New Yorker* 41 (November 27, 1965): 65–68.

Melano, Beatriz. "The Influence of Dietrich Bonhoeffer, Paul Lehmann, and Richard Shaull in Latin America." *Princeton Seminary Bulletin* 22:1 (2001): 65–84.

Miller, Ed L., and Stanley J. Grenz. *Fortress Introduction to Contemporary Theologies.* Minneapolis: Fortress Press, 1998.

Miller, Kevin A. "A Man for Others." Review of *A Testament to Freedom: The Essential Writings of Dietrich Bonhoeffer,* edited by Geffrey B. Kelly and F. Burton Nelson. *Christianity Today* 35 (July 22, 1991): 58–59.

Miller, Susan Martins. *Dietrich Bonhoeffer.* Men of Faith Series. Minneapolis: Bethany House, 2002.

Minthe, Eckard. "Bonhoeffer's Influence on the Younger Generation of Ministers in Germany." *Andover Newton Quarterly* 2 (September 1961): 13–45.

Mitchell, Elvis. "Film in Review: *Bonhoeffer.*" *New York Times* (July 20, 2003), E14.

Moeller, Michael F. "The Child, the Fool, the Sufferer: Dietrich Bonhoeffer: A Reflection on His Life and Ministry," http://www.luther95.org/NELCA/internos/moeller.htm.

Mollenkott, Virginia Ramey. "A Call to Subversion." *The Other Side* 35:4 (July–August 1999), http://www.theotherside.org/archive/jul-aug99/mollenkott.html.

Moltmann, Jürgen, and Jürgen Weissbach. *Two Studies in the Theology of Bonhoeffer.* Translated by Reginald H. Fuller and Ilse Fuller. New York: Charles Scribner's Sons, 1967.

Morton, R. K. "Quo Vadis Bonhoeffer?" *Christianity Today* 12:12 (March 15, 1968): 29–30.

Mulder, Karen L. "Martyrs Carved in Stone." *Christianity Today* 43 (September 7, 1998), http://www.ctlibrary.com/ct/1998/sept7/8ta27c.html.

Nelson, F. Burton. "Bonhoeffer and the Spiritual Life: Some Reflections." *Journal of Theology for Southern Africa* 30 (March 1980): 34–38.

Niebuhr, Reinhold, "The Death of a Martyr." *Christianity and Crisis* 5:11 (June 25, 1945): 6–7.

Novak, Michael. "Bonhoeffer's Way." *Book Week* 4 (February 19, 1967): 5–6.

Novak, Michael. "Dietrich Bonhoeffer." *The Critic* 25 (June–July 1967): 38–45.

Oden, Thomas C. "Theology and Therapy: A New Look at Bonhoeffer." *Dialog* 5:2 (Spring 1966): 98–111.

Ogden, Greg. *Discipleship Essentials: A Guide to Building Your Life in Christ.* Downers Grove, Ill.: Intervarsity, 1998.

Ogletree, Thomas W. "The Church's Mission to the World in the Theology of Dietrich Bonhoeffer." *Encounter* 25 (utumn 1964): 457–69.

Olsen, Ted. "Weblog: Evangelical Support of Israel Isn't Just about Premillennialism." *Christianity Today* 46 (April 22, 2002), http://www.christianitytoday.com/ct/2002/115/12.0.html.

Ott, Heinrich. *Reality and Faith: The Theological Legacy of Dietrich Bonhoeffer.* Philadelphia: Fortress Press, 1972.

Paulose, Paulose Mar. *Encounter in Humanization: Insights for Christian–Marxist Dialogue and Cooperation,* http://www.religion–online.org/cgi-bin/researchd.dll/showbook?item_id=1572.

Pelikan, Jaroslav. "He Inspired the Death of God." *Saturday Review* 50 (March 18, 1967): 30-33.

Pejsa, Jane. *To Pomerania in Search of Dietrich Bonhoeffer: A Traveler's Companion and Guide for Those Who Venture East of the Oder River, Seeking Markers of Bonhoeffer's Life and Ministry—1935 through 1943.* Minneapolis: Kenwood Publishing, 1996.

Phillips, John A. *Christ for Us in the Theology of Dietrich Bonhoeffer.* New York: Harper, 1967.

Phillips John A. "The Killing of Brother Dietrich." *Christianity and Crisis* 29 (February 16, 1969): 24–26.

Phillips, Michael. *The Eleventh Hour*. Wheaton, Ill.: Tyndale House, 1993.

Pinnock, Sarah K., ed. *The Theology of Dorothy Sölle*. Harrisburg, PA: Trinity Press International, 2003.

"Prison Prophet." *Time* 87 (May 27, 1966): 58-59

Rand, Roberta. "Pundits and Poets on the Rewards of Long-Term Marriage," http://www.family.org/focusoverfifty/articles/a0019657.html.

Rasmussen, Larry L. *Dietrich Bonhoeffer: Reality and Resistance*. Studies in Christian Ethics. Nashville: Abingdon, 1972.

Rasmussen, Larry L., with Renate Bethge. *Dietrich Bonhoeffer—His Significance for North Americans*. Minneapolis: Fortress Press, 1990.

Raum, Elizabeth. *Dietrich Bonhoeffer: Called by God*. New York: Continuum, 2002.

Rausch, David A. *A Legacy of Hatred: Why Christians Must Not Forget the Holocaust*. Second edition. Grand Rapids, Mich.: Baker, 1984.

Reist, Benjamin A. *The Promise of Bonhoeffer*. Philadelphia: J. B. Lippincott, 1969.

Ridd, J. Carl. "A Message from Bonhoeffer." *Christian Century* 83 (June 29, 1966): 827–29.

Ringma, Charles. *Seize the Day with Dietrich Bonhoeffer*. Colorado Springs: Piñon Press, 2000.

Robertson, Edwin H. *Dietrich Bonhoeffer*. Richmond, Va.: John Knox, 1967.

Robertson, Edwin. *Dietrich Bonhoeffer*. Makers of Contemporary Theology. Philadelphia: John Knox, 1966.

Robertson, Edwin H., ed. *No Rusty Swords: Letters, Lectures and Notes, 1928–1936, from the Collected Works of Dietrich Bonhoeffer*. Vol. 1. Translated by Edwin H. Robertson and John Bowden.New York: Harper & Row, 1965.

Robertson, Edwin, ed. and trans. *My Soul Finds Rest: Reflections on the Psalms by Dietrich Bonhoeffer*. Grand Rapids, Mich.: Zondervan, 2002.

Robertson, Edwin, ed. and trans. *Voices in the Night: The Prison Poems of Dietrich Bonhoeffer*. Grand Rapids, Mich.: Zondervan, 1999.

Robinson, John A. T. *Honest to God*. Philadelphia: Westminster Press, 1963.

Robinson, Marilynne. *The Death of Adam: Essays on Modern Thought*. Boston: Houghton Mifflin, 1998.

Rose, Stephen C. "Bethge's Monument." *Christianity and Crisis* 30 (July 20, 1970): 154–55.

Rouner, Leroy S. "Bonhoeffer and the Seventies." *Christianity and Crisis* 29 (April 14, 1969): 104–5.

Rubenstein, Richard L. "Was Dietrich Bonhoeffer a 'Righteous Gentile'?" Paper presented at the AAR/SBL Annual Meeting, Nashville, November 20, 2000.

Runia, K. "Dietrich Bonhoeffer: The Man and His Beliefs." *Eternity* 16 (December 1965): 11–13.

S., R. N. "Prominent German Pastor Was Executed by Nazis." *Christianity and Crisis* 5 (June 25, 1945): 8.

Schaff, Philip, ed. A *Select Library of the Nicene and Post–Nicene Fathers of the Christian Church Series.* 8 Vols. Grand Rapids, Mich.: Eerdmans, 1955.

Schalk, A. "A Second Look at a Modern Martyr." *U.S. Catholic* 37:7 (July 1972): 19–26.

Schönherr, Albrecht. "Dietrich Bonhoeffer: The Message of a Life." *Christian Century* 102 (November 27, 1985): 1090–94.

Scott, Jamie S. *Christians and Tyrants: The Prison Testimonies of Boethius, Thomas More and Dietrich Bonhoeffer.* Toronto Studies in Religion 19. New York: Peter Lang, 1995.

Shaffer, G. "The Transition of Dietrich Bonhoeffer." *Lutheran Forum* 3 (September 1969): 8–11.

Shelly, Rubel. "Biographers Needed! Please Apply," http://www.ibelieve.com/content.asp?cid=16342.

Sherman, Franklin. "Death of a Modern Martyr: The Witness of Dietrich Bonhoeffer." *Expository Times* 76 (April 1965): 204–7.

Shinn, R. L. "Dietrich Bonhoeffer: 1906–1945." *Christianity and Crisis* 25 (April 19, 1965): 75.

Siemon-Netto, Uwe. *The Acquittal of God: A Theology for Vietnam Veterans.* New York: Pilgrim Press, 1990.

Slane, Craig J. *Bonhoeffer as Martyr: Social Responsibility and Modern Christian Commitment.* Grand Rapids, Mich.: Brazos, 2003.

Smith, Harry E. *Secularization and the University.* Richmond, Va.: John Knox Press, 1968.

Smith, Ronald Gregor. *The New Man: Christianity and Man's Coming of Age.* New York: Harper & Brothers, 1956.

Smith, Ronald Gregor, ed. *World Come of Age.* Philadelphia: Fortress Press, 1967.

Smith, Ronald Gregor, and Wolf-Dieter Zimmerman, eds. *I Knew Dietrich Bonhoeffer.* Translated by Käthe Gregor Smith. New York: Harper & Row, 1966.

Smolik, Josef. "The Church without Privileges." *Ecumenical Review* 28: 2 (April 1976): 174–87.

Sölle, Dorothee. *Christ the Representative: An Essay after the 'Death of God.'* Translated by David Lewis. Philadelphia: Fortress Press, 1967.

Stassen, Glen. "Incarnating Ethics: We're Called to Faithful Discipleship, Not Creedal Rigidity." *Sojourners* 28:2 (March–April 1999): 14.

Sternhell, Zeev. *Neither Right Nor Left: Fascist Ideology In France.* Translated by David Maisel (English translation of *Ni Droite, Ni Gauche*). Berkeley: University of California Press, 1986.

"The Ten Most Influential Christians of the Twentieth Century," *Christian History,* http://www.ctlibrary.com/ch/2000/65/16.44.html.

"Theologian of Life." *Time* 75 (May 9, 1960): 53–54.

Thiemann, Ronald. "Waiting for God's Own Time: Dietrich Bonhoeffer as Public Intellectual." 88–107. In *Die Gehalt des Christentums im 21. Jahrhundert.* Edited by Christian Gremmels and Wolfgang Huber. Gürtersloher Verlagshaus, 2002.

Thornton, Martin. *The Rock and the River: An Encounter between Traditional Spirituality and Modern Thought.* New York: Morehouse-Barlow, 1965.

Vahanian, Gabriel. *No Other Name.* New York: George Braziller, 1966.

Vahanian, Gabriel. *The Death of God: The Culture of Our Post–Christian Era.* New York: Braziller, 1961.

van Buren, Paul. *The Secular Meaning of the Gospel: Based on An Analysis of Its Language.* New York: Macmillan, 1963.

van Dyke, Michael. *Dietrich Bonhoeffer: Opponent of the Nazi Regime.* Heroes of the Faith Series. Ulrichsville, Ohio: Barbour Publishing, 2001.

van Til, Cornelius. "Dietrich Bonhoeffer: A Review Article." *Westminster Theological Journal* 34:2 (May 1972): 152–73.

Veith, Gene Edward, Jr. *Modern Fascism: Liquidating the Judeo-Christian Worldview.* St. Louis: Concordia Publishing House, 1993.

Visser 't Hooft, W. A. "Dietrich Bonhoeffer and the Self-Understanding of the Ecumenical Movement." *Ecumenical Review* 27: 2 (April 1976): 198–203.

Visser 't Hooft, W. A. "Dietrich Bonhoeffer, 1945–1965." *Ecumenical Review* 17 (July 1965): 224–31.

Vorkink, Peter, II, ed. *Bonhoeffer in a World Come of Age.* Philadelphia: Fortress Press, 1968.

Walsh, Michael, ed. *Butler's Lives of the Saints, Concise Edition.* San Francisco: Harper & Row, 1985.

Wearne, Gary. "Perspectives: A Dialogue with Bonhoeffer," http://www.members.ozone.com.au/~seccomn/dbonhl.htm.

Webb, J. F., ed. *Lives of the Saints: The Voyage of St. Brendan; Bede: Life of Cuthbert; Eddius Stephanus: Life of Wilfrid.* Baltimore: Penguin, 1964.

Weber, Manfred, ed. *Dietrich Bonhoeffer: Meditations on the Cross.* Translated by Douglas W. Stott. Louisville: Westminster John Knox, 1998.

Wedel, Theodore O. "Man Come of Age." *Union Seminary Quarterly Review* 18:4 (May 1963): 326–40.

Weikart, Richard. *The Myth of Dietrich Bonhoeffer: Is His Theology Really Evangelical?* San Francisco: International Scholars Publications, 1997.

Weiland, J. Sperna. *New Ways in Theology.* Translated by N. D. Smith. New York: Newman Press.

Wentz, Frederick K. "Lay Renaissance: Europe and America." *Christian Century* 76 (May 13, 1959): 576–79.

West, Charles C. *The Power to Be Human: Toward a Secular Theology.* New York: Macmillan, 1970.

Westmoreland-White, Michael, Glen Stassen, and David P. Gushee. "Disciples of the Incarnation: The Witness of Dietrich Bonhoeffer, Martin Luther King, Jr., and Christian Rescuers of Jews Informs our Discipleship Today." *Sojourners* 23:4 (May 1994): 26–30.

Wilmore, Gayraud S., and James H. Cone, eds. *Black Theology: A Documentary History 1966–1979.* Maryknoll, N.Y.: Orbis, 1979.

Wind, Renate. *Dietrich Bonhoeffer: A Spoke in the Wheel.* Translated by John Bowden. Grand Rapids, Mich.: Eerdmans, 1992.

Wink, Walter. "The Bonhoeffer Assumption." *Sojourners* 31:1 (January–February 2002): 33.

The Wisdom and Witness of Dietrich Bonhoeffer: Meditations by Wayne Whitson Floyd Jr. on Texts by Dietrich Bonhoeffer. Minneapolis: Fortress Press, 2000.

Wise, Stephen A. "Why Isn't Bonhoeffer Honored at Yad Vashem?" *Christian Century* 115 (February 25, 1998): 202–4.

Woelfel, James. *Bonhoeffer's Theology: Classical and Revolutionary.* Nashville: Abingdon, 1970.

Wright, H. Elliott. "Aftermath of Flossenburg: Bonhoeffer, 1945–1970: An Interview with Eberhard Bethge." *Christian Century* 87 (May 27, 1970): 656–59.

Wyschogrod, Edith. *Saints and Post-Modernism: Revisioning Moral Theory.* Chicago: Univ. of Chicago Press, 1990.

Yancey, Philip. "The Bible Jesus Read." *Christianity Today* 43 (January 11, 1999), http://www.ctlibrary.com/ct/1999/jan11/9t1062.html.

Young, Josiah Ulysses, III. *No Difference in the Fare: Dietrich Bonhoeffer and the Problem of Racism.* Grand Rapids, Mich.: Eerdmans, 1998.

Zanchettin, Leo, and Patricia Mitchell. *Great Cloud of Witnesses: The Stories of Sixteen Saints and Christian Heroes.* Ijamsville, Md.: The Word Among Us Press, 1998.

Zoba, Wendy Murray. "Decoding Generations." *Christianity Today* (April 2, 2001), http://www.christianitytoday.com/ct/2001/005/30.83.html.

INDEX

DATE DUE
